סִדּוּר
שְׁמַע יִשְׂרָאֵל
SIDDUR
SHEMA YISRAEL

סִדּוּר
שְׁמַע יִשְׂרָאֵל
SIDDUR
SHEMA YISRAEL

A SIDDUR FOR SABBATH AND FESTIVALS AND SOURCEBOOK FOR STUDENTS AND FAMILIES

Shoshana Silberman
Illustrations: Jonathan Kremer

THE UNITED SYNAGOGUE OF CONSERVATIVE JUDAISM
נר ה' נשמת אדם

Published by
The United Synagogue of Conservative Judaism
Commission on Jewish Education

Dr. Shoshana Silberman is the author of *A Family Haggadah, The Whole Megillah (almost!)*. Presently the educational director of the Jewish Center of Princeton (NJ), she has been involved in Jewish education as a teacher, principal, workshop leader, and curriculum writer. Dr. Silberman received a B.S. from Columbia University and a B.H.L. from Gratz College. She holds a M.S.T. from The University of Chicago and an Ed. D. from Temple University.

Fourth Printing 2006

International Standard Book Number: 0-8381-0196-8

Design and typography by Schaffzin & Schaffzin

ACKNOWLEDGEMENTS

We wish to thank the publishers and authors listed below for having granted us permission to print excerpts from the following works. Their works enhance and enrich this *siddur* and we are grateful to them. (Wherever possible we have indicated the title of the poem or piece in the acknowledgement as well as where it is found in this *siddur*. Attribution is also indicated in the footnotes.)

The translations for blessings recited at home are based on *A Family Haggadah* by Shoshanah Silberman published by Kar-Ben Copies, Inc. All rights reserved. Reprinted by permission of Kar-Ben Copies, Inc.

"Prayers before *Hadlakat Nerot* " [found on p. 4] from *The Sabbath Eve Service* by Chaim Raphael. Published by Behrman House, Inc., 1985. Reprinted by permission of Behrman House, Inc. 235 Watchung Ave., W. Orange, NJ 07052.

"Sabbath Eyes" [found on p. 4] by Nancy Lee Gossels in *Vetaher Libenu*, a *siddur* published by Congregation Beth El, Sudbury River Valley, 1980. Reprinted by permission of author.

"T'khine for Lighting Candles" [found on p. 5] and "*T'khine* of Sora, Rokhil and Laye" [found on p. 12] from *The Merit of Our Mothers: A Bilingual Anthology of Jewish Women's Prayers* by Tracy Guren Klirs, et al. Published by the Hebrew Union College Press, 1992. Reprinted by permission of the Hebrew Union College Press.

"Blessing the Children" [found on p. 8] from *Nine Entered Paradise Alive* by Danny Siegel. Published by The Town House Press, Spring Valley, NY, 1980. Reprinted by permission of The Town House Press.

"For *Kabbalat Shabbat*" [found on p. 31] from *HARVEST: Collected Poems and Prayers by Ruth Brin*. Published by The Reconstructionist Press, New York, 1986. Reprinted by permission of The Reconstructionist Press.

"By the Shores" [found on p. 39] by Geela Rayzel Raphael. Copyright © Geela Rayzel Raphael. All rights reserved. Reprinted by permission of Geela Rayzel Raphael.

"The darkness darts" [found on p. 40 by Janine is from *MIRACLES: Poems by Children of the English-Speaking World*. Edited by Richard Lewis and originally published by Simon and Schuster. ©1966, Richard Lewis. Presently distributed by The Touchstone Center, 141 E. 88 St., New York, NY 10128. Used by permission of Richard Lewis.

"The Creation of the World" [found on p. 50] and "Creation of Fish, Fowl and Cattle" [found on p. 60] from *Ladder of Angels: Stories From the Bible Illustrated by Children of the World* by Madeleine L'Engle. Copyright ©1979 by Keter Publishing House of Jerusalem, Ltd. Text by Madeleine L'Engle, copyright ©1979 by Crosswicks, Ltd. Reprinted by permission of HarperCollins Publishers, Inc.

"Where Heaven and Earth Touch So Closely, They Appear To Be Kissing" [found on p. 77] from *A Hearing Heart* by Danny Siegel. Published by The Town House Press, Pittsboro, North Carolina, 1992. Reprinted by permission of The Town House Press.

"Morning Has Broken" [found on p. 91]. Copyright ©1957 by Eleanor Farjean. Reprinted by permission of Harold Ober Associates Incorporated.

"*Shalom Ba'olam*" [found on p. 128] from *Tov Lichtov* published by the Histadruth Ivrith of America.

"Reflections V" [found on p. 148] from *Munbaz II and Other Mitzvah Heroes* by Danny Siegel. Published by The Town House Press, Spring Valley, New York, 1988. Reprinted by permission of The Town House Press.

"Portions" [found on p. 169 by Rami Shapiro. Reprinted with permission.

"Merger Poem" [found on p. 178]. © Judy Chicago, 1988. Reprinted with permission.

Dedication

This *siddur* and source book is lovingly dedicated

in memory of my father, Samuel Ribner, ז״ל, a man of deep convictions and broad vision;

in honor of our daughter Lisa's marriage to Daniel Mordecai Brenner;

with appreciation to a wonderful family and with gratitude to the *Ḥavurah minyan* at The Jewish Center in Princeton for helping to make *Shabbat* and *Yontev* a time of *menuḥah v'simḥah* — a time of rest and joy.

Table of Contents

שַׁבָּת וְיוֹם טוֹב

TO THE LEADER

- As in *Tiku Shofar*, we continue, here, adapting an old tradition of using the word to decorate liturgical works. Jonathan Kremer has created illustrations to engage today's young people and involve them in interpretation.
- In placing Hebrew and English translation we have tried to keep the *siddur* "user friendly." We have sought to provide both flexibility and enhance the flow of the service. Most often the English follows the Hebrew but when deemed appropriate, it precedes it.
- To enhance aesthetics and the leader's ability to direct the eyes and minds of participants to specific content, we have limited the amount of text found on any one page.
- To further aid in the use of this *siddur* we have used the following visual cues:
  - Hebrew prayers and their translations appear in black.
  - Stories and poems are boxed and are lightly shaded in blue. At the top of the box is a graphic symbol.
  - Some explanations and other supplementary materials are also in blue and boxed, but do not have a symbol nor are they shaded.
  - Thoughts and comments appear in blue.
  - In transliterating, we have used the "ḥ" for both ח and כ. The "ḥ" is pronounced as in Ḥanukkah. The letters "ei" are pronounced like the long "a" in "state." An apostrophe between vowels indicates that the vowels are each pronounced separately.

Introduction

In many synagogues today, tradition and change sit comfortably together, though there is a great variation as to how services are conducted, especially services that include and involve children. In some congregations, a full service is held, while for at least part of the time, a junior congregation service goes on simultaneously. Other congregations hold regular or occasional family services that are somewhat abbreviated and use English as well as Hebrew. *Siddur Shema Yisrael* was planned with these needs in mind.

Siddur Shema Yisrael is targeted for children above eight years of age who are familiar with the basics of Hebrew reading, as well as for family services. Besides a substantial Hebrew text, there are selected transliterations and a simple gender sensitive translation of prayers that is meant to encourage both understanding and participation. As in *Tiku Shofar—A High Holy Day Maḥzor and Sourcebook for Students and Families*, the translation was done with both a deep respect for the authentic meaning of the prayers and a commitment to searching modern minds and hearts. The goal was not a verbatim translation, but one that captured the essence of the prayer.

The graphics done by artist Jonathan Kremer were commissioned not only to enhance the prayer book, but to spark interest in the text. Poetry, stories, commentaries, and questions were added to create thought provoking moments. These can be read privately or used by the service leader as a *kavanah*, focus. These additions can also be used by teachers and parents to prepare children for *Shabbat* services. For schools that emphasize prayer in the curriculum, *Siddur Shema Yisrael* can be a teaching text as well as a prayer book.

Siddur Shema Yisrael includes *Kabbalat Shabbat* and *Ma'ariv* as well as a home table service for Friday evening. It continues with a *Shabbat* morning service and includes the prayers for festivals.

It is hoped that *Siddur Shema Yisrael* will help students and parents not only feel more comfortable at services, but will also help them find meaning in the prayers of our people.

Special thanks to Rabbi Robert Abramson for his enthusiasm and diligence on working with this manuscript. Every submission received his full attention. He has the ability to be both challenging and supportive — wonderful traits for an editor.

Shabbat Shalom and *Ḥag Same'aḥ*!

Shoshana Silberman

SHABBAT

Shabbat is so important that the *mitzvah* to keep *Shabbat* is repeated twelve times in the Torah! Only *Shabbat*, of all the holidays, was included in the Ten Commandments. It is impossible to imagine a Jewish way of life without *Shabbat*.

Throughout the ages, keeping *Shabbat* has made us stronger as a people and has brought us closer together. The writer Aḥad Ha'Am once explained this by stating: "More than Israel has kept the Sabbath, the Sabbath has kept Israel."

Shabbat is not only meaningful to our people as a whole, but it can also be meaningful to each of us as individuals. It is a time for putting our worries and regrets aside and experiencing joy and inner harmony. It is a time to feel closer to God and to share special moments with family and friends. This is why the prophet Isaiah teaches us to "call *Shabbat* a delight" (Isaiah 58:13).

Shabbat is a gift that is passed on from generation to generation. The *Talmud* teaches us that, indeed, this was intended: "I have a precious gift in my treasury, said God to Moses. '*Shabbat*' is its name; go and tell Israel that I wish to present it to them." It is a gift each Jew can have and experience fifty-two times a year.

PREPARING FOR *SHABBAT*

"The *Shabbat* is the choicest fruit and flower of the week, the queen whose coming changes the humblest home into a palace."

Preparing for *Shabbat* helps us to be in the right mood for receiving our "guest," the Sabbath Queen, and enjoying her visit.

Shabbat preparation includes cooking and baking for our *Shabbat* meals, buying or baking *ḥallot,* and buying candles and wine — all of the things we need to observe *Shabbat* properly.

There is much to do to get ready for *Shabbat* and all preparations must be finished before candlelighting. It is customary to light candles eighteen minutes before sundown, by which time all shopping, cooking, baking and cleaning must cease. Our work is over; we now can welcome and enjoy *Shabbat*!

Preparing for *Shabbat* includes things that enhance or make *Shabbat* special. Examples are making decorations for *Shabbat*, giving *Tzedakah*, cleaning our houses and ourselves and inviting guests to our meals.

The *Midrash* teaches, "How does one honor *Shabbat*? With food, with drink and with festive clothing."

To honor *Shabbat*, it is customary to wear clean clothes, preferably clothes that we don't wear during the week.

Think of some other ways to make *Shabbat* special or different from the rest of the week.

Think about what you can wear and/or how you can decorate the house or set the table to make *Shabbat* more festive.

The Roman Emperor Hadrian once asked Rabbi Joshua ben Hanania why the food on *Shabbat* tasted so delicious. Rabbi Joshua told him that it was because of the Sabbath spice. Hadrian immediately asked him for some. Rabbi Joshua replied, "It only works for those who keep the Sabbath."

What did Rabbi Joshua mean by the "Sabbath spice"?

סֵדֶר לְלֵיל שַׁבָּת וּלְיוֹם טוֹב

Shabbat and Festival Evening Home Table Service

The Most Beautiful Thing to Paint

Once a restless artist went on a search to find the most beautiful thing in the world to paint. His search took him many miles through numerous towns and villages. Months later, he came to a lovely park where he sat down to relax. There he overheard a young couple speaking tenderly to each other. The look of love in their eyes inspired him to paint this scene. Convinced that he had found the most beautiful thing in the world to paint, he started for home.

On his journey, he came to a bridge. A guard ordered him to halt so some soldiers could cross first. As they approached, the artist asked one of the soldiers where he was going. "Home," he replied, "the fighting has ended; there is peace at last." Tears of joy filled the soldiers eyes. The artist was so moved that he began to paint.

The artist took the picture of love and the picture of peace and continued on his way until he found an inn for lodging. After a comfortable night's sleep, he awoke early and found himself on a small country road. As he passed a tiny cottage, he saw in the window an old man wearing a *tallit* and *tefillin*, praying with all his heart. He quickly rushed to capture this expression of faith on his canvas. He added this painting to the others and headed for home.

The artist arrived just before the beginning of *Shabbat*. Through the window, he watched his wife light the candles and bless their two children. Sweetly, they recited the *Kiddush*, washed their hands and said the *Motzi* over the *ḥallah*. He felt the presence of the *Sheḥinah* enter their house. He realized that, although he had found the three most beautiful things — love, peace and faith — on his journey, they were also right here where he lived. From then on, he celebrated each *Shabbat* with his family with great joy and thanksgiving.

FRIDAY EVENING HOME CEREMONIES

It is a *mitzvah* to light candles to usher in *Shabbat*. The candles are lit eighteen minutes before sunset.

We light the candles by drawing our hands to our face three times in a circular motion, inviting *Shabbat* to enter. After the third circle, our hands cover our eyes while the appropriate blessing is said. We do this because a *braḥah* is said before doing a *mitzvah*. The *mitzvah* we are doing is lighting the *Shabbat* candles. When we say the *braḥah* we are also announcing the start of *Shabbat*, after which we are not permitted to light fire. Therefore, we first cover our eyes and say the *braḥah*, and then open them to see the light of the candles.

The candles not only provide light to eat by, but are also a symbol of the light and joy that we experience on *Shabbat*.

There are two versions of the fourth commandment. In the book of Exodus it is written, "Remember the Sabbath day and keep it holy" (*Exodus* 20:8). In the book of *Deuteronomy* it says, "Observe the Sabbath day" (*Deuteronomy* 5:12). Some say we light two candles for *Shabbat* for the two versions of the fourth commandment.

In some homes, candles are lit for each member of the family.

Why begin *Shabbat* with candle lighting? One interpretation is because God began creation by saying, "Let there be light."

Prayers before *Hadlakat Nerot*
(Lighting the *Shabbat* Candles)

Merciful One, bestow Your
loving-kindness on me and my
loved ones, near and dear to me.
May peace and light and joy abide
forever in our home, for with
You is the fountain of life; in
Your light, we see light. Amen.

Sabbath Eyes

Holy One of Being
Help us replace
The earthbound things,
Confines of space,
With Sabbath eyes,
With Sabbath heart.

Help us to climb,
To reach that place
In sacred time
Where we can find our Sabbath soul.

Help us, we pray,
To recognize
Your Holiness,
To sanctify
And to embrace
The Sabbath day,
Your precious gift,
With love and grace.

T'khine for Lighting Candles

(This is to be said with complete *kavone* when lighting candles for *Shabbes* and *Yontev*.)

You have chosen the *Shabbes* alone for rest, for honor, and for blessing, for lighting candles and for joy and delight in Your service. Today is Your *Shabbes Koydesh*, which we are obliged to maintain with great care as a *ḥosn* cares for his *kale*. Almighty God, give me and my husband and my children and my household this *Shabbes Koydesh* for rest, for holiness and for blessedness.

Transliteration follows Yiddish pronunciation:
T'khine = a request of God
kavone = feeling
ḥosn = groom; *kale* = bride
Shabbes = Yiddish pronunciation of Sabbath
Shabbes Koydesh = Holy Sabbath

CANDLE LIGHTING

On the eve of *Shabbat*, before sunset, candles are lit at home using the following blessing:

בָּרוּךְ אַתָּה יְיָ אֱלֹהֵינוּ מֶלֶךְ הָעוֹלָם, אֲשֶׁר קִדְּשָׁנוּ
בְּמִצְוֹתָיו וְצִוָּנוּ לְהַדְלִיק נֵר שֶׁל שַׁבָּת.

We praise You, *Adonai* our God, Ruler of the Universe, Who makes us holy by Your *mitzvot* and commands us to light the Sabbath lights.

Baruḥ atah Adonai Eloheinu Meleḥ ha'olam, asher kid'deshanu b'mitzvotav v'tzivanu l'hadlik ner shel Shabbat.

On the eve of a festival, *Yom Tov*, which falls on a *Shabbat*, before sunset, candles are lit at home using the following blessing. When Yom Tov falls on a weekday the words in parenthesis are not said:

בָּרוּךְ אַתָּה יְיָ אֱלֹהֵינוּ מֶלֶךְ הָעוֹלָם, אֲשֶׁר קִדְּשָׁנוּ
בְּמִצְוֹתָיו וְצִוָּנוּ לְהַדְלִיק נֵר שֶׁל (שַׁבָּת וְשֶׁל) יוֹם טוֹב.

We praise You, *Adonai* our God, Ruler of the Universe, Who makes us holy by Your *mitzvot* and commands us to light the [*Shabbat* and] *Yom Tov* lights.

Baruḥ atah Adonai Eloheinu Meleḥ ha'olam, asher kid'deshanu b'mitzvotav v'tzivanu l'hadlik ner shel (Shabbat v'shel) Yom Tov.

AT THE TABLE

At the dinner table, it is customary to bless the children in the family. The parent(s) place both hands on the head of each child. The traditional blessings are:

For girls:

Y'simeḥ Elohim k'Sarah	יְשִׂימֵךְ אֱלֹהִים כְּשָׂרָה,
Rivkah, Leah v'Raḥel.	רִבְקָה, לֵאָה וְרָחֵל.

May you be like Sarah, Rebecca, Leah and Rachel.

For boys:

Y'simḥa Elohim	יְשִׂמְךָ אֱלֹהִים
k'Efra'im v'ḥiM'nasheh.	כְּאֶפְרַיִם וְכִמְנַשֶּׁה.

May you be like Ephraim and Manasseh.

It is also appropriate for parents to add their own wishes and blessings. Parents conclude blessing all children with the threefold blessing:

Y'vareḥeḥa Adonai v'yish'mereḥa.	יְבָרֶכְךָ יְיָ וְיִשְׁמְרֶךָ.
Ya'er Adonai panav eileḥa viḥuneka.	יָאֵר יְיָ פָּנָיו אֵלֶיךָ וִיחֻנֶּךָּ.
Yisa Adonai panav eileḥa	יִשָּׂא יְיָ פָּנָיו אֵלֶיךָ,
v'yasem l'ḥa Shalom	וְיָשֵׂם לְךָ שָׁלוֹם.

May *Adonai* bless and protect you.

May *Adonai* shine upon you with graciousness.

May *Adonai* look upon you with favor and grant you peace.

If you are concerned about gender stereotyping, one suggestion is to add an additional blessing to the traditional one. For example: (for boys) "...and may God make you as hospitable as Sarah and a judicious leader like Deborah"; (for girls) "...and may God make you as wise as Solomon and a caring leader like Moses." Another idea is to say the traditional blessings for both boys and girls.

A child once described the receiving of a blessing as being "zapped," but "in a good way." What do you think he meant?

BLESSING THE CHILDREN: II

May you be as Henrietta Szold,
raising and building,
that your People
need not suffer
the loneliness of pain.

may you be as Herzl and Ben Yehuda,
stung and raving with visions
for the sake of Israel
and the Jews.

And may our family be together
as Sholom Aleichem and his children,
passing on our stories to each other
with a radiance of joy
and a laugh of love.

SHALOM ALEIḤEM

שָׁלוֹם עֲלֵיכֶם, מַלְאֲכֵי הַשָּׁרֵת, מַלְאֲכֵי עֶלְיוֹן
מִמֶּלֶךְ מַלְכֵי הַמְּלָכִים, הַקָּדוֹשׁ בָּרוּךְ הוּא.
בּוֹאֲכֶם לְשָׁלוֹם, מַלְאֲכֵי הַשָּׁלוֹם, מַלְאֲכֵי עֶלְיוֹן
מִמֶּלֶךְ מַלְכֵי הַמְּלָכִים, הַקָּדוֹשׁ בָּרוּךְ הוּא.
בָּרְכוּנִי לְשָׁלוֹם, מַלְאֲכֵי הַשָּׁלוֹם, מַלְאֲכֵי עֶלְיוֹן
מִמֶּלֶךְ מַלְכֵי הַמְּלָכִים, הַקָּדוֹשׁ בָּרוּךְ הוּא.
צֵאתְכֶם לְשָׁלוֹם, מַלְאֲכֵי הַשָּׁלוֹם, מַלְאֲכֵי עֶלְיוֹן
מִמֶּלֶךְ מַלְכֵי הַמְּלָכִים, הַקָּדוֹשׁ בָּרוּךְ הוּא.

Peace to you, messengers, angels of the Most High, from the Ruler of rulers, the Holy One praised be God.

Come in peace, messengers of peace, angels of the Most High, from the Ruler of rulers, the Holy One praised be God.

Bless me with peace, messengers of peace, angels of the Most High, from the Ruler of rulers, the Holy One praised be God.

Go in peace, messengers of peace, angels of the Most High, from the Ruler of rulers, the Holy One praised be God.

S'fas Emes explains that the opening verse of *Shalom Aleiḥem* is a greeting to the angels who have come to be with us on *Shabbat*, while the closing stanza is a farewell to those angels who have been with us throughout the week and are now leaving.

In Praise of the Spouse

Traditionally, husbands recited a passage from the book of *Proverbs* at the *Shabbat* table to their wives. These verses entitled "A Woman of Valor" can be found in *Proverbs* 31:10-31.

אֵשֶׁת חַיִל מִי יִמְצָא, וְרָחֹק מִפְּנִינִים מִכְרָהּ. בָּטַח בָּהּ לֵב בַּעְלָהּ, וְשָׁלָל לֹא יֶחְסָר. גְּמָלַתְהוּ טוֹב וְלֹא רָע, כֹּל יְמֵי חַיֶּיהָ. כַּפָּהּ פָּרְשָׂה לֶעָנִי, וְיָדֶיהָ שִׁלְּחָה לָאֶבְיוֹן. עוֹז וְהָדָר לְבוּשָׁהּ, וַתִּשְׂחַק לְיוֹם אַחֲרוֹן. פִּיהָ פָּתְחָה בְחָכְמָה, וְתוֹרַת־חֶסֶד עַל לְשׁוֹנָהּ. צוֹפִיָּה הֲלִיכוֹת בֵּיתָהּ, וְלֶחֶם עַצְלוּת לֹא תֹאכֵל. קָמוּ בָנֶיהָ וַיְאַשְּׁרוּהָ, בַּעְלָהּ וַיְהַלְלָהּ. רַבּוֹת בָּנוֹת עָשׂוּ חָיִל, וְאַתְּ עָלִית עַל כֻּלָּנָה. שֶׁקֶר הַחֵן וְהֶבֶל הַיֹּפִי, אִשָּׁה יִרְאַת יְיָ הִיא תִתְהַלָּל. תְּנוּ לָהּ מִפְּרִי יָדֶיהָ, וִיהַלְלוּהָ בַשְּׁעָרִים מַעֲשֶׂיהָ.

EISHET ḤAYIL

A good wife, who can find? She is precious far beyond rubies. Her husband trusts in her and, therefore, lacks nothing. She renders him good and not evil all the days of her life. She opens her hand to the needy and extends her hand to the poor. She is robed in strength and dignity and cheerfully faces the future. She opens her mouth with wisdom; her tongue is guided by kindness. She tends to the affairs of her household and eats not the bread of idleness. Her children come forward and bless her; her husband praises her, "Many women have done superbly, but you surpass them all. Charm is deceit and beauty is vain, but a God-revering woman is much to be praised. Give her honor for the fruit of her hands; wherever people gather, her deeds speak her praise."

Adapted from Proverbs 31

If a wife wishes to respond to *Eishet Ḥayil* with a passage from scripture, it is suggested that she recite selections from Psalm 1 and Psalm 34.

אַשְׁרֵי הָאִישׁ אֲשֶׁר לֹא הָלַךְ בַּעֲצַת רְשָׁעִים
וּבְדֶרֶךְ חַטָּאִים לֹא עָמָד וּבְמוֹשַׁב לֵצִים לֹא יָשָׁב.
כִּי אִם בְּתוֹרַת יְהוָה חֶפְצוֹ וּבְתוֹרָתוֹ יֶהְגֶּה יוֹמָם
וָלָיְלָה. וְהָיָה כְּעֵץ שָׁתוּל עַל־פַּלְגֵי מָיִם אֲשֶׁר פִּרְיוֹ
יִתֵּן בְּעִתּוֹ וְעָלֵהוּ לֹא־יִבּוֹל וְכֹל אֲשֶׁר־יַעֲשֶׂה יַצְלִיחַ.

Happy is the man who does not follow the advice of the world, the path of the sinner or the ways of the scorner. But his desire is in God's Torah which guides him both day and night. He shall be like a tree replanted by streams of water that yields its fruit in due season and whose leaf never withers. And all that he does will succeed.

Psalm 1

מִי הָאִישׁ הֶחָפֵץ חַיִּים, אֹהֵב יָמִים לִרְאוֹת טוֹב. נְצֹר לְשׁוֹנְךָ
מֵרָע וּשְׂפָתֶיךָ מִדַּבֵּר מִרְמָה. סוּר מֵרָע וַעֲשֵׂה טוֹב, בַּקֵּשׁ
שָׁלוֹם וְרָדְפֵהוּ.

Who is the man who wants life, who desires good? He keeps his tongue from evil, and his lips from speaking falsely. He avoids evil and does good; Seeks peace and chases after it.

Psalm 34

SOME THOUGHTS ON *KIDDUSH*

For *Kiddush*, a large cup is filled to overflowing to show that our hearts are overflowing with joy.

Why was wine chosen to announce the holiness of *Shabbat*? When you see or taste a grape, it is a regular fruit but the juice inside can ferment and become wine. This is like a person who looks a certain way on the outside but hidden inside is the part of a person that can make him or her special.

Shabbat is like a weekly awards ceremony. We praise God for the greatness of creation. Imagine presenting God with an award. What would you say in your speech? How does the *Kiddush* praise God?

The world that God creates is not the end of creation. The final act of creation is a special day, *Shabbat* — a day that brings the six days not only to an end (finish), but also to their end (destination).

Shabbat is the day when God and people celebrate the creation of the world. It is a time for God and people to be together.

Each Jew is required to view the Exodus from Egypt as something that personally happened to him or her. By remembering our slavery as we recite *Kiddush*, we each will be committed to working for the freedom of others.

Each week, *Shabbat* reminds us to value and work for freedom. This may be why tyrants throughout the ages prohibited the observance of *Shabbat*.

Shabbat is a sign of the covenant between God and the people Israel. Observing *Shabbat*, even when it is sometimes difficult to do, shows our loyalty to God.

T'khine of *Sora*, *Rivke*, *Rokhil* and *Laye*

"*Riboyne shel Oylem*, Almighty God, You created heaven and earth and all creatures with great compassion within six days and with only ten words. And on the seventh day, which is *Shabbes Koydesh*, You rested from Your work. And You also commanded Your beloved people, *Yisro'el*, that they, too, should rest on *Shabbes koydesh* from all work...."

Shabbes Koydesh = Yiddish for Holy Sabbath

On *Shabbat*, we recite the *Kiddush* blessing for wine:

וַיְהִי עֶרֶב וַיְהִי־בֹקֶר יוֹם הַשִּׁשִּׁי. וַיְכֻלּוּ הַשָּׁמַיִם וְהָאָרֶץ
וְכָל־צְבָאָם. וַיְכַל אֱלֹהִים בַּיּוֹם הַשְּׁבִיעִי מְלַאכְתּוֹ אֲשֶׁר עָשָׂה,
וַיִּשְׁבֹּת בַּיּוֹם הַשְּׁבִיעִי מִכָּל־מְלַאכְתּוֹ אֲשֶׁר עָשָׂה. וַיְבָרֶךְ
אֱלֹהִים אֶת־יוֹם הַשְּׁבִיעִי וַיְקַדֵּשׁ אֹתוֹ, כִּי בוֹ שָׁבַת
מִכָּל־מְלַאכְתּוֹ אֲשֶׁר בָּרָא אֱלֹהִים לַעֲשׂוֹת.

On the sixth day, the heavens and the earth were completed. On the seventh day, God finished the work of creation and rested. God blessed the seventh day and called it holy, because on that day God rested from the work of creation.

Va'y'hi erev va'y'hi voker yom hashishi. Va'y'ḥulu hashamayim v'ha'aretz v'ḥol tz'va'am. Va'y'ḥal Elohim bayom hash'vi'i m'laḥto asher asah. Vayishbot bayom hash'vi'i mikol m'laḥto asher asah. Va'y'vareḥ Elohim et yom hash'vi'i va'y'kadesh oto, ki vo shavat mikol m'laḥto asher bara Elohim la'asot.

סַבְרִי מָרָנָן
בָּרוּךְ אַתָּה יְיָ אֱלֹהֵינוּ מֶלֶךְ הָעוֹלָם, בּוֹרֵא פְּרִי הַגָּפֶן.

We praise You, *Adonai* our God, Ruler of the Universe, Who creates the fruit of the vine.

Savri Maranan
Baruḥ atah Adonai Eloheinu Meleḥ ha'olam borei p'ri hagafen.

בָּרוּךְ אַתָּה יְיָ אֱלֹהֵינוּ מֶלֶךְ הָעוֹלָם, אֲשֶׁר קִדְּשָׁנוּ בְּמִצְוֹתָיו
וְרָצָה בָנוּ, וְשַׁבַּת קָדְשׁוֹ בְּאַהֲבָה וּבְרָצוֹן הִנְחִילָנוּ, זִכָּרוֹן
לְמַעֲשֵׂה בְרֵאשִׁית. כִּי הוּא יוֹם תְּחִלָּה לְמִקְרָאֵי־קֹדֶשׁ, זֵכֶר
לִיצִיאַת מִצְרָיִם. כִּי בָנוּ בָחַרְתָּ וְאוֹתָנוּ קִדַּשְׁתָּ מִכָּל־הָעַמִּים,
וְשַׁבַּת קָדְשְׁךָ בְּאַהֲבָה וּבְרָצוֹן הִנְחַלְתָּנוּ.
בָּרוּךְ אַתָּה יְיָ מְקַדֵּשׁ הַשַּׁבָּת.

We praise You, *Adonai* our God, Ruler of the Universe, Who has made us holy through Your *mitzvot* and lovingly has given us the gift of *Shabbat* as a reminder of creation. It is the first among the holy days reminding us of our going out of Egypt. You have chosen us with the gift of the *Shabbat* to treasure for all generations. We praise You, *Adonai*, Who makes the *Shabbat* holy.

Baruḥ atah Adonai Eloheinu Meleḥ ha'olam, asher kid'deshanu b'mitzvotav v'ratzah vanu, v'Shabbat kod'sho b'ahavah uv'ratzon hinḥilanu, zikaron l'ma'aseh v'reishit. Ki hu yom teḥilah l'mikra'ei kodesh, zeḥer litzi'at mitzrayim. Ki vanu vaḥarta v'otanu kidashta mikol ha'amim, v'Shabbat kodsheḥa b'ahavah uv'ratzon hinḥaltanu. Baruḥ atah Adonai m'kadesh haShabbat.

KIDDUSH L'YOM TOV
FESTIVAL EVENINGS

On *Shabbat*, begin with "*Va'y'hi erev va'y'hi voker*" p.13 and then add the words in brackets.

סַבְרִי מָרָנָן

בָּרוּךְ אַתָּה יְיָ אֱלֹהֵינוּ מֶלֶךְ הָעוֹלָם, בּוֹרֵא פְּרִי הַגָּפֶן.

בָּרוּךְ אַתָּה יְיָ אֱלֹהֵינוּ מֶלֶךְ הָעוֹלָם, אֲשֶׁר בָּחַר בָּנוּ מִכָּל־עָם וְרוֹמְמָנוּ מִכָּל־לָשׁוֹן וְקִדְּשָׁנוּ בְּמִצְוֹתָיו. וַתִּתֶּן־לָנוּ יְיָ אֱלֹהֵינוּ בְּאַהֲבָה (שַׁבָּתוֹת לִמְנוּחָה וּ) מוֹעֲדִים לְשִׂמְחָה, חַגִּים וּזְמַנִּים לְשָׂשׂוֹן, אֶת־יוֹם (הַשַּׁבָּת הַזֶּה וְאֶת יוֹם)

On *Pesaḥ*: חַג הַמַּצּוֹת הַזֶּה, זְמַן חֵרוּתֵנוּ,

On *Shavuot*: חַג הַשָּׁבוּעוֹת הַזֶּה, זְמַן מַתַּן תּוֹרָתֵנוּ,

On *Sukkot*: חַג הַסֻּכּוֹת הַזֶּה, זְמַן שִׂמְחָתֵנוּ,

On *Sh'mini Atzeret* and on *Simḥat Torah*:

הַשְּׁמִינִי, חַג הָעֲצֶרֶת הַזֶּה, זְמַן שִׂמְחָתֵנוּ,

(בְּאַהֲבָה) מִקְרָא קֹדֶשׁ, זֵכֶר לִיצִיאַת מִצְרָיִם. כִּי בָנוּ בָחַרְתָּ וְאוֹתָנוּ קִדַּשְׁתָּ מִכָּל־הָעַמִּים [וְשַׁבָּת] וּמוֹעֲדֵי קָדְשְׁךָ (בְּאַהֲבָה וּבְרָצוֹן) בְּשִׂמְחָה וּבְשָׂשׂוֹן הִנְחַלְתָּנוּ. בָּרוּךְ אַתָּה יְיָ מְקַדֵּשׁ (הַשַּׁבָּת וְ) יִשְׂרָאֵל וְהַזְּמַנִּים.

We praise You, *Adonai* our God, Ruler of the Universe, Who creates the fruit of the vine.

We praise You, *Adonai* our God, Ruler of the Universe, Who has chosen us and made us holy through Your *mitzvot*. You lovingly have given us [Sabbaths for rest and] festivals for joy and holidays for happiness, among them this [*Shabbat* and this] day of the

On *Pesaḥ*: Festival of *Pesaḥ*, season of our freedom
On *Shavuot*: Festival of *Shavuot*, season of the giving of our Torah
On *Sukkot*: Festival of *Sukkot*, season of our joy
On *Sh'mini Atzeret* and on *Simḥat Torah*: Festival of *Sh'mini Atzeret*, season of our joy

a holy time to recall our going out of Egypt. You have chosen us for the gift of [*Shabbat* and] Your holy festivals [lovingly and willingly] in gladness to pass on for generations this gift. Praised are You, *Adonai*, Who makes holy [*Shabbat* and] the people Israel and the festivals.

Savri Maranan
Baruḥ atah Adonai Eloheinu Meleḥ ha'olam borei p'ri hagafen.

Baruḥ atah Adonai Eloheinu Meleḥ ha'olam asher baḥar banu mikol am, v'rom'manu mikol lashon, v'kid'deshanu b'mitzvotav. Vatiten lanu Adonai Eloheinu b'ahavah [Shabbat l'minuḥah,] mo'adim l'simḥa, ḥagim u'zmanim l'sason, [et yom haShabbat hazeh v'] et yom

On *Pesaḥ: ḥag hamatzot hazeh, zman ḥeruteinu*
On *Shavuot: ḥag hashavu'ot hazeh, zman matan torateinu*
On *Sukkot: ḥag hasukkot hazeh, zman simḥateinu*
On *Sh'mini Atzeret* and *Simḥat Torah: hash'mini ḥag ha'atzeret hazeh, zman simḥateinu*

[b'ahava] mikrah kodesh, zeḥer l'yitzi'at Mitzrayim. Ki vanu vaḥarta, v'otanu kidashta mikol ha'amim [v'Shabbat] umo'adei kodsheḥa [b'ahavah uvratzon] b'simḥa u'vsason hinḥaltanu. Baruḥ atah Adonai, m'kadesh [haShabbat v'] Yisrael v'hazmanim.

On Saturday night only, we add *Havdalah*.

בָּרוּךְ אַתָּה יְיָ אֱלֹהֵינוּ מֶלֶךְ הָעוֹלָם, בּוֹרֵא מְאוֹרֵי הָאֵשׁ.
בָּרוּךְ אַתָּה יְיָ אֱלֹהֵינוּ מֶלֶךְ הָעוֹלָם, הַמַּבְדִּיל בֵּין קֹדֶשׁ לְחֹל, בֵּין
אוֹר לְחֹשֶׁךְ, בֵּין יִשְׂרָאֵל לָעַמִּים, בֵּין יוֹם הַשְּׁבִיעִי לְשֵׁשֶׁת יְמֵי
הַמַּעֲשֶׂה. בֵּין קְדֻשַּׁת שַׁבָּת לִקְדֻשַּׁת יוֹם טוֹב הִבְדַּלְתָּ, וְאֶת־יוֹם
הַשְּׁבִיעִי מִשֵּׁשֶׁת יְמֵי הַמַּעֲשֶׂה קִדַּשְׁתָּ, הִבְדַּלְתָּ וְקִדַּשְׁתָּ אֶת־עַמְּךָ
יִשְׂרָאֵל בִּקְדֻשָּׁתֶךָ. בָּרוּךְ אַתָּה יְיָ הַמַּבְדִּיל בֵּין קֹדֶשׁ לְקֹדֶשׁ.

Praised are You, *Adonai* our God, Ruler of the Universe, Who makes a distinction between the holy and the ordinary, light and darkness, the uniqueness of the Jewish people and the uniqueness of other peoples, the seventh day and the six days for work. You have made a distinction between the holiness of *Shabbat* and the holiness of the holidays. Praised are You, *Adonai*, Who makes a distinction between holy times.

Baruḥ atah Adonai Eloheinu Meleḥ ha'olam, borei m'orei ha'eish.
Baruḥ atah Adonai Eloheinu Meleḥ ha'olam, hamavdil bein kodesh l'ḥol, bein or l'ḥosheh, bein Yisrael l'amim, bein yom hashvi'i l'sheshet y'mei hama'aseh, bein kedushat Shabbat l'kedushat yom tov hivdalta, v'et yom hashvi'i mi'sheshet y'mei hama'aseh kidashta, hivdalta v'kidashta et am'ḥa yisrael bikdushateḥa. Baruḥ atah Adonai, hamavdil bein kodesh l'kodesh.

On the first two nights of *Sukkot*, if we are in a *sukkah*, we say the blessing for being in the *sukkah* at this time.

בָּרוּךְ אַתָּה יְיָ אֱלֹהֵינוּ מֶלֶךְ הָעוֹלָם, אֲשֶׁר קִדְּשָׁנוּ בְּמִצְוֹתָיו
וְצִוָּנוּ לֵישֵׁב בַּסֻּכָּה.

We praise You, *Adonai* our God, Ruler of the Universe, Who has made us holy by Your *mitzvot* and commands us to be in the *sukkah*.

Baruḥ atah Adonai, Eloheinu Meleḥ ha'olam, asher kid'deshanu b'mitzvotav v'tzvivanu leishev basukkah.

Omit on the last two nights of *Pesaḥ*.

בָּרוּךְ אַתָּה יְיָ אֱלֹהֵינוּ מֶלֶךְ הָעוֹלָם, שֶׁהֶחֱיָנוּ וְקִיְּמָנוּ
וְהִגִּיעָנוּ לַזְּמַן הַזֶּה.

We praise You, *Adonai* our God, Ruler of the Universe, Who has kept us alive and well so that we can celebrate this special time.

Baruḥ Atah Adonai Eloheinu Meleḥ ha'olam, sheheḥeyanu v'ki'yi'manu, v'higi'anu la'zman hazeh.

We wash our hands for the meal and say this blessing:

בָּרוּךְ אַתָּה יְיָ אֱלֹהֵינוּ מֶלֶךְ הָעוֹלָם, אֲשֶׁר קִדְּשָׁנוּ בְּמִצְוֹתָיו
וְצִוָּנוּ עַל נְטִילַת יָדָיִם.

We praise You, *Adonai* our God, Ruler of the Universe, Who has made us holy by Your *mitzvot* and commands us to wash our hands.

Baruḥ atah Adonai Eloheinu Meleḥ ha'olam asher kid'deshanu b'mitzvotav v'tzivanu al n'tilat yadayim.

The *Motzi* (blessing for bread) is recited over two *ḥallot*:

בָּרוּךְ אַתָּה יְיָ אֱלֹהֵינוּ מֶלֶךְ הָעוֹלָם, הַמּוֹצִיא לֶחֶם מִן הָאָרֶץ.

We praise You, *Adonai* our God, Ruler of the Universe, Who brings forth bread from the earth.

Baruḥ atah Adonai, Eloheinu Meleḥ ha'olam hamotzi leḥem min ha'aretz.

SOME THOUGHTS ON *SHABBAT* MEALS

During the time the Jewish people wandered in the desert before entering Israel (The Promised Land), they were sent manna which miraculously fell from the sky each day. On Friday, a double portion of manna fell. This enabled the people to have enough for all of *Shabbat*, without having to gather food. This is why we put out two loaves of *ḥallah* at our *Shabbat* table.

Some say that we cover the *ḥallah* so as not to embarrass it since we say the *Kiddush* blessing first. This teaches us that if we wouldn't shame the *ḥallah*, surely we should not shame other people.

When we say the *motzi*, we praise God for the bread that comes from the ground. Yet it is people who must take the grain, make it into flour and bake the bread. By using the resources God gives us, we become partners with God. Can you think of other gifts God gives us that we use to sustain or enhance our lives?

All *Shabbat* meals should be eaten in a festive mood. The special foods prepared for these meals should be eaten slowly so we can truly enjoy each meal. There should be no discussion of business or school "work"—grades, tests or assignments. However, it is a time to talk about things learned during the week.

In *Sefer Ḥasidim*, it is written: "Tell nothing (on *Shabbat*) which will draw tears."

It was during the Middle Ages that the custom of singing *z'mirot* (table songs) began. This custom is based on Psalm 92:1-2 — "A psalm, a song, for the Sabbath day. It is good to thank You, *Adonai*, and to sing (*l'zamer*) praises to Your exalted name." *Shabbat* meals are a time to sing. The meal should conclude with *Birkat haMazon* (the Blessings After the Meal).

קַבָּלַת שַׁבָּת וְעַרְבִית

Shabbat Evening Service

KABBALAT SHABBAT

In Palestine of the third century, we learn from the *Talmud* that Rabbi Hanina would put on his finest clothes and at sunset on *erev Shabbat* would say "Come, let us go out to welcome the Sabbath Queen." Rabbi Yannai, a colleague of his, would say, "Come, oh Bride! Come, oh Bride!"

In the sixteenth century, the Jews of *Tzefat* left the synagogue and marched to the fields at the outskirts of the city and there sang psalms in honor of this "guest" who each week was entering their lives. This was the beginning of *Kabbalat Shabbat* — a service for welcoming the *Shabbat*.

***K**abbalat Shabbat* consists of six psalms, one for each weekday and then the *L'ḥa Dodi*, a prayer-poem which welcomes *Shabbat*. This is followed by Psalm 92, "A Psalm for the Sabbath Day." These psalms, written 2,500-3,000 years ago, still move us with their powerful words and images. The psalms speak of God as both the Creator and Ruler of the universe. They also assure us that God's presence is always with us.

Selections of Psalms before *L'ḥa Dodi*

Psalm 95

לְכוּ נְרַנְּנָה לַיְיָ, נָרִיעָה לְצוּר יִשְׁעֵנוּ. נְקַדְּמָה פָנָיו בְּתוֹדָה, בִּזְמִרוֹת נָרִיעַ לוֹ.

Let us sing to *Adonai* and rejoice in the Rock of our strength, greeting the Holy One with psalms of praise and thanks.

Psalm 96

יִשְׂמְחוּ הַשָּׁמַיִם וְתָגֵל הָאָרֶץ, יִרְעַם הַיָּם וּמְלֹאוֹ.

Let the heavens rejoice; let the earth be glad. Let the sea and all in it roar praise.

Psalm 97

יְיָ מָלָךְ תָּגֵל הָאָרֶץ, יִשְׂמְחוּ אִיִּים רַבִּים: עָנָן וַעֲרָפֶל סְבִיבָיו, צֶדֶק וּמִשְׁפָּט מְכוֹן כִּסְאוֹ.

Adonai rules; let the whole earth and even the small islands be glad. Cloud and darkness surround God; righteousness and justice are the foundation of God's throne.

Psalm 98

רָאוּ כָל־אַפְסֵי אָרֶץ אֵת יְשׁוּעַת אֱלֹהֵינוּ. הָרִיעוּ לַיְיָ כָּל־הָאָרֶץ, פִּצְחוּ וְרַנְּנוּ וְזַמֵּרוּ.

The whole world has seen the helping power of God. Therefore, let all the inhabitants of the earth shout for joy and break into song.

Psalm 99

רוֹמְמוּ יְיָ אֱלֹהֵינוּ
וְהִשְׁתַּחֲווּ לְהַר קָדְשׁוֹ,
כִּי קָדוֹשׁ יְיָ אֱלֹהֵינוּ.

Praise *Adonai*, our God, and worship at God's holy mountain, for *Adonai* our God is holy.

Psalm 29

יְיָ לַמַּבּוּל יָשָׁב, וַיֵּשֶׁב יְיָ מֶלֶךְ לְעוֹלָם.
יְיָ עֹז לְעַמּוֹ יִתֵּן, יְיָ יְבָרֵךְ אֶת־עַמּוֹ בַשָּׁלוֹם.

At the great Flood, *Adonai* ruled. *Adonai* will remain our Ruler forever. *Adonai* will give strength to the people and bless them with peace.

L'ḤA DODI

In "*L'ḥa Dodi*" it says: "*Shamor* and *Zaḥor* in a single command." This points to the two versions of the fourth commandment. *Exodus* 20:8-11 instructs us: "Remember the Sabbath day." *Deuteronomy* 5:12-15 tells us: "Observe the Sabbath day." The purpose of both remembering and observing is to make *Shabbat* "*kodesh*" (holy).

The Torah tells us to "Remember the *Shabbat*." It appears, though, that the Hebrews already had a seven-day week, unlike many ancient peoples who had a ten-day week. The commandment, however, tells us why we should do it. We are to imitate God who rested on the seventh day. Being told that God rested, teaches us that God was not controlled by other forces. Rest is a sign of freedom. What does our rest mean?

Who wrote, "*L'ḥa Dodi* "? The author is Shlomo HaLevi Alkabetz who lived in *Tzefat* in the 16th century. We know he composed *L'ḥa Dodi* because he reveals his name, *Shlomo HaLevi*, in the form of an acrostic. He spells out his name with the beginning letter of each verse of the poem.

During the next week, try to write a psalm or poem using the letters of your own name.

1, 2, 3, 5
LAST
over 26

L'ḥa dod	לְכָה דוֹדִי לִקְרַאת כַּלָּה,
p'nei Sh	פְּנֵי שַׁבָּת נְקַבְּלָה.
Shamor	שָׁמוֹר וְזָכוֹר בְּדִבּוּר אֶחָד
hishmi-anu el ha'meyuḥad.	הִשְׁמִיעָנוּ אֵל הַמְיֻחָד.
Adonai eḥad u'sh'mo eḥad,	יְיָ אֶחָד וּשְׁמוֹ אֶחָד
L'sheim u'letiferet u'lit'hilah.	לְשֵׁם וּלְתִפְאֶרֶת וְלִתְהִלָּה.
L'ḥa dodi...	לְכָה דוֹדִי לִקְרַאת כַּלָּה, פְּנֵי שַׁבָּת נְקַבְּלָה.
Likrat Shabbat l'ḥu v'nelḥa,	לִקְרַאת שַׁבָּת לְכוּ וְנֵלְכָה
Ki hi m'kor hab'raḥah.	כִּי הִיא מְקוֹר הַבְּרָכָה.
Meirosh mikedem n'suḥah,	מֵרֹאשׁ מִקֶּדֶם נְסוּכָה
Sof ma'aseh b'maḥshavah t'ḥilah.	סוֹף מַעֲשֶׂה בְּמַחֲשָׁבָה תְּחִלָּה.
L'ḥa dodi...	לְכָה דוֹדִי לִקְרַאת כַּלָּה, פְּנֵי שַׁבָּת נְקַבְּלָה.
Mikdash Meleḥ ir m'luḥah	מִקְדַּשׁ מֶלֶךְ עִיר מְלוּכָה,
kumi tse'i mitoḥ hahafeiḥa	קוּמִי צְאִי מִתּוֹךְ הַהֲפֵכָה.
rav laḥ shevet b'emek habaḥah	רַב לָךְ שֶׁבֶת בְּעֵמֶק הַבָּכָא,
ve'hu yaḥamol alayiḥ ḥemlah	וְהוּא יַחֲמוֹל עָלַיִךְ חֶמְלָה.
L'ḥa dodi...	לְכָה דוֹדִי לִקְרַאת כַּלָּה, פְּנֵי שַׁבָּת נְקַבְּלָה.

הִתְעוֹרְרִי הִתְעוֹרְרִי	*Hit'or'ri, hit'or'ri*
כִּי בָא אוֹרֵךְ קוּמִי אוֹרִי.	*Ki va oreḥ, kumi, ori.*
עוּרִי עוּרִי שִׁיר דַּבֵּרִי,	*Uri, uri, shir dabeiri*
כְּבוֹד יְיָ עָלַיִךְ נִגְלָה.	*K'vod Adonai alayiḥ niglah.*
לְכָה דוֹדִי לִקְרַאת כַּלָּה, פְּנֵי שַׁבָּת נְקַבְּלָה.	*L'ḥa dodi...*

(We rise)

בּוֹאִי בְשָׁלוֹם עֲטֶרֶת בַּעְלָהּ,	*Bo'i v'shalom, ateret ba'alah*
גַּם בְּשִׂמְחָה וּבְצָהֳלָה,	*gam b'simḥa uv'tzohalah.*
תּוֹךְ אֱמוּנֵי עַם סְגֻלָּה,	*Toḥ emunei, am s'gula,*
בּוֹאִי כַלָּה, בּוֹאִי כַלָּה.	*Bo'i ḥala, bo'i ḥala!*
לְכָה דוֹדִי לִקְרַאת כַּלָּה, פְּנֵי שַׁבָּת נְקַבְּלָה.	*L'ḥa dodi...*

L'ḥa Dodi
(Selected verses)

Chorus: Come, dear friend.
Let us greet the bride.
Let us welcome the *Shabbat*.

"Keep" and "remember" in a single command,
The one the Holy One made us hear.
Adonai is One, the Holy name, One.
And to the One belongs glory and praise.

Let us go and greet *Shabbat*
For she is the source of blessing.
From the very beginning it was to be:
Last in creation, first in God's plan.

O holy city, O royal place,
Rise up from disgrace.
No longer sit in a valley of tears,
Now God your voice will hear!

Awake, awake, awaken yourself
for your light has come!
Arise and sing, for the Eternal's
Glory is shown to you.

Come in peace, crown of her mate.
Enter with rejoicing and gladness
among the faithful ones.
Come O bride, O *Shabbat* Queen.

Chorus:

מִזְמוֹר שִׁיר לְיוֹם הַשַּׁבָּת.
טוֹב לְהֹדוֹת לַייָ, וּלְזַמֵּר לְשִׁמְךָ עֶלְיוֹן.
לְהַגִּיד בַּבֹּקֶר חַסְדֶּךָ, וֶאֱמוּנָתְךָ בַּלֵּילוֹת.
עֲלֵי עָשׂוֹר וַעֲלֵי נָבֶל, עֲלֵי הִגָּיוֹן בְּכִנּוֹר.
כִּי שִׂמַּחְתַּנִי יְיָ בְּפָעֳלֶךָ, בְּמַעֲשֵׂי יָדֶיךָ אֲרַנֵּ
מַה גָּדְלוּ מַעֲשֶׂיךָ יְיָ, מְאֹד עָמְקוּ מַחְשְׁבֹתֶי
אִישׁ בַּעַר לֹא יֵדָע, וּכְסִיל לֹא יָבִין אֶת־זֹא
צַדִּיק כַּתָּמָר יִפְרָח, כְּאֶרֶז בַּלְּבָנוֹן יִשְׂגֶּה.
שְׁתוּלִים בְּבֵית יְיָ, בְּחַצְרוֹת אֱלֹהֵינוּ יַפְרִיחוּ.
עוֹד יְנוּבוּן בְּשֵׂיבָה, דְּשֵׁנִים וְרַעֲנַנִּים יִהְיוּ.
לְהַגִּיד כִּי יָשָׁר יְיָ, צוּרִי וְלֹא עַוְלָתָה בּוֹ.

(A Selection)

Psalm 92

It is good to give thanks to *Adonai*
And to sing praises to Your supreme name,

Telling of Your kindness in the morning
And Your faithfulness each night,

To the music of lyre and lute
And with melodies on the harp.

You raise me with Your deeds.
I sing for joy at the work of Your hands.

How incredible are Your acts, *Adonai*!
How incredible are Your thoughts!

This the foolish person cannot know,
Nor the empty-headed one understand.

For though the wicked multiply like weeds
And those who do evil thrive,

It is so in the end,
they'll be destroyed forever.

But You, *Adonai*, are always supreme.
See, Your enemies are lost and all evil ones will be scattered.

You raise my power like that of a strong ox;
I am anointed with fresh oil.

My eyes shall gaze in victory over my enemies.
My ears shall hear of their doom.

The righteous shall thrive like the palm tree
And grow mighty like a cedar tree from Lebanon.

Planted in the house of *Adonai*,
They shall thrive and bear fruit.

Even in old age they shall reproduce
And be fresh and vigorous.

Ready to tell that *Adonai* is just,
My Rock, Who is without fault.

Ma'ariv

THE *SHEMA* AND ITS BLESSINGS

We rise.

Leader:

בָּרְכוּ אֶת־יְיָ הַמְבֹרָךְ.

Let us praise.

Barḥu et Adonai ham'voraḥ

Congregation then Leader:

בָּרוּךְ יְיָ הַמְבֹרָךְ לְעוֹלָם וָעֶד.

Praised are You, *Adonai*, the Source of all blessings, forever and ever.

Baruḥ Adonai ham'voraḥ l'olam va'ed.

We are seated.

For *Kabbalat Shabbat*

Praised be You, Eternal One our God, Ruler of the Universe,
Who with Your word brings on the evening twilight....
rolling away the light before the darkness.

The trees are silent, and the earth is still,
the sun makes no sound; no voice has the hill.

The earth rolls in silence, the stars pierce the sky,
the moon will not whisper, the clouds cannot sigh.

And though God has bid them, we have not heard,
this night has fallen without sound of God's word.

Yet Your law sends the stars across the night,
the earth turns surely from darkness to light.

How then shall we praise God who silently gives?
Each silently praises who righteously lives.

Our stillness is praise when our ears have heard
the command of love: God's unspoken word.

בָּרוּךְ אַתָּה יְיָ אֱלֹהֵינוּ מֶלֶךְ הָעוֹלָם, אֲשֶׁר בִּדְבָרוֹ מַעֲרִיב
עֲרָבִים. בְּחָכְמָה פּוֹתֵחַ שְׁעָרִים, וּבִתְבוּנָה מְשַׁנֶּה עִתִּים
וּמַחֲלִיף אֶת־הַזְּמַנִּים, וּמְסַדֵּר אֶת־הַכּוֹכָבִים בְּמִשְׁמְרוֹתֵיהֶם
בָּרָקִיעַ כִּרְצוֹנוֹ. בּוֹרֵא יוֹם וָלָיְלָה, גּוֹלֵל אוֹר מִפְּנֵי חֹשֶׁךְ
וְחֹשֶׁךְ מִפְּנֵי אוֹר, וּמַעֲבִיר יוֹם וּמֵבִיא לָיְלָה, וּמַבְדִּיל בֵּין
יוֹם וּבֵין לָיְלָה, יְיָ צְבָאוֹת שְׁמוֹ. אֵל חַי וְקַיָּם, תָּמִיד יִמְלֹךְ
עָלֵינוּ לְעוֹלָם וָעֶד. בָּרוּךְ אַתָּה יְיָ הַמַּעֲרִיב עֲרָבִים.

TO 34

We pra[illegible] *Adonai* our God, Ruler of the Universe, Whose word brings [illegible] the gates of dawn with wisdom and with u[illegible] time, cause the seasons to change and a[illegible] all according to Your will. Creator of da[illegible] away from darkness and darkness away [illegible] ay to pass and night to come, dividing d[illegible] ot, Ruler of the heavens is Your name. Eternal God, [illegible] s now and always. Praised are You, *Adonai*, Who makes the evenings fall.

THE NEED FOR ORDER

What problems would we have if the sun did not rise and set regularly or the seasons did not come in order? What if the stars changed their place each night or fish swam in the air? How are we dependent on the regularity of the universe?

PRAYERS WITH PROBLEMS

What's the problem with the prayers below?

Dear God...

Please don't have the sun rise tomorrow.

Please make sure that my friend Sonny gets a bad grade on his test.

My mom's pregnant. Please let her have a girl.

Please give me an A on my math test even if I didn't have time to study.

AN EVENING PRAYER FOR *SHABBAT*

We praise You, *Adonai* our God, Ruler of the Universe,
Who completed creation on the seventh day and named it
"Holy *Shabbat*," lasting from evening to evening.

You gave it as rest and holiness to the Jewish people.

Creator of day and night, You cause light to give way before darkness and darkness before light.

The One who brings day and night, Who separates between day and night, You are known as *Adonai Tzva'ot*.

Eternal God, You will rule over us forever.
Praised are You, *Adonai*, who brings each evening.

This special *Shabbat* version of the Evening Prayer used by Italian Jews has continued to be said by some Jews for well over a thousand years.

בָּרוּךְ אַתָּה יְיָ אֱלֹהֵינוּ מֶלֶךְ הָעוֹלָם אֲשֶׁר כִּלָּה מַעֲשָׂיו
בַּיּוֹם הַשְּׁבִיעִי וַיִּקְרָאֵהוּ שַׁבָּת קֹדֶשׁ מֵעֶרֶב וְעַד עֶרֶב וּנְתָנוֹ
מְנוּחָה לְעַמּוֹ יִשְׂרָאֵל בִּקְדוּשָּׁתוֹ. בּוֹרֵא יוֹמָם וָלַיְלָה גּוֹלֵל
אוֹר מִפְּנֵי חֹשֶׁךְ וְחֹשֶׁךְ מִפְּנֵי אוֹר הַמַּעֲבִיר יוֹם וּמֵבִיא
לַיְלָה הַמַּבְדִּיל בֵּין יוֹם וּבֵין לַיְלָה יְיָ צְבָאוֹת שְׁמוֹ וּשְׁמוֹ
אֵל חַי וְקַיָּם תָּמִיד הוּא יִמְלוֹךְ עָלֵינוּ לְעוֹלָם וָעֶד.
בָּרוּךְ אַתָּה יְיָ הַמַּעֲרִיב עֲרָבִים.

אַהֲבַת עוֹלָם בֵּית יִשְׂרָאֵל עַמְּךָ אָהָבְתָּ. תּוֹרָה וּמִצְוֹת חֻקִּים
וּמִשְׁפָּטִים אוֹתָנוּ לִמַּדְתָּ. עַל כֵּן יְיָ אֱלֹהֵינוּ בְּשָׁכְבֵנוּ וּבְקוּמֵנוּ
נָשִׂיחַ בְּחֻקֶּיךָ, וְנִשְׂמַח בְּדִבְרֵי תוֹרָתֶךָ וּבְמִצְוֹתֶיךָ לְעוֹלָם וָעֶד.
כִּי הֵם חַיֵּינוּ וְאֹרֶךְ יָמֵינוּ וּבָהֶם נֶהְגֶּה יוֹמָם וָלָיְלָה. וְאַהֲבָתְךָ
אַל תָּסִיר מִמֶּנּוּ לְעוֹלָמִים. בָּרוּךְ אַתָּה יְיָ אוֹהֵב עַמּוֹ יִשְׂרָאֵל.

With unending love You have loved Israel, Your people, teaching us Torah, commandments, laws and judgments. Therefore, *Adonai* our God, before we go to sleep and when we arise, we will concentrate on Your teachings. We will forever rejoice in Your commandments, for they are our life and give meaning to our days. May You never take away Your love from us. Praised are You, *Adonai*, who loves the people Israel.

How many times can you find the root, "אהב," in the prayer *Ahavat Olam*?

God has shown *ahavah* (love) for the Jewish people by giving us the Torah. By following the Torah, we show God that this gift is precious to us.

Ahavat olam beit Yisrael amḥa ahavta
Torah u'mitzvot, ḥukim u'mishpatim
otanu limadta. Al kein, Adonai Eloheinu
b'shoḥveinu uv'kumeinu nasi'aḥ b'ḥukeḥa
v'nismaḥ b'divrei torateḥa
uv'mitzvoteḥa l'olam va'ed.
Ki heim ḥayenu v'oreḥ yameinu
u'vahem neh'geh yomam valailah.
V'a'havat'ḥa al tasir mimenu l'olamim.
Baruḥ ata Adonai, ohev amo Yisrael.

שְׁמַע יִשְׂרָאֵל יְהוָה אֱלֹהֵינוּ יְהוָה ׀ אֶחָד׃

Hear O Israel:
Adonai our God, *Adonai* is ONE.
Shema Yisrael, Adonai Eloheinu, Adonai Eḥad

In a whisper:

בָּרוּךְ שֵׁם כְּבוֹד מַלְכוּתוֹ לְעוֹלָם וָעֶד.

We praise God Whose glorious presence is with us now and forever.
Baruḥ shem k'vod malḥuto l'olam va'ed

וְאָהַבְתָּ אֵת יְהוָה אֱלֹהֶיךָ בְּכָל־לְבָבְךָ וּבְכָל־נַפְשְׁךָ
וּבְכָל־מְאֹדֶךָ׃ וְהָיוּ הַדְּבָרִים הָאֵלֶּה אֲשֶׁר אָנֹכִי מְצַוְּךָ הַיּוֹם
עַל־לְבָבֶךָ׃ וְשִׁנַּנְתָּם לְבָנֶיךָ וְדִבַּרְתָּ בָּם בְּשִׁבְתְּךָ בְּבֵיתֶךָ
וּבְלֶכְתְּךָ בַדֶּרֶךְ וּבְשָׁכְבְּךָ וּבְקוּמֶךָ׃ וּקְשַׁרְתָּם לְאוֹת
עַל־יָדֶךָ וְהָיוּ לְטֹטָפֹת בֵּין עֵינֶיךָ׃ וּכְתַבְתָּם עַל־מְזֻזוֹת
בֵּיתֶךָ וּבִשְׁעָרֶיךָ׃

+36, 37

You shall l… all your heart, with all your soul and w… …ese words which I command you today, … …art. Teach them to your children. Spe… …t home and when you are away. Repeat them when you lie down at night and when you rise up in the morning. Bind them as a sign upon your arm and place them as a reminder between your eyes. Write them on the doorposts of your houses and on your gates.

וְהָיָ֗ה אִם־שָׁמֹ֤עַ תִּשְׁמְעוּ֙ אֶל־מִצְוֺתַ֔י אֲשֶׁ֧ר אָנֹכִ֛י מְצַוֶּ֥ה אֶתְכֶ֖ם

הַיּ֑וֹם לְאַהֲבָ֞ה אֶת־יְהֹוָ֤ה אֱלֹֽהֵיכֶם֙ וּלְעָבְד֔וֹ בְּכָל־לְבַבְכֶ֖ם

וּבְכָל־נַפְשְׁכֶֽם: וְנָתַתִּ֧י מְטַֽר־אַרְצְכֶ֛ם בְּעִתּ֖וֹ יוֹרֶ֣ה וּמַלְק֑וֹשׁ

וְאָסַפְתָּ֣ דְגָנֶ֔ךָ וְתִירֹשְׁךָ֖ וְיִצְהָרֶֽךָ: וְנָתַתִּ֛י עֵ֥שֶׂב בְּשָׂדְךָ֖ לִבְהֶמְתֶּ֑ךָ

וְאָכַלְתָּ֖ וְשָׂבָֽעְתָּ: הִשָּֽׁמְר֣וּ לָכֶ֔ם פֶּן־יִפְתֶּ֖ה לְבַבְכֶ֑ם וְסַרְתֶּ֗ם

וַעֲבַדְתֶּם֙ אֱלֹהִ֣ים אֲחֵרִ֔ים וְהִשְׁתַּחֲוִיתֶ֖ם לָהֶֽם: וְחָרָ֨ה אַף־יְהֹוָ֜ה

בָּכֶ֗ם וְעָצַ֤ר אֶת־הַשָּׁמַ֙יִם֙ וְלֹֽא־יִהְיֶ֣ה מָטָ֔ר וְהָ֣אֲדָמָ֔ה לֹ֥א תִתֵּ֖ן

אֶת־יְבוּלָ֑הּ וַאֲבַדְתֶּ֣ם מְהֵרָ֗ה מֵעַל֙ הָאָ֣רֶץ הַטֹּבָ֔ה אֲשֶׁ֥ר יְהֹוָ֖ה

נֹתֵ֣ן לָכֶֽם: וְשַׂמְתֶּם֙ אֶת־דְּבָרַ֣י אֵ֔לֶּה עַל־לְבַבְכֶ֖ם וְעַֽל־נַפְשְׁכֶ֑ם

וּקְשַׁרְתֶּ֨ם אֹתָ֤ם לְאוֹת֙ עַל־יֶדְכֶ֔ם וְהָי֥וּ לְטוֹטָפֹ֖ת בֵּ֥ין עֵינֵיכֶֽם:

וְלִמַּדְתֶּ֥ם אֹתָ֛ם אֶת־בְּנֵיכֶ֖ם לְדַבֵּ֣ר בָּ֑ם בְּשִׁבְתְּךָ֤ בְּבֵיתֶ֙ךָ֙

וּבְלֶכְתְּךָ֣ בַדֶּ֔רֶךְ וּֽבְשָׁכְבְּךָ֖ וּבְקוּמֶֽךָ: וּכְתַבְתָּ֛ם עַל־מְזוּז֥וֹת

בֵּיתֶ֖ךָ וּבִשְׁעָרֶֽיךָ: לְמַ֨עַן יִרְבּ֤וּ יְמֵיכֶם֙ וִימֵ֣י בְנֵיכֶ֔ם עַ֚ל הָֽאֲדָמָ֔ה

אֲשֶׁ֨ר נִשְׁבַּ֧ע יְהֹוָ֛ה לַאֲבֹתֵיכֶ֖ם לָתֵ֣ת לָהֶ֑ם כִּימֵ֥י הַשָּׁמַ֖יִם

עַל־הָאָֽרֶץ:

If you sincerely follow My commandments, then I will favor your land with rain at the proper season. Then you will have a full harvest of grain, wine and oil and there will be grass in the fields for your cattle. You will eat and be satisfied. But if you turn from God's ways, there will be no rain and the earth will not bring forth its produce. In the end, you will even disappear from the good land which *Adonai* has given you. Therefore, place these words of Mine in your heart and in your soul. Bind them as a sign upon your arm and as a reminder between your eyes. Teach them to your children. Speak of them when you are at home and when you are away. Repeat them when you lie down at night and when you rise up in the morning. Write them on the doorposts of your houses and on your gates. They will make your days and the days of your descendants fuller when you live in the land that God promised your ancestors.

וַיֹּאמֶר יְהֹוָה אֶל־מֹשֶׁה לֵּאמֹר: דַּבֵּר אֶל־בְּנֵי יִשְׂרָאֵל
וְאָמַרְתָּ אֲלֵהֶם וְעָשׂוּ לָהֶם צִיצִת עַל־כַּנְפֵי בִגְדֵיהֶם
לְדֹרֹתָם וְנָתְנוּ עַל־צִיצִת הַכָּנָף פְּתִיל תְּכֵלֶת: וְהָיָה לָכֶם
לְצִיצִת וּרְאִיתֶם אֹתוֹ וּזְכַרְתֶּם אֶת־כָּל־מִצְוֹת יְהֹוָה וַעֲשִׂיתֶם
אֹתָם וְלֹא תָתוּרוּ אַחֲרֵי לְבַבְכֶם וְאַחֲרֵי עֵינֵיכֶם אֲשֶׁר־אַתֶּם
זֹנִים אַחֲרֵיהֶם: לְמַעַן תִּזְכְּרוּ וַעֲשִׂיתֶם אֶת־כָּל־מִצְוֹתָי
וִהְיִיתֶם קְדֹשִׁים לֵאלֹהֵיכֶם: אֲנִי יְהֹוָה אֱלֹהֵיכֶם אֲשֶׁר
הוֹצֵאתִי אֶתְכֶם מֵאֶרֶץ מִצְרַיִם לִהְיוֹת לָכֶם לֵאלֹהִים
אֲנִי יְהֹוָה אֱלֹהֵיכֶם:

And *Adonai* spoke to Moses: Speak to the Israelites and tell them
to put fringes on the corners of their garments and bind a thread of
blue in the fringe of each corner. When you look at these fringes
you will be reminded of all the commandments of God and you will
do them and not be tempted to go in other directions. Then you
will be dedicated and do all my *mitzvot* and you will be holy to your
God. I am *Adonai*, your God, who brought you out of *Mitzrayim* to
be your God. I, *Adonai*, am your God.

Leader:

יְהֹוָה אֱלֹהֵיכֶם אֱמֶת.

Adonai, your God, is Truth.

וְרָאוּ בָנָיו גְּבוּרָתוֹ, שִׁבְּחוּ וְהוֹדוּ לִשְׁמוֹ. וּמַלְכוּתוֹ בְּרָצוֹן קִבְּלוּ עֲלֵיהֶם. מֹשֶׁה וּבְנֵי יִשְׂרָאֵל לְךָ עָנוּ שִׁירָה בְּשִׂמְחָה רַבָּה, וְאָמְרוּ כֻלָּם:

מִי כָמֹכָה בָּאֵלִם יְיָ, מִי כָּמֹכָה נֶאְדָּר בַּקֹּדֶשׁ, נוֹרָא תְהִלֹּת עֹשֵׂה פֶלֶא.

Seeing God's might before them, the people Israel sang praises and thanks and willingly accepted God's rule. Then Moses and all the people burst into joyous song and all said together as one:

"Who is like You, *Adonai*,
among the mighty?
Who is like You, *Adonai*,
glorious in holiness,
awesome in splendor,
the Maker of Miracles?"

מַלְכוּתְךָ רָאוּ בָנֶיךָ, בּוֹקֵעַ יָם לִפְנֵי מֹשֶׁה. זֶה אֵלִי עָנוּ וְאָמְרוּ: יְיָ יִמְלֹךְ לְעֹלָם וָעֶד.
וְנֶאֱמַר: כִּי פָדָה יְיָ אֶת־יַעֲקֹב, וּגְאָלוֹ מִיַּד חָזָק מִמֶּנּוּ. בָּרוּךְ אַתָּה יְיָ גָּאַל יִשְׂרָאֵל.

Your children saw Your majesty when You parted the sea before Moses. "This is my God!" they shouted, and then said: "*Adonai* shall rule forever and ever."
And it is said: "*Adonai* has saved Jacob from a strong, powerful people. Praised are You, *Adonai*, Who has helped the people Israel.

BY THE SHORES

(Based on Exodus 15:20)

"Then Miriam the prophetess, Aaron's sister, took a timbrel in her hand, and all the women went out after her in dance with timbrels."

By the shores, by the shores,
of the Red, Red Sea,
By the shores of the Red, Red Sea;
The light of day lit up the night
The children, they were free.

Chorus:
And Miriam took her timbrel out and all the women danced.
vatikaḥ Miriam han'vi'ah et hatof b'yadah vateitzena kol hanashim aḥareha!

They danced, they danced
Oh, how they danced
They danced the night away
Clapped their hands and stamped their feet
With voices loud they praised.

They danced with joy
They danced with grace
They danced on nimble feet
Kicked up their heels, threw back their heads
Hypnotic with the beat.

Chorus

They danced so hard, they danced so fast;
They danced with movement strong
Laughed and cried, brought out alive
They danced until the dawn.

• • •

Chorus

As they watched, and they clapped, they began to sway
Drawn to ride the wave
and all our brothers began to dance
They dance with us today!

They danced, we dance
Sheḥinah dance
They danced the night away
And all the women began to sing
They're singing 'til this day!

Chorus

הַשְׁכִּיבֵנוּ יְיָ אֱלֹהֵינוּ לְשָׁלוֹם, וְהַעֲמִידֵנוּ מַלְכֵּנוּ לְחַיִּים, וּפְרֹשׂ
עָלֵינוּ סֻכַּת שְׁלוֹמֶךָ, וְתַקְּנֵנוּ בְּעֵצָה טוֹבָה מִלְּפָנֶיךָ, וְהוֹשִׁיעֵנוּ
לְמַעַן שְׁמֶךָ. וְהָגֵן בַּעֲדֵנוּ וְהָסֵר מֵעָלֵינוּ אוֹיֵב דֶּבֶר וְחֶרֶב וְרָעָב
וְיָגוֹן, וְהָסֵר שָׂטָן מִלְּפָנֵינוּ וּמֵאַחֲרֵינוּ. וּבְצֵל כְּנָפֶיךָ תַּסְתִּירֵנוּ כִּי
אֵל שׁוֹמְרֵנוּ וּמַצִּילֵנוּ אָתָּה, כִּי אֵל מֶלֶךְ חַנּוּן וְרַחוּם אָתָּה.
וּשְׁמוֹר צֵאתֵנוּ וּבוֹאֵנוּ לְחַיִּים וּלְשָׁלוֹם מֵעַתָּה וְעַד עוֹלָם.
וּפְרוֹשׂ עָלֵינוּ סֻכַּת שְׁלוֹמֶךָ. בָּרוּךְ אַתָּה יְיָ הַפּוֹרֵשׂ סֻכַּת שָׁלוֹם
עָלֵינוּ וְעַל כָּל־עַמּוֹ יִשְׂרָאֵל וְעַל יְרוּשָׁלָיִם.

Help us, *Adonai* our God, to lie down peacefully and then wake us again as new. Spread over us Your shelter of peace and guide us with Your good advice. Help us for Your own sake and be like a shield around us, protecting us from enemies, disease, violence, hunger and sorrow. Shelter us in the shadow of Your wings, for You are our compassionate Ruler. Guard us as we come and go so that we may live peacefully now and forever. Praised are You, *Adonai*, Who spreads a shelter of peace over us and Jerusalem.

The darkness darts. The moon curls up,
Everybody goes to sleep. The stars come here.
The stars dance all over the place.
Every daylight, candlelight and candles go out.
They have tea before they go to bed.
The darkness stays until the morning.
Then the darkness goes and the sunshine comes.

(Janine, a young child from England.)

ADVICE AND PROTECTION

Have you ever reached deep within yourself for advice or help to make a decision? Did you ever reach deep within yourself to find the strength to do what was right or to persuade others to do the right thing?

The words, *sukkat shalom*, "shelter of peace," feel very comforting. If we were in this *sukkat shalom*, from what would we be protected? How can we make the world safer?

On *Shabbat*:

וְשָׁמְרוּ בְנֵי־יִשְׂרָאֵל אֶת־הַשַּׁבָּת לַעֲשׂוֹת אֶת־הַשַּׁבָּת לְדֹרֹתָם
בְּרִית עוֹלָם: בֵּינִי וּבֵין בְּנֵי יִשְׂרָאֵל אוֹת הִיא לְעֹלָם
כִּי־שֵׁשֶׁת יָמִים עָשָׂה יְיָ אֶת־הַשָּׁמַיִם וְאֶת־הָאָרֶץ וּבַיּוֹם
הַשְּׁבִיעִי שָׁבַת וַיִּנָּפַשׁ:

The people of Israel ... observing it throughout the generations as a ... is a sign between Me and the people, Isra... *Adonai* made the heavens and the ear..., *Adonai* rested and was refreshed.

V'shamru v'nei Yisrael et haShabbat la'asot et haShabbat le'dorotam berit olam. Beini uvein b'nei Yisrael ot hi l'olam ki sheishet yamim asah Adonai et hashamayim v'et ha'aretz u'vayom ha'shvi'i shavat va'yi'nafash.

On Festivals:

וַיְדַבֵּר מֹשֶׁה אֶת־מֹעֲדֵי יְיָ אֶל בְּנֵי יִשְׂרָאֵל:

And Moses spoke to the people Israel concerning the festivals.

Vay'daber Moshe et mo'adei Adonai el b'nei Yisrael.

THOUGHTS ON OBSERVING THE *SHABBAT*

"And the children of Israel shall observe the *Shabbat* to make the *Shabbat*." (*Exodus* 31:16) *Shabbat* cannot happen unless we make it happen. How do we do that?

"***S**hamor*" is usually translated as "keep" or "guard." It can also be translated as "watchful anticipation." This means that we should eagerly look forward to the arrival of *Shabbat* each week.

"It is a sign between Me and the children of Israel forever." (*Exodus* 31:17) This implies that the *Shabbat* will never disappear from Israel.

L'dorotam (throughout the generations) — The covenant between God and Israel is for all time. It was not just with our ancestors that God made this covenant, but with us and all future generations.

Once *Shabbat* came to God to complain: "Every day of the week has a partner: Sunday goes with Monday, Tuesday goes with Wednesday and Thursday goes with Friday. Only I don't have a partner." God replied, "The people of Israel will be your partner."

"Six days shall you labor and do all your work; but the seventh day is a *Shabbat* unto *Adonai*, your God." (*Exodus* 20:9) The duty to work for six days is just as much a part of God's plan for us as the commandment to not work on the *Shabbat*. Our work is something we should value and love.

If school is the "job" of children, how should children feel about school? How can adults create schools that children feel good about?

חֲצִי קַדִּישׁ

Ḥatzi Kaddish

Leader:

יִתְגַּדַּל וְיִתְקַדַּשׁ שְׁמֵהּ רַבָּא בְּעָלְמָא דִּי בְרָא כִרְעוּתֵהּ,
וְיַמְלִיךְ מַלְכוּתֵהּ בְּחַיֵּיכוֹן וּבְיוֹמֵיכוֹן וּבְחַיֵּי דְכָל־בֵּית
יִשְׂרָאֵל בַּעֲגָלָא וּבִזְמַן קָרִיב, וְאִמְרוּ אָמֵן.

Congregation and Leader answer:

יְהֵא שְׁמֵהּ רַבָּא מְבָרַךְ לְעָלַם וּלְעָלְמֵי עָלְמַיָּא.

Y'hei shmei rabba m'voraḥ l'olam u'l'olmei almay'ya.

Leader:

יִתְבָּרַךְ וְיִשְׁתַּבַּח וְיִתְפָּאַר וְיִתְרוֹמַם וְיִתְנַשֵּׂא וְיִתְהַדַּר
וְיִתְעַלֶּה וְיִתְהַלַּל שְׁמֵהּ דְּקֻדְשָׁא

Congregation and Leader answer:

בְּרִיךְ הוּא.

Briḥ hu.

Leader:

לְעֵלָּא [לְעֵלָּא מִכָּל־] מִן כָּל־בִּרְכָתָא וְשִׁירָתָא תֻּשְׁבְּחָתָא
וְנֶחֱמָתָא דַּאֲמִירָן בְּעָלְמָא, וְאִמְרוּ אָמֵן.

To 47

The version of th… …ich speaks of our forefathers

The version whic… …nothers is found on page 47.

Amidah for *Shabbat* Evening

Adonai, open my lips that my mouth may declare Your praise.

אֲדֹנָי, שְׂפָתַי תִּפְתָּח וּפִי יַגִּיד תְּהִלָּתֶךָ.

בָּרוּךְ אַתָּה יְיָ אֱלֹהֵינוּ וֵאלֹהֵי אֲבוֹתֵינוּ, אֱלֹהֵי אַבְרָהָם
אֱלֹהֵי יִצְחָק וֵאלֹהֵי יַעֲקֹב, הָאֵל הַגָּדוֹל הַגִּבּוֹר וְהַנּוֹרָא אֵל
עֶלְיוֹן גּוֹמֵל חֲסָדִים טוֹבִים וְקוֹנֵה הַכֹּל, וְזוֹכֵר חַסְדֵי אָבוֹת
וּמֵבִיא גוֹאֵל לִבְנֵי בְנֵיהֶם לְמַעַן שְׁמוֹ בְּאַהֲבָה.

On *Shabbat* before *Yom Kippur* we say:

זָכְרֵנוּ לְחַיִּים מֶלֶךְ חָפֵץ בַּחַיִּים,
וְכָתְבֵנוּ בְּסֵפֶר הַחַיִּים לְמַעַנְךָ אֱלֹהִים חַיִּים.

מֶלֶךְ עוֹזֵר וּמוֹשִׁיעַ וּמָגֵן. בָּרוּךְ אַתָּה יְיָ מָגֵן אַבְרָהָם.

אַתָּה גִּבּוֹר לְעוֹלָם אֲדֹנָי מְחַיֵּה מֵתִים אַתָּה רַב לְהוֹשִׁיעַ.

From *Sh'mini Atzeret* to *Pesaḥ* we say:

מַשִּׁיב הָרוּחַ וּמוֹרִיד הַגֶּשֶׁם.

מְכַלְכֵּל חַיִּים בְּחֶסֶד מְחַיֵּה מֵתִים בְּרַחֲמִים רַבִּים, סוֹמֵךְ
נוֹפְלִים וְרוֹפֵא חוֹלִים וּמַתִּיר אֲסוּרִים וּמְקַיֵּם אֱמוּנָתוֹ
לִישֵׁנֵי עָפָר. מִי כָמוֹךָ בַּעַל גְּבוּרוֹת וּמִי דוֹמֶה לָּךְ, מֶלֶךְ
מֵמִית וּמְחַיֶּה וּמַצְמִיחַ יְשׁוּעָה.

On *Shabbat* before *Yom Kippur* we say:

מִי כָמְוֹךָ אַב הָרַחֲמִים, זוֹכֵר יְצוּרָיו לְחַיִּים בְּרַחֲמִים.

וְנֶאֱמָן אַתָּה לְהַחֲיוֹת מֵתִים. בָּרוּךְ אַתָּה יְיָ מְחַיֵּה הַמֵּתִים.

אַתָּה קָדוֹשׁ וְשִׁמְךָ קָדוֹשׁ, וּקְדוֹשִׁים בְּכָל־יוֹם יְהַלְלוּךָ סֶּלָה.

On *Shabbat* before *Yom Kippur* we say the words below
and not the line which follows:

בָּרוּךְ אַתָּה יְיָ הַמֶּלֶךְ הַקָּדוֹשׁ.

בָּרוּךְ אַתָּה יְיָ הָאֵל הַקָּדוֹשׁ.

Adonai, open my lips that my mouth may declare Your praise.

Blessed are You, *Adonai*, our God and God of our ancestors,
God of Abraham, God of Isaac and God of Jacob.
Supreme God who responds with kindness,
You remember the good deeds of our ancestors and
lovingly bring help to us.

On the *Shabbat* before *Yom Kippur* add:

Remember us for life, Ruler, Who desires life, and write us in Your book of life, for Your sake, ever-living God.

Ruler, Supporter, Helper and Shield, praised are You, *Adonai*,
Who protects Abraham.

You are powerful, Almighty One.
You renew life with Your saving acts.

From *Sh'mini Atzeret* to *Pesaḥ* we say:

You cause the wind to blow and the rain to fall.

You sustain the living with loving-kindness and with mercy, renew life. You support the falling, heal the sick, free the captives and remember those who have passed on. Who can compare to You, Almighty God? Who resembles You, the Source of life and death, the Source of blossoming hope?

On the *Shabbat* before *Yom Kippur* add:

Who is like You, merciful Parent?
You remember with mercy all creatures for life.

You are faithful in giving life to all. Praised are You, Who renews life.

You are holy and Your name is holy and those who strive to be holy praise you each day,

On *Shabbat* before *Yom Kippur* we say the words below
and not the line which follows:

Praised are You, holy Ruler.

Praised are You, holy God.

Amidah for *Shabbat* Evening

Adonai, open my lips that my mouth may declare Your praise.

אדֹנָי, שְׂפָתַי תִּפְתָּח וּפִי יַגִּיד תְּהִלָּתֶךָ.

בָּרוּךְ אַתָּה יְיָ אֱלֹהֵינוּ וֵאלֹהֵי אֲבוֹתֵינוּ, אֱלֹהֵי אַבְרָהָם אֱלֹהֵי יִצְחָק וֵאלֹהֵי יַעֲקֹב, אֱלֹהֵי שָׂרָה אֱלֹהֵי רִבְקָה אֱלֹהֵי רָחֵל וֵאלֹהֵי לֵאָה, הָאֵל הַגָּדוֹל הַגִּבּוֹר וְהַנּוֹרָא אֵל עֶלְיוֹן גּוֹמֵל חֲסָדִים טוֹבִים וְקוֹנֵה הַכֹּל, וְזוֹכֵר חַסְדֵי אָבוֹת וּמֵבִיא גוֹאֵל לִבְנֵי בְנֵיהֶם לְמַעַן שְׁמוֹ בְּאַהֲבָה.

On *Shabbat* before *Yom Kippur* we say:

זָכְרֵנוּ לְחַיִּים מֶלֶךְ חָפֵץ בַּחַיִּים,
וְכָתְבֵנוּ בְּסֵפֶר הַחַיִּים לְמַעַנְךָ אֱלֹהִים חַיִּים.

מֶלֶךְ עוֹזֵר וּפוֹקֵד וּמוֹשִׁיעַ [illegible] אַבְרָהָם וּפוֹקֵד שָׂרָה.

אַתָּה גִּבּוֹר לְעוֹלָם אֲדֹנָי [illegible]וֹשִׁיעַ.

From *Sh'mini Atzeret* to *Pesaḥ* we say:

מַשִּׁיב הָרוּחַ וּמוֹרִיד הַגֶּשֶׁם.

מְכַלְכֵּל חַיִּים בְּחֶסֶד מְחַיֵּה מֵתִים בְּרַחֲמִים רַבִּים, סוֹמֵךְ נוֹפְלִים וְרוֹפֵא חוֹלִים וּמַתִּיר אֲסוּרִים וּמְקַיֵּם אֱמוּנָתוֹ לִישֵׁנֵי עָפָר. מִי כָמוֹךָ בַּעַל גְּבוּרוֹת וּמִי דוֹמֶה לָּךְ, מֶלֶךְ מֵמִית וּמְחַיֶּה וּמַצְמִיחַ יְשׁוּעָה.

On *Shabbat* before *Yom Kippur* we say:

מִי כָמוֹךָ אַב הָרַחֲמִים, זוֹכֵר יְצוּרָיו לְחַיִּים בְּרַחֲמִים.

וְנֶאֱמָן אַתָּה לְהַחֲיוֹת מֵתִים. בָּרוּךְ אַתָּה יְיָ מְחַיֵּה הַמֵּתִים.

אַתָּה קָדוֹשׁ וְשִׁמְךָ קָדוֹשׁ, וּקְדוֹשִׁים בְּכָל־יוֹם יְהַלְלוּךָ סֶּלָה.

On *Shabbat* before *Yom Kippur* we say the words below
and not the line which follows:

בָּרוּךְ אַתָּה יְיָ הַמֶּלֶךְ הַקָּדוֹשׁ.

בָּרוּךְ אַתָּה יְיָ הָאֵל הַקָּדוֹשׁ.

Adonai, open my lips that my mouth may declare Your praise.

Blessed are You, *Adonai*, our God and God of our ancestors,
God of Abraham, God of Isaac and God of Jacob,
God of Sarah, God of Rebecca, God of Leah and God of Rachel.
Supreme God who responds with kindness,
You remember the good deeds of our ancestors and
lovingly bring help to us.

On the *Shabbat* before *Yom Kippur* add:

> Remember us for life, Ruler, Who desires life, and write us in Your book of life, for Your sake, ever-living God.

Ruler, Supporter, Helper and Shield, praised are You, *Adonai*,
Who protects Abraham and remembers Sarah.

You are powerful, Almighty One.
You renew life with Your saving acts.

From *Sh'mini Atzeret* to *Pesaḥ* we say:

> You cause the wind to blow and the rain to fall.

You sustain the living with loving-kindness, and with mercy, renew life. You support the falling, heal the sick, free the captives and remember those who have passed on. Who can compare to You, Almighty God? Who resembles You, the Source of life and death, the Source of blossoming hope?

On the *Shabbat* before *Yom Kippur* add:

> Who is like You, merciful Parent?
> You remember with mercy all creatures for life.

You are faithful in giving life to all. Praised are You, Who renews life.

On *Shabbat* before *Yom Kippur* we say the words below
and not the line which follows:

> Praised are You, holy Ruler.

Praised are You, holy God.

THE CREATION OF THE WORLD

There was nothing.
There was chaos.
The spirit of God brooded over darkness,
unbroken darkness.
Then a mass, single, dense,
and suddenly an explosion,
a bursting forth of light,
stars, suns to make the brilliance of day
against the cool of night,
day sky and night sky,
and then water, and from the water, land,
and from the land grass and trees and flowers
and fish and fowl and butterflies and behemoths.
There was nothing.
And then God, in His infinite joy,
Created.

You make the seventh day holy...as it is written in Your Torah:
On the sixth day, the heavens and the earth were completed. On the seventh day, God finished the work of creation and rested. God blessed the seventh day and called it holy, because on that day God rested from the work of creation.

וַיְכֻלּוּ הַשָּׁמַיִם וְהָאָרֶץ וְכָל־צְבָאָם. וַיְכַל אֱלֹהִים בַּיּוֹם הַשְּׁבִיעִי
מְלַאכְתּוֹ אֲשֶׁר עָשָׂה, וַיִּשְׁבֹּת בַּיּוֹם הַשְּׁבִיעִי מִכָּל־מְלַאכְתּוֹ
אֲשֶׁר עָשָׂה. וַיְבָרֶךְ אֱלֹהִים אֶת־יוֹם הַשְּׁבִיעִי וַיְקַדֵּשׁ אֹתוֹ, כִּי
בוֹ שָׁבַת מִכָּל־מְלַאכְתּוֹ אֲשֶׁר בָּרָא אֱלֹהִים לַעֲשׂוֹת.

Some rabbis translate "*la'asot*" as "to do." When we look at the Biblical text, we can interpret it to mean, "And God blessed the seventh day and made it holy because on it God ceased all the work which [God] created [for humans] to do." God's job was done. The world was handed over to humans. We can use the resources God gave us — materials, energy, intelligence to complete the task. It's up to us to do this wisely.

אֱלֹהֵינוּ וֵאלֹהֵי אֲבוֹתֵינוּ, רְצֵה בִמְנוּחָתֵנוּ קַדְּשֵׁנוּ בְּמִצְוֹתֶיךָ וְתֵן
חֶלְקֵנוּ בְּתוֹרָתֶךָ, שַׂבְּעֵנוּ מִטּוּבֶךָ וְשַׂמְּחֵנוּ בִּישׁוּעָתֶךָ, וְטַהֵר
לִבֵּנוּ לְעָבְדְּךָ בֶּאֱמֶת. וְהַנְחִילֵנוּ יְיָ אֱלֹהֵינוּ בְּאַהֲבָה וּבְרָצוֹן
שַׁבַּת קָדְשֶׁךָ, וְיָנוּחוּ בָהּ יִשְׂרָאֵל מְקַדְּשֵׁי שְׁמֶךָ. בָּרוּךְ אַתָּה יְיָ
מְקַדֵּשׁ הַשַּׁבָּת.

Our God and God of our ancestors, be pleased with our rest. Let Your *mitzvot* lead us to holy deeds and the study of Torah. Let us find happiness in Your blessings and joy in Your supporting power. Let our hearts be pure to serve You with sincerity. With Your gracious love, let us continue our holy tradition of keeping the *Shabbat*. Let the people Israel rest on *Shabbat* and honor Your name. We praise You, *Adonai*, Who makes *Shabbat* holy.

רְצֵה יְיָ אֱלֹהֵינוּ בְּעַמְּךָ יִשְׂרָאֵל וּבִתְפִלָּתָם וְהָשֵׁב אֶת־הָעֲבוֹדָה לִדְבִיר בֵּיתֶךָ וּתְפִלָּתָם בְּאַהֲבָה תְקַבֵּל בְּרָצוֹן וּתְהִי לְרָצוֹן תָּמִיד עֲבוֹדַת יִשְׂרָאֵל עַמֶּךָ.

Be pleased, *Adonai*, our God, with Your people Israel and their prayers. May our worship always be acceptable to You.

On *Rosh Ḥodesh* and *Ḥol Hamo'ed* we say:

אֱלֹהֵינוּ וֵאלֹהֵי אֲבוֹתֵינוּ, יַעֲלֶה וְיָבֹא וְיַגִּיעַ, וְיֵרָאֶה וְיֵרָצֶה וְיִשָּׁמַע, וְיִפָּקֵד וְיִזָּכֵר זִכְרוֹנֵנוּ וּפִקְדוֹנֵנוּ, וְזִכְרוֹן אֲבוֹתֵינוּ, וְזִכְרוֹן מָשִׁיחַ בֶּן־דָּוִד עַבְדֶּךָ, וְזִכְרוֹן יְרוּשָׁלַיִם עִיר קָדְשֶׁךָ, לְחֵן וּלְחֶסֶד וּלְרַחֲמִים, לְחַיִּים וּלְשָׁלוֹם בְּיוֹם

On Rosh Ḥodesh: רֹאשׁ הַחֹדֶשׁ

On Pesaḥ: חַג הַמַּצּוֹת

On Sukkot: חַג הַסֻּכּוֹת

הַזֶּה. זָכְרֵנוּ יְיָ אֱלֹהֵינוּ בּוֹ לְטוֹבָה, וּפָקְדֵנוּ בוֹ לִבְרָכָה, וְהוֹשִׁיעֵנוּ בוֹ לְחַיִּים.

Our God and God of our ancestors, may Your remembering us, our ancestors, Jerusalem the holy city, and Your promises for our future allow You to grant us happiness, peace and life on this day of

Rosh Ḥodesh:	*Pesaḥ:*	*Sukkot:*
New Moon	The Feast of *Matzah*	The Festival of *Sukkot*

וְתֶחֱזֶינָה עֵינֵינוּ בְּשׁוּבְךָ לְצִיּוֹן בְּרַחֲמִים. בָּרוּךְ אַתָּה יְיָ הַמַּחֲזִיר שְׁכִינָתוֹ לְצִיּוֹן.

May we witness your merciful return to Zion. Praised are You, *Adonai*, Who seeks closeness to us. May we feel Your closeness in Zion.

מוֹדִים אֲנַחְנוּ לָךְ שָׁאַתָּה הוּא יְיָ אֱלֹהֵינוּ וֵאלֹהֵי אֲבוֹתֵינוּ לְעוֹלָם וָעֶד, צוּר חַיֵּינוּ מָגֵן יִשְׁעֵנוּ אַתָּה הוּא לְדוֹר וָדוֹר. נוֹדֶה לְּךָ וּנְסַפֵּר תְּהִלָּתֶךָ, עַל חַיֵּינוּ הַמְּסוּרִים בְּיָדֶךָ וְעַל נִשְׁמוֹתֵינוּ הַפְּקוּדוֹת לָךְ וְעַל נִסֶּיךָ שֶׁבְּכָל־יוֹם עִמָּנוּ וְעַל נִפְלְאוֹתֶיךָ וְטוֹבוֹתֶיךָ שֶׁבְּכָל־עֵת, עֶרֶב וָבֹקֶר וְצָהֳרָיִם. הַטּוֹב כִּי לֹא כָלוּ רַחֲמֶיךָ, וְהַמְרַחֵם כִּי לֹא תַמּוּ חֲסָדֶיךָ, מֵעוֹלָם קִוִּינוּ לָךְ.

How grateful we are to You, God of our ancestors, the Eternal One. You are the source of our strength just as You have been the protecting shield of each generation.

We thank You for our lives which are in Your hands and our souls which are in Your care. We thank You for Your miracles which surround us all the time and the wondrous acts of Your kindness that we experience each morning, noon and night. You are the source of never-ending loving-kindness. You are our hope forever.

On *Ḥanukkah* we say:

עַל הַנִּסִּים וְעַל הַפֻּרְקָן, וְעַל הַגְּבוּרוֹת, וְעַל הַתְּשׁוּעוֹת, וְעַל הַמִּלְחָמוֹת שֶׁעָשִׂיתָ לַאֲבוֹתֵינוּ בַּיָּמִים הָהֵם וּבִזְּמַן הַזֶּה.

בִּימֵי מַתִּתְיָהוּ בֶּן־יוֹחָנָן כֹּהֵן גָּדוֹל, חַשְׁמוֹנַי וּבָנָיו, כְּשֶׁעָמְדָה מַלְכוּת יָוָן הָרְשָׁעָה עַל עַמְּךָ יִשְׂרָאֵל לְהַשְׁכִּיחָם תּוֹרָתֶךָ וּלְהַעֲבִירָם מֵחֻקֵּי רְצוֹנֶךָ, וְאַתָּה בְּרַחֲמֶיךָ הָרַבִּים עָמַדְתָּ לָהֶם בְּעֵת צָרָתָם, רַבְתָּ אֶת־רִיבָם, דַּנְתָּ אֶת־דִּינָם, נָקַמְתָּ אֶת־נִקְמָתָם, מָסַרְתָּ גִבּוֹרִים בְּיַד חַלָּשִׁים, וְרַבִּים בְּיַד מְעַטִּים, וּטְמֵאִים בְּיַד טְהוֹרִים, וּרְשָׁעִים בְּיַד צַדִּיקִים, וְזֵדִים בְּיַד עוֹסְקֵי תוֹרָתֶךָ. וּלְךָ עָשִׂיתָ שֵׁם גָּדוֹל וְקָדוֹשׁ בְּעוֹלָמֶךָ, וּלְעַמְּךָ יִשְׂרָאֵל עָשִׂיתָ תְּשׁוּעָה גְדוֹלָה וּפֻרְקָן כְּהַיּוֹם הַזֶּה. וְאַחַר כֵּן בָּאוּ בָנֶיךָ לִדְבִיר בֵּיתֶךָ וּפִנּוּ אֶת־הֵיכָלֶךָ, וְטִהֲרוּ אֶת־מִקְדָּשֶׁךָ, וְהִדְלִיקוּ נֵרוֹת בְּחַצְרוֹת קָדְשֶׁךָ, וְקָבְעוּ שְׁמוֹנַת יְמֵי חֲנֻכָּה אֵלּוּ לְהוֹדוֹת וּלְהַלֵּל לְשִׁמְךָ הַגָּדוֹל.

On *Ḥanukkah* we say:

We thank You for the miracles, the triumphs, the heroism, the help You gave to our ancestors in days past and in our own time.

In the days of the High Priest, Mattathias, and his sons (known as the Maccabees) a cruel government, the Syrian Greeks, rose up against Israel, demanding that they abandon the Torah and *mitzvot*. You, with great mercy, stood by Your people in their time of trouble. You championed their cause, defended their rights and punished their enemies. You delivered the strong into the hands of the weak, the many into the hands of the few, the corrupt into the hands of the pure, the wicked into the hands of the righteous, and the arrogant into the hands of students of Torah. You have made great victories for Your people Israel to this day, showing Your glory and holiness to the world. Then Your children came to Your shrine, cleaned Your temple, made Your sanctuary pure and lit candles in Your sacred courts. They set aside these eight days to give thanks and praise to Your holy name.

וְעַל כֻּלָּם יִתְבָּרַךְ וְיִתְרוֹמַם שִׁמְךָ מַלְכֵּנוּ תָּמִיד לְעוֹלָם וָעֶד.

On *Shabbat Shuvah,* before *Yom Kippur* add:

וּכְתֹב לְחַיִּים טוֹבִים כָּל־בְּנֵי בְרִיתֶךָ.

וְכֹל הַחַיִּים יוֹדוּךָ סֶּלָה, וִיהַלְלוּ אֶת־שִׁמְךָ בֶּאֱמֶת הָאֵל יְשׁוּעָתֵנוּ
וְעֶזְרָתֵנוּ סֶלָה. בָּרוּךְ אַתָּה יְיָ הַטּוֹב שִׁמְךָ וּלְךָ נָאֶה לְהוֹדוֹת.

For all these blessings, may Your name be praised and exalted forever.

On *Shabbat Shuvah,* before *Yom Kippur*, add:

May we all look forward to a good year of life.

Praised are You, *Adonai*, who deserves our praise.

שָׁלוֹם רָב עַל יִשְׂרָאֵל עַמְּךָ וְעַל כָּל־יוֹשְׁבֵי תֵבֵל תָּשִׂים
לְעוֹלָם, כִּי אַתָּה הוּא מֶלֶךְ אָדוֹן לְכָל־הַשָּׁלוֹם. וְטוֹב בְּעֵינֶיךָ
לְבָרֵךְ אֶת־עַמְּךָ יִשְׂרָאֵל בְּכָל־עֵת וּבְכָל־שָׁעָה בִּשְׁלוֹמֶךָ.

Grant a lasting peace to Israel and to all others who share this earth, for You are the Supreme One. May it please You to bless us in every season and at all times with Your precious gift of peace.

On *Shabbat Shuvah*, before *Yom Kippur* we substitute these words:

בְּסֵפֶר חַיִּים בְּרָכָה וְשָׁלוֹם וּפַרְנָסָה טוֹבָה נִזָּכֵר וְנִכָּתֵב לְפָנֶיךָ אֲנַחְנוּ
וְכָל־עַמְּךָ בֵּית יִשְׂרָאֵל לְחַיִּים טוֹבִים וּלְשָׁלוֹם.
בָּרוּךְ אַתָּה יְיָ עוֹשֵׂה הַשָּׁלוֹם.

בָּרוּךְ אַתָּה יְיָ הַמְבָרֵךְ אֶת־עַמּוֹ יִשְׂרָאֵל בַּשָּׁלוֹם.

Blessed are You, *Adonai*, who blesses the people Israel with peace.

Shalom Rav is very simple. It just says, "Peace, please...Pass the peace, please." Everything can be fit into "*Shalom*," it sums up everything we have been asking for.

We sing:

Oseh shalom bimromov	עֹשֶׂה שָׁלוֹם בִּמְרוֹמָיו,
Hu ya'aseh shalom aleinu	הוּא יַעֲשֶׂה שָׁלוֹם עָלֵינוּ
v'al kol Yisrael	וְעַל כָּל־יִשְׂרָאֵל,
v'imru: Amen.	וְאִמְרוּ אָמֵן.

We say while standing:

וַיְכֻלּוּ הַשָּׁמַיִם וְהָאָרֶץ וְכָל־צְבָאָם. וַיְכַל אֱלֹהִים בַּיּוֹם הַשְּׁבִיעִי מְלַאכְתּוֹ אֲשֶׁר עָשָׂה, וַיִּשְׁבֹּת בַּיּוֹם הַשְּׁבִיעִי מִכָּל־מְלַאכְתּוֹ אֲשֶׁר עָשָׂה. וַיְבָרֶךְ אֱלֹהִים אֶת־יוֹם הַשְּׁבִיעִי וַיְקַדֵּשׁ אֹתוֹ, כִּי בוֹ שָׁבַת מִכָּל־מְלַאכְתּוֹ אֲשֶׁר בָּרָא אֱלֹהִים לַעֲשׂוֹת.

The following three paragraphs are said only with a *minyan:*

Leader says:

בָּרוּךְ אַתָּה יְיָ אֱלֹהֵינוּ וֵאלֹהֵי אֲבוֹתֵינוּ, אֱלֹהֵי אַבְרָהָם אֱלֹהֵי יִצְחָק וֵאלֹהֵי יַעֲקֹב, הָאֵל הַגָּדוֹל הַגִּבּוֹר וְהַנּוֹרָא, אֵל עֶלְיוֹן, קוֹנֵה שָׁמַיִם וָאָרֶץ.

All say:

מָגֵן אָבוֹת בִּדְבָרוֹ, מְחַיֵּה מֵתִים בְּמַאֲמָרוֹ, הָאֵל [הַמֶּלֶךְ] הַקָּדוֹשׁ שֶׁאֵין כָּמוֹהוּ, הַמֵּנִיחַ לְעַמּוֹ בְּיוֹם שַׁבַּת קָדְשׁוֹ, כִּי בָם רָצָה לְהָנִיחַ לָהֶם. לְפָנָיו נַעֲבוֹד בְּיִרְאָה וָפַחַד, וְנוֹדֶה לִשְׁמוֹ בְּכָל־יוֹם תָּמִיד מֵעֵין הַבְּרָכוֹת. אֵל הַהוֹדָאוֹת, אֲדוֹן הַשָּׁלוֹם, מְקַדֵּשׁ הַשַּׁבָּת וּמְבָרֵךְ שְׁבִיעִי, וּמֵנִיחַ בִּקְדֻשָּׁה לְעַם מְדֻשְּׁנֵי־עֹנֶג, זֵכֶר לְמַעֲשֵׂה בְרֵאשִׁית.

Leader says:

אֱלֹהֵינוּ וֵאלֹהֵי אֲבוֹתֵינוּ, רְצֵה בִמְנוּחָתֵנוּ קַדְּשֵׁנוּ בְּמִצְוֹתֶיךָ וְתֵן חֶלְקֵנוּ בְּתוֹרָתֶךָ, שַׂבְּעֵנוּ מִטּוּבֶךָ וְשַׂמְּחֵנוּ בִּישׁוּעָתֶךָ, וְטַהֵר לִבֵּנוּ לְעָבְדְּךָ בֶּאֱמֶת. וְהַנְחִילֵנוּ יְיָ אֱלֹהֵינוּ בְּאַהֲבָה וּבְרָצוֹן שַׁבַּת קָדְשֶׁךָ, וְיָנוּחוּ בָהּ יִשְׂרָאֵל מְקַדְּשֵׁי שְׁמֶךָ. בָּרוּךְ אַתָּה יְיָ מְקַדֵּשׁ הַשַּׁבָּת.

KADDISH SHALEM

קַדִּישׁ שָׁלֵם

Leader:

יִתְגַּדַּל וְיִתְקַדַּשׁ שְׁמֵהּ רַבָּא בְּעָלְמָא דִּי בְרָא כִרְעוּתֵהּ,
וְיַמְלִיךְ מַלְכוּתֵהּ בְּחַיֵּיכוֹן וּבְיוֹמֵיכוֹן וּבְחַיֵּי דְכָל־בֵּית יִשְׂרָאֵל,
בַּעֲגָלָא וּבִזְמַן קָרִיב, וְאִמְרוּ אָמֵן.

Congregation and Leader answer:

יְהֵא שְׁמֵהּ רַבָּא מְבָרַךְ לְעָלַם וּלְעָלְמֵי עָלְמַיָּא.

Y'hei shmei rabba m'vorah̩ l'olam u'l'olmei almay'ya.

Leader:

יִתְבָּרַךְ וְיִשְׁתַּבַּח וְיִתְפָּאַר וְיִתְרוֹמַם וְיִתְנַשֵּׂא, וְיִתְהַדַּר וְיִתְעַלֶּה
וְיִתְהַלַּל שְׁמֵהּ דְּקֻדְשָׁא,

Congregation and Leader answer:

בְּרִיךְ הוּא.

Brih̩ hu.

Leader:

לְעֵלָּא [לְעֵלָּא מִכָּל־] מִן כָּל־בִּרְכָתָא וְשִׁירָתָא תֻּשְׁבְּחָתָא
וְנֶחֱמָתָא דַּאֲמִירָן בְּעָלְמָא, וְאִמְרוּ אָמֵן.

תִּתְקַבַּל צְלוֹתְהוֹן וּבָעוּתְהוֹן דְּכָל־יִשְׂרָאֵל קֳדָם אֲבוּהוֹן דִּי
בִשְׁמַיָּא, וְאִמְרוּ אָמֵן.

יְהֵא שְׁלָמָא רַבָּא מִן שְׁמַיָּא וְחַיִּים עָלֵינוּ וְעַל כָּל־יִשְׂרָאֵל,
וְאִמְרוּ אָמֵן.

עוֹשֶׂה שָׁלוֹם בִּמְרוֹמָיו, הוּא יַעֲשֶׂה שָׁלוֹם עָלֵינוּ וְעַל
כָּל־יִשְׂרָאֵל, וְאִמְרוּ אָמֵן.

KIDDUSH FOR *SHABBAT*

We stand and sing in Hebrew:

בָּרוּךְ אַתָּה יְיָ אֱלֹהֵינוּ מֶלֶךְ הָעוֹלָם, בּוֹרֵא פְּרִי הַגָּפֶן.

בָּרוּךְ אַתָּה יְיָ אֱלֹהֵינוּ מֶלֶךְ הָעוֹלָם, אֲשֶׁר קִדְּשָׁנוּ בְּמִצְוֹתָיו
וְרָצָה בָנוּ, וְשַׁבַּת קָדְשׁוֹ בְּאַהֲבָה וּבְרָצוֹן הִנְחִילָנוּ, זִכָּרוֹן
לְמַעֲשֵׂה בְרֵאשִׁית. כִּי הוּא יוֹם תְּחִלָּה לְמִקְרָאֵי־קֹדֶשׁ, זֵכֶר
לִיצִיאַת מִצְרָיִם. כִּי בָנוּ בָחַרְתָּ וְאוֹתָנוּ קִדַּשְׁתָּ מִכָּל־הָעַמִּים,
וְשַׁבַּת קָדְשְׁךָ בְּאַהֲבָה וּבְרָצוֹן הִנְחַלְתָּנוּ.
בָּרוּךְ אַתָּה יְיָ מְקַדֵּשׁ הַשַּׁבָּת.

We praise You, *Adonai*, our God, Ruler of the Universe, Who creates the fruit of the vine.

We praise You, *Adonai*, our God, Ruler of the Universe, Who has made us holy through Your *mitzvot* and lovingly has given us the gift of *Shabbat* as a reminder of creation. It is the first among the holy days, reminding us of our going out of Egypt. You have chosen us with the gift of the *Shabbat* to treasure for all generations. We praise You, *Adonai*, Who makes the *Shabbat* holy.

Baruḥ atah Adonai, Eloheinu, Meleḥ ha'olam borei p'ri hagafen.
Baruḥ atah Adonai, Eloheinu, Meleḥ ha'olam asher kid'deshanu b'mitzvotav v'ratzah vanu, v'Shabbat kod'sho, b'ahavah uv'ratzon hinḥilanu, zikaron l'ma'aseh v'reishit. Ki hu yom t'ḥila, l'mikra'ei kodesh, zeḥer litzi'at Mitzrayim. Ki vanu vaḥarta v'otanu kidashta mikol ha'amim, v'Shabbat kodsheḥa b'ahavah uv'ratson hinḥaltanu.
Baruḥ atah Adonai, m'kadesh haShabbat.

CREATION OF FISH, FOWL, AND CATTLE

Be!
Be, caterpillar and comet,
be porcupine and planet,
sea sand and solar system,
sing with us,
dance with us,
rejoice with us
for the glory of creation,
sea gulls and seraphim,
angle worms and angel host,
chrysanthemum and cherubim
Be!
Sing for the glory
of the living and the loving
the flaming of Creation
sing with us
dance with us
be with us
Be!

The *Omer* is counted each day from the second day of *Pesaḥ* until the holiday of *Shavuot*.

I am about to fulfill the *mitzvah* of counting the *omer*, as it is written in the Torah: “You shall count from the day following the day of rest, from the day that you brought an omer of grain as an offering, seven full weeks shall be counted. You shall count fifty days to the day following the seventh week.” (*Leviticus* 23:15-16)

בָּרוּךְ אַתָּה יְיָ אֱלֹהֵינוּ מֶלֶךְ הָעוֹלָם, אֲשֶׁר קִדְּשָׁנוּ בְּמִצְוֹתָיו וְצִוָּנוּ עַל סְפִירַת הָעֹמֶר.

Praised are You, *Adonai*, Ruler of the Universe, Who taught us the way of holiness and commanded us to count the days of the *omer*.

Baruḥ atah Adonai Eloheinu Meleḥ ha'olam asher kid'deshanu b'mitzvotav v'tzivanu al s'firat ha'omer.

Here we specify the day:

Today is the _____ day of the *omer*.

In Hebrew we use the following forms.

Day 1

הַיּוֹם יוֹם אֶחָד לָעֹמֶר

Day 2-6

הַיּוֹם ___ יָמִים לָעֹמֶר

Day 7

הַיּוֹם שִׁבְעָה יָמִים, שֶׁהֵם שָׁבוּעַ אֶחָד לָעֹמֶר

Day 8

הַיּוֹם שְׁמוֹנָה יָמִים, שֶׁהֵם שָׁבוּעַ אֶחָד וְיוֹם אֶחָד לָעֹמֶר

Day 9-10

הַיּוֹם ___ יָמִים, שֶׁהֵם שָׁבוּעַ אֶחָד וּ___ יָמִים לָעֹמֶר

Day 11-13

הַיּוֹם ___ ___ יוֹם, שֶׁהֵם שָׁבוּעַ אֶחָד וְ___ יָמִים לָעֹמֶר

Each full week

הַיּוֹם ________ יוֹם, שֶׁהֵם ___ שָׁבוּעוֹת לָעֹמֶר

Day after each full week

הַיּוֹם ___ ___ יוֹם, שֶׁהֵם ___ שָׁבוּעוֹת וְיוֹם אֶחָד לָעֹמֶר

Day 2-6 of each full week

הַיּוֹם ___ ___ יוֹם, שֶׁהֵם ___ שָׁבוּעוֹת וְ/וּ___ יָמִים לָעֹמֶר

We rise:

עָלֵינוּ לְשַׁבֵּחַ לַאֲדוֹן הַכֹּל, לָתֵת גְּדֻלָּה לְיוֹצֵר בְּרֵאשִׁית,
שֶׁלֹּא עָשָׂנוּ כְּגוֹיֵי הָאֲרָצוֹת וְלֹא שָׂמָנוּ כְּמִשְׁפְּחוֹת הָאֲדָמָה,
שֶׁלֹּא שָׂם חֶלְקֵנוּ כָּהֶם וְגוֹרָלֵנוּ כְּכָל־הֲמוֹנָם. וַאֲנַחְנוּ
כּוֹרְעִים וּמִשְׁתַּחֲוִים וּמוֹדִים לִפְנֵי מֶלֶךְ מַלְכֵי הַמְּלָכִים
הַקָּדוֹשׁ בָּרוּךְ הוּא, שֶׁהוּא נוֹטֶה שָׁמַיִם וְיוֹסֵד אָרֶץ וּמוֹשַׁב
יְקָרוֹ בַּשָּׁמַיִם מִמַּעַל וּשְׁכִינַת עֻזּוֹ בְּגָבְהֵי מְרוֹמִים. הוּא
אֱלֹהֵינוּ אֵין עוֹד. אֱמֶת מַלְכֵּנוּ אֶפֶס זוּלָתוֹ, כַּכָּתוּב
בְּתוֹרָתוֹ: וְיָדַעְתָּ הַיּוֹם וַהֲשֵׁבֹתָ אֶל לְבָבֶךָ כִּי יְיָ הוּא
הָאֱלֹהִים בַּשָּׁמַיִם מִמַּעַל וְעַל הָאָרֶץ מִתָּחַת, אֵין עוֹד.

It is for us to praise the Ruler of all and to glorify the Creator of the world for giving us a special heritage and a unique destiny.

Before our Supreme Ruler, we bend the knee and bow in devotion.

As it is written in the Torah, "Accept this day with both mind and heart. Know that God's presence fills creation."

Because we believe in You, we hope for the day when Your majesty will triumph and all will work to mend the world and live according to Your ways. For it is written in the Torah, "*Adonai* shall rule for ever and ever."

Aleinu l'shabei'aḥ la'adon hakol, latet g'dulah l'yotzer b'reishit,
shelo asanu k'goyei ha'aratzot, v'lo samanu k'mishp'ḥot ha'adamah,
shelo sam ḥelkeinu kahem, v'goraleinu k'ḥol hamonam.

Va'anaḥnu korim umishtaḥavim umodim, lifnei Meleḥ malḥei ham'laḥim haKadosh baruḥ Hu.

עַל כֵּן נְקַוֶּה לְךָ יְיָ אֱלֹהֵינוּ לִרְאוֹת מְהֵרָה בְּתִפְאֶרֶת עֻזֶּךָ,
לְהַעֲבִיר גִּלּוּלִים מִן הָאָרֶץ וְהָאֱלִילִים כָּרוֹת יִכָּרֵתוּן,
לְתַקֵּן עוֹלָם בְּמַלְכוּת שַׁדַּי וְכָל־בְּנֵי בָשָׂר יִקְרְאוּ בִשְׁמֶךָ,
לְהַפְנוֹת אֵלֶיךָ כָּל רִשְׁעֵי אָרֶץ. יַכִּירוּ וְיֵדְעוּ כָּל־יוֹשְׁבֵי
תֵבֵל כִּי לְךָ תִּכְרַע כָּל־בֶּרֶךְ תִּשָּׁבַע כָּל־לָשׁוֹן. לְפָנֶיךָ יְיָ
אֱלֹהֵינוּ יִכְרְעוּ וְיִפֹּלוּ וְלִכְבוֹד שִׁמְךָ יְקָר יִתֵּנוּ, וִיקַבְּלוּ
כֻלָּם אֶת־עֹל מַלְכוּתֶךָ וְתִמְלֹךְ עֲלֵיהֶם מְהֵרָה לְעוֹלָם וָעֶד,
כִּי הַמַּלְכוּת שֶׁלְּךָ הִיא וּלְעוֹלְמֵי עַד תִּמְלוֹךְ בְּכָבוֹד,
כַּכָּתוּב בְּתוֹרָתֶךָ: יְיָ יִמְלֹךְ לְעֹלָם וָעֶד.

וְנֶאֱמַר: וְהָיָה יְיָ לְמֶלֶךְ עַל כָּל־הָאָרֶץ, בַּיּוֹם הַהוּא יִהְיֶה יְיָ
אֶחָד וּשְׁמוֹ אֶחָד.

V'ne'emar, v'hayah Adonai l'Meleḥ al kol ha'aretz.
Bayom hahu yih'yeh Adonai eḥad ush'mo eḥad.

MOURNER'S *KADDISH*

Mourners and those observing a memorial day rise and say:

יִתְגַּדַּל וְיִתְקַדַּשׁ שְׁמֵהּ רַבָּא בְּעָלְמָא דִּי בְרָא כִרְעוּתֵהּ,
וְיַמְלִיךְ מַלְכוּתֵהּ בְּחַיֵּיכוֹן וּבְיוֹמֵיכוֹן וּבְחַיֵּי דְכָל־בֵּית יִשְׂרָאֵל
בַּעֲגָלָא וּבִזְמַן קָרִיב, וְאִמְרוּ אָמֵן.

The congregation says together with the mourners:

יְהֵא שְׁמֵהּ רַבָּא מְבָרַךְ לְעָלַם וּלְעָלְמֵי עָלְמַיָּא.

Y'hei shmei rabba m'voraḥ l'olam u'l'olmei almay'ya.

Mourners continue:

יִתְבָּרַךְ וְיִשְׁתַּבַּח וְיִתְפָּאַר וְיִתְרוֹמַם וְיִתְנַשֵּׂא וְיִתְהַדָּר וְיִתְעַלֶּה
וְיִתְהַלָּל שְׁמֵהּ דְּקֻדְשָׁא

Congregation together with the mourners:

בְּרִיךְ הוּא.

Briḥ hu.

לְעֵלָּא (לְעֵלָּא מִכָּל־) מִן כָּל־בִּרְכָתָא וְשִׁירָתָא תֻּשְׁבְּחָתָא
וְנֶחֱמָתָא דַּאֲמִירָן בְּעָלְמָא, וְאִמְרוּ אָמֵן.

יְהֵא שְׁלָמָא רַבָּא מִן שְׁמַיָּא וְחַיִּים עָלֵינוּ וְעַל כָּל־יִשְׂרָאֵל,
וְאִמְרוּ אָמֵן.

עוֹשֶׂה שָׁלוֹם בִּמְרוֹמָיו הוּא יַעֲשֶׂה שָׁלוֹם עָלֵינוּ וְעַל
כָּל־יִשְׂרָאֵל, וְאִמְרוּ אָמֵן.

יִגְדַּל אֱלֹהִים חַי וְיִשְׁתַּבַּח נִמְצָא וְאֵין עֵת אֶל מְצִיאוּתוֹ.
אֶחָד וְאֵין יָחִיד כְּיִחוּדוֹ נֶעְלָם וְגַם אֵין סוֹף לְאַחְדּוּתוֹ.
אֵין לוֹ דְמוּת הַגּוּף וְאֵינוֹ גוּף לֹא נַעֲרוֹךְ אֵלָיו קְדֻשָּׁתוֹ.
קַדְמוֹן לְכָל־דָּבָר אֲשֶׁר נִבְרָא רִאשׁוֹן וְאֵין רֵאשִׁית לְרֵאשִׁיתוֹ.
הִנּוֹ אֲדוֹן עוֹלָם, וְכָל־נוֹצָר יוֹרֶה גְדֻלָּתוֹ וּמַלְכוּתוֹ.
שֶׁפַע נְבוּאָתוֹ נְתָנוֹ אֶל אַנְשֵׁי סְגֻלָּתוֹ וְתִפְאַרְתּוֹ.
לֹא קָם בְּיִשְׂרָאֵל כְּמשֶׁה עוֹד נָבִיא וּמַבִּיט אֶת־תְּמוּנָתוֹ.
תּוֹרַת אֱמֶת נָתַן לְעַמּוֹ אֵל עַל יַד נְבִיאוֹ נֶאֱמַן בֵּיתוֹ.
לֹא יַחֲלִיף הָאֵל, וְלֹא יָמִיר דָּתוֹ לְעוֹלָמִים לְזוּלָתוֹ.
צוֹפֶה וְיוֹדֵעַ סְתָרֵינוּ מַבִּיט לְסוֹף דָּבָר בְּקַדְמָתוֹ.
גּוֹמֵל לְאִישׁ חֶסֶד כְּמִפְעָלוֹ נוֹתֵן לְרָשָׁע רָע כְּרִשְׁעָתוֹ.
יִשְׁלַח לְקֵץ יָמִין מְשִׁיחֵנוּ לִפְדּוֹת מְחַכֵּי קֵץ יְשׁוּעָתוֹ.
מֵתִים יְחַיֶּה אֵל בְּרֹב חַסְדּוֹ בָּרוּךְ עֲדֵי עַד שֵׁם תְּהִלָּתוֹ.

Yigdal is a summary of the thirteen principles of faith written by Maimonides in his commentary on the *Mishnah* (*Sanhedrin* 10:1). The poem in its present form was written by Daniel Judah of Rome in the fourteenth century.

In the Hebrew, one rhyme runs through the poem. Can you tell what it is?

Do you agree with every principle stated?

1. God exists and God's existence is beyond time.
2. God is One and God is unknowable.
3. God has no physical form.
4. God was first, before creation.
5. Every creature must declare God's greatness and majesty.
6. God granted the gift of prophecy to those specially chosen.
7. Never has there been a prophet like Moses, who saw God's image.
8. God gave a Torah of truth to the people Israel, through God's faithful servant, Moses.
9. God's laws are eternal.
10. God understands our innermost thoughts.
11. God rewards the good people for their deeds and repays the evil ones for their evil.
12. At the end of days, God will send a Messiah to save all those who wait for this final help.
13. God, with great mercy, will revive the dead.

Blessed be God's glorious name forever.

If you were composing a list of statements about God, what would you include?

שַׁחֲרִית לְשַׁבָּת וּלְיוֹם טוֹב

Morning Service for *Shabbat* and Festivals

מַה טֹּבוּ אֹהָלֶיךָ יַעֲקֹב, מִשְׁכְּנֹתֶיךָ יִשְׂרָאֵל.
וַאֲנִי בְּרֹב חַסְדְּךָ אָבוֹא בֵיתֶךָ,
אֶשְׁתַּחֲוֶה אֶל הֵיכַל קָדְשְׁךָ בְּיִרְאָתֶךָ.

How beautiful are your tents,
O people of Jacob,
And your dwelling places,
O Israelites!

Ma tovu ohaleḥa Ya'akov, mishkenoteḥa Yisrael.
Va'ani b'rov ḥasdeḥa, avo veiteḥa,
eshtaḥaveh el heiḥal kod'sheḥa b'yirateḥa.

Through Your loving-kindness, I enter Your house to pray.
Here in this special place, I will bow before You.
Accept my prayers, *Elohim*, and answer me with mercy.
Teach me Your ways of truth.

How many times can you find/count the words "I," "me" or "my" in the *Mah Tovu* prayer? Why do you think this prayer is in the singular?

It is easy for us to take our synagogues for granted, since religious freedom is part of our country's law and tradition. Yet there were times when we were forbidden to pray together as Jews. Do you know of any such times? How is your synagogue important to you, to your famiy and to your community?

TZITZIT

I will wrap myself in a *tallit* with *tzitzit* (fringes) to fulfill the *mitzvah* written in the Torah: "They shall put fringes on the corners of their garments in every generation" (*Numbers* 15:38)

בָּרוּךְ אַתָּה יְיָ אֱלֹהֵינוּ מֶלֶךְ הָעוֹלָם, אֲשֶׁר קִדְּשָׁנוּ בְּמִצְוֹתָיו
וְצִוָּנוּ לְהִתְעַטֵּף בַּצִּיצִית.

Praised are You, *Adonai*, Ruler of the Universe, Who has made us holy by Your *mitzvot* and commands us to wrap ourselves in *tzitzit*.

The House That Expanded

A farmer, his wife, and their seven children all lived together in their small, crowded hut. "What shall we do?" cried the exasperated wife. "There's hardly room to breathe!" "Let's ask the rabbi's advice," suggested the farmer.

To their surprise, the rabbi told them to bring their three chickens into the hut. The chickens' squawking was unbearable, as was their flying about bumping into everyone.

"Rabbi, the situation is worse! Now what should we do?" asked the farmer.

"Bring your two goats into the hut," he replied.

The two goats ate the tablecloth and the pile of laundry waiting to be washed. "Good heavens, Rabbi," cried the wife, "the situation is even worse! Now what should we do?" "You must bring Batya the cow into your hut."

Now the parents and children could not even all squeeze into their own home. When Batya kicked over the baby's cradle, they all had had enough.

"Rabbi, Rabbi, what should we do now? Could anything be worse?" The rabbi told them, "Remove the chickens, goats and cow and your problem will be solved." They did; it was!

Commentary:

It is tempting to be envious of what others have. We sometimes wish we had a bigger house, faster bike, newer sneakers, or a better baseball glove. It takes a lot of will power to put aside our jealousies. We can help ourselves do this by counting the many blessings that we do have.

ON SAYING BLESSINGS AT THE BEGINNING OF THE DAY

In *Birḥot Hashaḥar*, we repeat the words, "*Baruḥ atah Adonai*," sixteen times! Why not just say it once at the beginning?

When we say a blessing, we are reminded that we are partners with God. If we say, for example, that God frees those who are captives, then we must be inspired to help free those in our world who are not free.

Rabbi Levi Isaac of Berdichev taught, "Whenever a person lifts his/her hands to do a deed, that person should consider the hands as messengers of God."

Challenge yourself:

Try to say 100 *braḥot* in one day! You can find *braḥot* listed in a complete prayerbook such as *Siddur Sim Shalom*.

בִּרְכוֹת הַשַּׁחַר

בָּרוּךְ אַתָּה יְיָ אֱלֹהֵינוּ מֶלֶךְ הָעוֹלָם, אֲשֶׁר נָתַן לַשֶּׂכְוִי בִינָה לְהַבְחִין בֵּין יוֹם וּבֵין לָיְלָה:

בָּרוּךְ אַתָּה יְיָ אֱלֹהֵינוּ מֶלֶךְ הָעוֹלָם, שֶׁעָשַׂנִי בְּצַלְמוֹ:

בָּרוּךְ אַתָּה יְיָ אֱלֹהֵינוּ מֶלֶךְ הָעוֹלָם, שֶׁעָשַׂנִי בֶּן־[בַּת־] חוֹרִין:

בָּרוּךְ אַתָּה יְיָ אֱלֹהֵינוּ מֶלֶךְ הָעוֹלָם, שֶׁעָשַׂנִי יִשְׂרָאֵל:

בָּרוּךְ אַתָּה יְיָ אֱלֹהֵינוּ מֶלֶךְ הָעוֹלָם, פּוֹקֵחַ עִוְרִים:

בָּרוּךְ אַתָּה יְיָ אֱלֹהֵינוּ מֶלֶךְ הָעוֹלָם, מַלְבִּישׁ עֲרֻמִּים:

בָּרוּךְ אַתָּה יְיָ אֱלֹהֵינוּ מֶלֶךְ הָעוֹלָם, מַתִּיר אֲסוּרִים:

בָּרוּךְ אַתָּה יְיָ אֱלֹהֵינוּ מֶלֶךְ הָעוֹלָם, זוֹקֵף כְּפוּפִים:

בָּרוּךְ אַתָּה יְיָ אֱלֹהֵינוּ מֶלֶךְ הָעוֹלָם, רוֹקַע הָאָרֶץ עַל הַמָּיִם:

בָּרוּךְ אַתָּה יְיָ אֱלֹהֵינוּ מֶלֶךְ הָעוֹלָם, שֶׁעָשָׂה לִי כָּל־צָרְכִּי:

בָּרוּךְ אַתָּה יְיָ אֱלֹהֵינוּ מֶלֶךְ הָעוֹלָם, הַמֵּכִין מִצְעֲדֵי־גָבֶר:

בָּרוּךְ אַתָּה יְיָ אֱלֹהֵינוּ מֶלֶךְ הָעוֹלָם, אוֹזֵר יִשְׂרָאֵל בִּגְבוּרָה:

בָּרוּךְ אַתָּה יְיָ אֱלֹהֵינוּ מֶלֶךְ הָעוֹלָם, עוֹטֵר יִשְׂרָאֵל בְּתִפְאָרָה:

בָּרוּךְ אַתָּה יְיָ אֱלֹהֵינוּ מֶלֶךְ הָעוֹלָם, הַנּוֹתֵן לַיָּעֵף כֹּחַ:

בָּרוּךְ אַתָּה יְיָ אֱלֹהֵינוּ מֶלֶךְ הָעוֹלָם, הַמַּעֲבִיר שֵׁנָה מֵעֵינַי וּתְנוּמָה מֵעַפְעַפָּי:

As we bless the Source of life, so we are blessed.
And the blessing gives us strength and makes our vision clear.
And the blessing gives us peace, and the courage to dare.

Thank You, *Adonai* our God, Source of blessing, for letting me see a new day.
Thank You, *Adonai* our God, Source of blessing, for forming me in Your image.
Thank You, *Adonai* our God, Source of blessing, for granting me freedom.
Thank You, *Adonai* our God, Source of blessing, for making me a Jewish person.
Thank You, *Adonai* our God, Source of blessing, for opening our eyes to all that is around us.
Thank You, *Adonai* our God, Source of blessing, for giving clothes to protect us.
Thank You, *Adonai* our God, Source of blessing, for releasing the oppressed.
Thank You, *Adonai* our God, Source of blessing, for strengthening those who are tired or afraid.
Thank You, *Adonai* our God, Source of blessing, for creating heaven and earth.
Thank You, *Adonai* our God, Source of blessing, for providing me with all my needs.
Thank You, *Adonai* our God, Source of blessing, for offering guidance and hope.
Thank You, *Adonai* our God, Source of blessing, for giving us courage.
Thank You, *Adonai* our God, Source of blessing, for crowning us with glory.
Thank You, *Adonai* our God, Source of blessing, for restoring our energy.
Thank You, *Adonai* our God, Source of blessing, for removing sleep from my eyes and slumber from my eyelids.

בָּרוּךְ שֶׁאָמַר

בָּרוּךְ שֶׁאָמַר וְהָיָה הָעוֹלָם, בָּרוּךְ הוּא,
בָּרוּךְ עֹשֶׂה בְרֵאשִׁית, בָּרוּךְ אוֹמֵר וְעוֹשֶׂה,
בָּרוּךְ גּוֹזֵר וּמְקַיֵּם, בָּרוּךְ מְרַחֵם עַל הָאָרֶץ,
בָּרוּךְ מְרַחֵם עַל הַבְּרִיּוֹת, בָּרוּךְ מְשַׁלֵּם שָׂכָר טוֹב לִירֵאָיו,
בָּרוּךְ חַי לָעַד וְקַיָּם לָנֶצַח,
בָּרוּךְ פּוֹדֶה וּמַצִּיל, בָּרוּךְ שְׁמוֹ.
בָּרוּךְ אַתָּה יְיָ אֱלֹהֵינוּ מֶלֶךְ הָעוֹלָם, הָאֵל הָאָב הָרַחֲמָן.
הַמְהֻלָּל בְּפִי עַמּוֹ, מְשֻׁבָּח וּמְפֹאָר בִּלְשׁוֹן חֲסִידָיו וַעֲבָדָיו.
בָּרוּךְ אַתָּה יְיָ מֶלֶךְ מְהֻלָּל בַּתִּשְׁבָּחוֹת.

Blessed is the One Who spoke and the world was created.
Blessed is the One Who cares for the earth and all its creatures.
Blessed is the One Who keeps promises.
Blessed is the One Who judges and rewards.
Blessed is the One Who lives forever.
Blessed is Your holy name.

Your faithful ones will bless You, *Adonai*, and will sing hymns to Your glory.

Where Heaven and Earth Touch
So Closely, They Appear to be Kissing

In birth, in love,
and in death;
at the horizon (of course),
in the sun's warming the earth so we may live,
in the green leaves' edges
rusting and turning to gold in the Fall,
in bread and its grains and the rains that raise the seed;
in the sapphire and ruby, the emerald and the diamond uncut;
in fingers barely intertwined;
in the red of blood,
the yellow-on-black of the pansies,
the blue of night waters under the rising and the risen moon,
the flesh of flesh;
in Torah, in Mitzvahs,
in candles and forgiveness,
in your never-ending care.

Prayer Warm-Up

If you were going to run in a race, you'd first have to do warm-up exercises to get your body ready. It's like that with prayer, too. Reading psalms helps us get in the mood for praying. They help us get ready for the main part of the service.

We can also add our own prayers to help us get ready for the main part of the service. Try creating a prayer-poem by completing one of these sentence stems:

Sing to *Adonai*...
Let all peoples praise *Adonai*...
The earth declares God's glory...

Why is praying with *kavanah* (feeling) easier for someone who prays regularly?

A selection from Psalm 34:

לְכוּ בָנִים שִׁמְעוּ לִי, יִרְאַת יְיָ אֲלַמֶּדְכֶם.
מִי הָאִישׁ הֶחָפֵץ חַיִּים, אֹהֵב יָמִים לִרְאוֹת טוֹב.
נְצֹר לְשׁוֹנְךָ מֵרָע וּשְׂפָתֶיךָ מִדַּבֵּר מִרְמָה.
סוּר מֵרָע וַעֲשֵׂה טוֹב, בַּקֵּשׁ שָׁלוֹם וְרָדְפֵהוּ.

Come children; listen to me, and I will teach you to be in awe of God.

Who is the person who wants life, who desires good? Keep your tongue from evil, and your lips from speaking falsely. Avoid evil and do good; Seek peace and chase after it.

Selections from Psalm 136:

הודו לַיְיָ כִּי טוב	כִּי לְעוֹלָם חַסְדּוֹ.
הודו לֵאלֹהֵי הָאֱלֹהִים	כִּי לְעוֹלָם חַסְדּוֹ.
הודו לַאֲדֹנֵי הָאֲדֹנִים	כִּי לְעוֹלָם חַסְדּוֹ.
לְעֹשֵׂה נִפְלָאוֹת גְּדֹלוֹת לְבַדּוֹ	כִּי לְעוֹלָם חַסְדּוֹ.
לְעֹשֵׂה הַשָּׁמַיִם בִּתְבוּנָה	כִּי לְעוֹלָם חַסְדּוֹ.
לְרֹקַע הָאָרֶץ עַל הַמָּיִם	כִּי לְעוֹלָם חַסְדּוֹ.
לְעֹשֵׂה אוֹרִים גְּדֹלִים	כִּי לְעוֹלָם חַסְדּוֹ.
נֹתֵן לֶחֶם לְכָל־בָּשָׂר	כִּי לְעוֹלָם חַסְדּוֹ.
הודו לְאֵל הַשָּׁמָיִם	כִּי לְעוֹלָם חַסְדּוֹ.

Leader	Congregation
Give thanks to *Adonai* for God is good.	God's love is forever.
Give thanks to the Supreme God.	*Ki l'olam ḥasdo.*
Give thanks to the Ruler of rulers.	*Ki l'olam ḥasdo.*
Give thanks to the One Who alone does wonders.	*Ki l'olam ḥasdo.*
Give thanks to the One Who spread the earth over waters.	*Ki l'olam ḥasdo.*
Give thanks to the One Who made great lights.	*Ki l'olam ḥasdo.*
Give thanks to the One who feeds all creatures.	*Ki l'olam ḥasdo.*
Give thanks to the God of the Universe.	*Ki l'olam ḥasdo.*

A selection from Psalm 92

מִזְמוֹר שִׁיר לְיוֹם הַשַּׁבָּת.
טוֹב לְהֹדוֹת לַיְיָ, וּלְזַמֵּר לְשִׁמְךָ עֶלְיוֹן.
לְהַגִּיד בַּבֹּקֶר חַסְדֶּךָ, וֶאֱמוּנָתְךָ בַּלֵּילוֹת.
עֲלֵי עָשׂוֹר וַעֲלֵי נָבֶל, עֲלֵי הִגָּיוֹן בְּכִנּוֹר.
כִּי שִׂמַּחְתַּנִי יְיָ בְּפָעֳלֶךָ, בְּמַעֲשֵׂי יָדֶיךָ אֲרַנֵּן.
מַה גָּדְלוּ מַעֲשֶׂיךָ יְיָ, מְאֹד עָמְקוּ מַחְשְׁבֹתֶיךָ.
צַדִּיק כַּתָּמָר יִפְרָח, כְּאֶרֶז בַּלְּבָנוֹן יִשְׂגֶּה.
שְׁתוּלִים בְּבֵית יְיָ, בְּחַצְרוֹת אֱלֹהֵינוּ יַפְרִיחוּ.
עוֹד יְנוּבוּן בְּשֵׂיבָה, דְּשֵׁנִים וְרַעֲנַנִּים יִהְיוּ.
לְהַגִּיד כִּי יָשָׁר יְיָ, צוּרִי וְלֹא עַוְלָתָה בּוֹ.

(A Selection)

It is good to give thanks to *Adonai*
And to sing praises to Your supreme name,

Telling of Your kindness in the morning
And Your faithfulness each night,

To the music of lyre and lute
And with melodies on the harp.

You raise me with Your deeds.
I sing for joy at the work of Your hands.

How incredible are Your acts, *Adonai*!
How incredible are Your thoughts!

The righteous shall thrive like the palm tree
And grow mighty like a cedar tree from Lebanon.

Planted in the house of *Adonai*,
They shall thrive and bear fruit.

Even in old age they shall reproduce
And be fresh and vigorous.

Ready to tell that *Adonai* is just,
My Rock, Who is without fault.

(A Selection)

הַלְלוּיָהּ. הַלְלוּ אֵל בְּקָדְשׁוֹ, הַלְלוּהוּ בִּרְקִיעַ עֻזּוֹ.
הַלְלוּהוּ בִגְבוּרֹתָיו, הַלְלוּהוּ כְּרֹב גֻּדְלוֹ.
הַלְלוּהוּ בְּתֵקַע שׁוֹפָר, הַלְלוּהוּ בְּנֵבֶל וְכִנּוֹר.
הַלְלוּהוּ בְתֹף וּמָחוֹל, הַלְלוּהוּ בְּמִנִּים וְעֻגָב.
הַלְלוּהוּ בְצִלְצְלֵי־שָׁמַע, הַלְלוּהוּ בְּצִלְצְלֵי תְרוּעָה.
כֹּל הַנְּשָׁמָה תְּהַלֵּל יָהּ. הַלְלוּיָהּ.
כֹּל הַנְּשָׁמָה תְּהַלֵּל יָהּ. הַלְלוּיָהּ.

Halleluyah!
Praise God in the holy place.
Praise God in the heavens.
Sing praises for mighty acts .
Blast the shofar -
Strum the strings -
Toot the flutes -
Clang the cymbals -
Beat the drums -
Let everything that breathes sing praise.
Halleluyah!

Halleluhu v'tziltz'lei shama, halleluhu b'tziltz'lei t'ruah.
Kol han'shamah t'hallel ya, halleluyah.

Songs of Praise

When King David went to sleep at night, he would place his golden harp by his bed. At midnight, the breeze from the open window would cause the harp to make lovely sounds. This music would awaken King David and inspire him to write the beautiful psalms for which he would become famous.

One night after he completed a psalm, he was so proud of himself that he went to the open window and shouted boastingly: "O God, is there anyone in the whole wide world who has ever sung Your praises so well? Can any living creature match my psalms?"

Imagine King David's shock when a frog jumped out of the water and croaked, "Stop your bragging. For thousands of years my ancestors have been raising their voices to praise God. And you can hear our song of praise all day and night, if you just listen with your heart." Then the Holy One spoke. "All living things have the power to praise, each in their own way. To me the voices of the poets and the voices of the frogs are equal."

Having learned his lesson, Kind David sat down and wrote, "Happy are they that dwell in Your house, they are ever praising You."

נִשְׁמַת

Nishmat is said only on *Shabbat* and *Yom Tov* because they are days when we are not working or busy at school. This gives us the time to think about the prayer's message, that "the breath of all that lives" points to God's greatness.

נִשְׁמַת כָּל־חַי תְּבָרֵךְ אֶת־שִׁמְךָ יְיָ אֱלֹהֵינוּ, וְרוּחַ כָּל־בָּשָׂר
תְּפָאֵר וּתְרוֹמֵם זִכְרְךָ מַלְכֵּנוּ תָּמִיד. מִן הָעוֹלָם וְעַד הָעוֹלָם
אַתָּה אֵל, וּמִבַּלְעָדֶיךָ אֵין לָנוּ מֶלֶךְ גּוֹאֵל וּמוֹשִׁיעַ, פּוֹדֶה
וּמַצִּיל וּמְפַרְנֵס וּמְרַחֵם בְּכָל־עֵת צָרָה וְצוּקָה. אֵין לָנוּ מֶלֶךְ
אֶלָּא אָתָּה.

The breath of all that lives shall bless Your name, *Adonai*, and shall sing of Your greatness. Since the beginning of time to the end of days, You are our God; we have no other. You help us when we are in trouble and guide us in times of stress. God of all generations, to You alone we give thanks.

אִלּוּ פִינוּ מָלֵא שִׁירָה כַּיָּם
וּלְשׁוֹנֵנוּ רִנָּה כַּהֲמוֹן גַּלָּיו
וְשִׂפְתוֹתֵינוּ שֶׁבַח כְּמֶרְחֲבֵי רָקִיעַ
וְעֵינֵינוּ מְאִירוֹת כַּשֶּׁמֶשׁ וְכַיָּרֵחַ
וְיָדֵינוּ פְרוּשׂוֹת כְּנִשְׁרֵי שָׁמָיִם
וְרַגְלֵינוּ קַלּוֹת כָּאַיָּלוֹת
אֵין אֲנַחְנוּ מַסְפִּיקִים לְהוֹדוֹת לְךָ יְיָ אֱלֹהֵינוּ וֵאלֹהֵי אֲבוֹתֵינוּ
וּלְבָרֵךְ אֶת־שִׁמְךָ עַל אַחַת מֵאֶלֶף אַלְפֵי אֲלָפִים וְרִבֵּי רְבָבוֹת
פְּעָמִים הַטּוֹבוֹת שֶׁעָשִׂיתָ עִם אֲבוֹתֵינוּ וְעִמָּנוּ.

Even if our mouths were filled with as much song as the oceans hold water
And even if our lips could form enough words to fill an endless sky,
We would still be unable to thank You for all the good
You have done for our ancestors and for us.
Stay with us, *Adonai*,
And we will bless Your Holy name.

On a festival, *Yom Tov*, the leader begins aloud here:

הָאֵל בְּתַעֲצֻמוֹת עֻזֶּךָ, הַגָּדוֹל בִּכְבוֹד שְׁמֶךָ, הַגִּבּוֹר לָנֶצַח
וְהַנּוֹרָא בְּנוֹרְאוֹתֶיךָ, הַמֶּלֶךְ יוֹשֵׁב עַל כִּסֵּא רָם וְנִשָּׂא.

You are God by the strength of Your might. You are God by the glory by which You are known, powerful forever by Your awesome deeds. You, our Ruler, sit within our mind's eye as on a majestic throne on high.

On *Shabbat*, the leader begins here:

שׁוֹכֵן עַד, מָרוֹם וְקָדוֹשׁ שְׁמוֹ.
וְכָתוּב: רַנְּנוּ צַדִּיקִים בַּייָ
לַיְשָׁרִים נָאוָה תְהִלָּה.
בְּפִי יְשָׁרִים תִּתְהַלָּל
וּבְדִבְרֵי צַדִּיקִים תִּתְבָּרַךְ
וּבִלְשׁוֹן חֲסִידִים תִּתְרוֹמָם
וּבְקֶרֶב קְדוֹשִׁים תִּתְקַדָּשׁ.

You are honored by the mouth of the upright.
You are blessed by the words of the righteous.
You are declared holy by the tongue of the faithful.
You are praised in the hearts of good and kind people.

וּבְמַקְהֲלוֹת רִבְבוֹת עַמְּךָ בֵּית יִשְׂרָאֵל בְּרִנָּה יִתְפָּאַר שִׁמְךָ
מַלְכֵּנוּ בְּכָל־דּוֹר וָדוֹר. שֶׁכֵּן חוֹבַת כָּל־הַיְצוּרִים לְפָנֶיךָ יְיָ
אֱלֹהֵינוּ וֵאלֹהֵי אֲבוֹתֵינוּ לְהוֹדוֹת לְהַלֵּל לְשַׁבֵּחַ לְפָאֵר לְרוֹמֵם
לְהַדֵּר לְבָרֵךְ לְעַלֵּה וּלְקַלֵּס עַל כָּל־דִּבְרֵי שִׁירוֹת וְתִשְׁבְּחוֹת
דָּוִד בֶּן־יִשַׁי עַבְדְּךָ מְשִׁיחֶךָ.

In every generation, Your people Israel gathers to sing Your praises, adding songs to those written by King David, Your dedicated servant.

יִשְׁתַּבַּח שִׁמְךָ לָעַד, מַלְכֵּנוּ, הָאֵל הַמֶּלֶךְ הַגָּדוֹל וְהַקָּדוֹשׁ
בַּשָּׁמַיִם וּבָאָרֶץ. כִּי לְךָ נָאֶה, יְיָ אֱלֹהֵינוּ וֵאלֹהֵי אֲבוֹתֵינוּ, שִׁיר
וּשְׁבָחָה הַלֵּל וְזִמְרָה, עֹז וּמֶמְשָׁלָה, נֶצַח גְּדֻלָּה וּגְבוּרָה, תְּהִלָּה
וְתִפְאֶרֶת, קְדֻשָּׁה וּמַלְכוּת, בְּרָכוֹת וְהוֹדָאוֹת מֵעַתָּה וְעַד
עוֹלָם. בָּרוּךְ אַתָּה יְיָ אֵל מֶלֶךְ גָּדוֹל בַּתִּשְׁבָּחוֹת, אֵל
הַהוֹדָאוֹת אֲדוֹן הַנִּפְלָאוֹת הַבּוֹחֵר בְּשִׁירֵי זִמְרָה, מֶלֶךְ אֵל חֵי
הָעוֹלָמִים.

May You be praised forever with songs that tell of Your strength, glory and holiness. We look to You for blessing as we offer You thanksgiving. Praised are You, *Adonai* our Ruler and Do-er of wonders, Who delights in our songs.

THE *KADDISH*

The *Kaddish* is recited only if there is a *minyan* (ten people).

No one is perfect. If we pray as a group, each person makes up for what the other is lacking. Each takes strength from the others.

Individuals play an important part, but only the community can guarantee the survival of the Jewish people.

Though mourners recite a version of the *Kaddish*, there is no mention of death in this prayer. The *Kaddish* praises God and asks for peace in the world. It enables us, despite our sadness, to continue living in a positive way, carrying the memory of our loved ones in our hearts and minds.

By answering "*amen*" at appropriate times during the *Kaddish*, we show our agreement with the words being said, indicate our participation in the community, and, during the Mourner's *Kaddish*, support those who mourn and affirm their words of prayer.

חֲצִי קַדִּישׁ
ḤATZI KADDISH

Leader:

יִתְגַּדַּל וְיִתְקַדַּשׁ שְׁמֵהּ רַבָּא בְּעָלְמָא דִּי בְרָא כִרְעוּתֵהּ,
וְיַמְלִיךְ מַלְכוּתֵהּ בְּחַיֵּיכוֹן וּבְיוֹמֵיכוֹן וּבְחַיֵּי דְכָל־בֵּית
יִשְׂרָאֵל בַּעֲגָלָא וּבִזְמַן קָרִיב, וְאִמְרוּ אָמֵן.

Congregation and Leader answer:

יְהֵא שְׁמֵהּ רַבָּא מְבָרַךְ לְעָלַם וּלְעָלְמֵי עָלְמַיָּא.

Y'hei shmei rabba m'voraḥ l'olam u'l'olmei almay'ya.

Leader:

יִתְבָּרַךְ וְיִשְׁתַּבַּח וְיִתְפָּאַר וְיִתְרוֹמַם וְיִתְנַשֵּׂא וְיִתְהַדַּר
וְיִתְעַלֶּה וְיִתְהַלָּל שְׁמֵהּ דְּקֻדְשָׁא

Congregation and Leader answer:

בְּרִיךְ הוּא.

Briḥ hu.

Leader:

לְעֵלָּא [לְעֵלָּא מִכָּל־] מִן כָּל־בִּרְכָתָא וְשִׁירָתָא תֻּשְׁבְּחָתָא
וְנֶחֱמָתָא דַּאֲמִירָן בְּעָלְמָא, וְאִמְרוּ אָמֵן.

The *Minyan*

The *bareḥu* is our official call to worship. It signals that the "warm-up" section of the service is over. Now the main prayers begin. The *bareḥu* is also our invitation to community prayer. We can't say it unless we have a *minyan* (ten people). We also can not publicly repeat the *Amidah* or do the Torah reading or recite the *Kaddish* without a *minyan*.

"All words of holiness require an invitation." (*Zohar* 43a, 192.1)

What is the importance of asking people to join together in prayer?

We rise:

Leader:

בָּרְכוּ אֶת־יְיָ הַמְבֹרָךְ.

Let us praise.
Barḥu et Adonai ham'voraḥ.

Congregation, then leader:

בָּרוּךְ יְיָ הַמְבֹרָךְ לְעוֹלָם וָעֶד.

Praised are You, *Adonai*, the Source of all blessings, forever and ever.
Baruḥ Adonai ham'voraḥ l'olam va'ed.

We are seated.

יוצר אור ובורא חושך

בָּרוּךְ אַתָּה יְיָ אֱלֹהֵינוּ מֶלֶךְ הָעוֹלָם, יוֹצֵר אוֹר וּבוֹרֵא
חֹשֶׁךְ עֹשֶׂה שָׁלוֹם וּבוֹרֵא אֶת־הַכֹּל.

Praised are You, *Adonai*, Source of all blessing, Who forms light and darkness, Who makes peace and creates all things.

Baruḥ atah Adonai, Eloheinu Meleḥ ha'olam, yotzer or u'vorei ḥosheh, oseh shalom u'vorei et hakol.

In the prayer, *"Yotzer Or,"* the words "*yotzer* (forms)," "*borei* (creates)," and "*oseh* (makes)" are in the present tense. What does that teach us about creation?

God creates things that can be seen and things that cannot be seen. Can you add to the list below?

Things we can see:
oceans
trees
animals

Things we cannot see:
love
loyalty
knowledge

How do we know that things we can't see exist?

There is a *midrash* about Adam and Eve's first day on earth. As the sun set, Adam and Eve were terrified of the dark. When the sun began to rise the next morning, their fears went away. They realized that the world had a plan; light would follow the dark.

In ancient times, people believed that one god created day and another god created night. Abraham was the first to teach us that there is one God, Who created the entire universe. Opposites, like light and darkness, are not in conflict, but are in harmony, as part of God's plan.

In the creation story, the first thing God created was light. When we wake up in the morning, the first thing we see is light. Is this a coincidence?

Imagine that you are waking up for the first time. Describe your sense of wonder and amazement.

MORNING HAS BROKEN

Morning has broken like the first morning
Blackbird has spoken like the first bird
Praise for the singing, praise for the morning
Praise for the springing fresh from the Word.

Sweet the rain's new fall sunlit from heaven
Like the first dew fall on the first grass
Praise for the sweetness of the wet garden
Sprung in completeness where God's feet pass.

Mine is the sunlight, mine is the morning
Born of the one light Eden saw play
Praise with elation, praise every morning
God's re-creation of the new day.

On a festival that takes place on a weekday, continue with *hame'ir la'aretz* — "In Your mercy, You give light," p. 95.

On *Shabbat* we say this:

הַכֹּל יוֹדְוּךָ, וְהַכֹּל יְשַׁבְּחְוּךָ, וְהַכֹּל יֹאמְרוּ: אֵין קָדוֹשׁ כַּיְיָ.
הַכֹּל יְרוֹמְמְוּךָ סֶּלָה, יוֹצֵר הַכֹּל, הָאֵל הַפּוֹתֵחַ בְּכָל־יוֹם
דַּלְתוֹת שַׁעֲרֵי מִזְרָח, וּבוֹקֵעַ חַלּוֹנֵי רָקִיעַ, מוֹצִיא חַמָּה
מִמְּקוֹמָהּ וּלְבָנָה מִמְּכוֹן שִׁבְתָּהּ, וּמֵאִיר לָעוֹלָם כֻּלּוֹ וּלְיוֹשְׁבָיו
שֶׁבָּרָא בְּמִדַּת רַחֲמִים. הַמֵּאִיר לָאָרֶץ וְלַדָּרִים עָלֶיהָ
בְּרַחֲמִים, וּבְטוּבוֹ מְחַדֵּשׁ בְּכָל־יוֹם תָּמִיד מַעֲשֵׂה בְרֵאשִׁית.

All shall thank You. All shall praise You. All shall say, "There is none holy like *Adonai*!" All shall honor You, the Creator of all. Each day, You open the gates of the east, parting the windows of the sky. You usher the sun from its place and the moon from its home, giving light to the whole world and to those created with Your mercy. In Your goodness, You renew the work of creation day by day.

The *Shabbat* is the weekly celebration of creation. *El Adon* is sung only on *Shabbat*, emphasizing God's power and goodness as Creator of the Universe.

אֵל אָדוֹן עַל כָּל־הַמַּעֲשִׂים, בָּרוּךְ וּמְבֹרָךְ בְּפִי כָּל־נְשָׁמָה.
גָּדְלוֹ וְטוּבוֹ מָלֵא עוֹלָם, דַּעַת וּתְבוּנָה סוֹבְבִים אוֹתוֹ.
הַמִּתְגָּאֶה עַל חַיּוֹת הַקֹּדֶשׁ, וְנֶהְדָּר בְּכָבוֹד עַל הַמֶּרְכָּבָה.
זְכוּת וּמִישׁוֹר לִפְנֵי כִסְאוֹ, חֶסֶד וְרַחֲמִים לִפְנֵי כְבוֹדוֹ.
טוֹבִים מְאוֹרוֹת שֶׁבָּרָא אֱלֹהֵינוּ, יְצָרָם בְּדַעַת בְּבִינָה וּבְהַשְׂכֵּל.
כֹּחַ וּגְבוּרָה נָתַן בָּהֶם, לִהְיוֹת מוֹשְׁלִים בְּקֶרֶב תֵּבֵל.
מְלֵאִים זִיו וּמְפִיקִים נֹגַה, נָאֶה זִיוָם בְּכָל־הָעוֹלָם.
שְׂמֵחִים בְּצֵאתָם וְשָׂשִׂים בְּבוֹאָם, עוֹשִׂים בְּאֵימָה רְצוֹן קוֹנָם.
פְּאֵר וְכָבוֹד נוֹתְנִים לִשְׁמוֹ, צָהֳלָה וְרִנָּה לְזֵכֶר מַלְכוּתוֹ.
קָרָא לַשֶּׁמֶשׁ וַיִּזְרַח אוֹר, רָאָה וְהִתְקִין צוּרַת הַלְּבָנָה.
שֶׁבַח נוֹתְנִים לוֹ כָּל־צְבָא מָרוֹם, תִּפְאֶרֶת וּגְדֻלָּה שְׂרָפִים
וְאוֹפַנִּים וְחַיּוֹת הַקֹּדֶשׁ.

El Adon — An Interpretation

God, the Creator of all,
is praised by every soul.
God's greatness and essence
enter the world, as wisdom
announces the Holy presence.

Your praises we laud
for we are so awed
by sun, moon and stars
that we view from afar,
created by You skillfully,
with energy and beauty.

Full of splendor they shine,
doing what is assigned
to them by their Maker.
They rejoice so proud,
singing praises aloud
of the Holy One, the Creator.

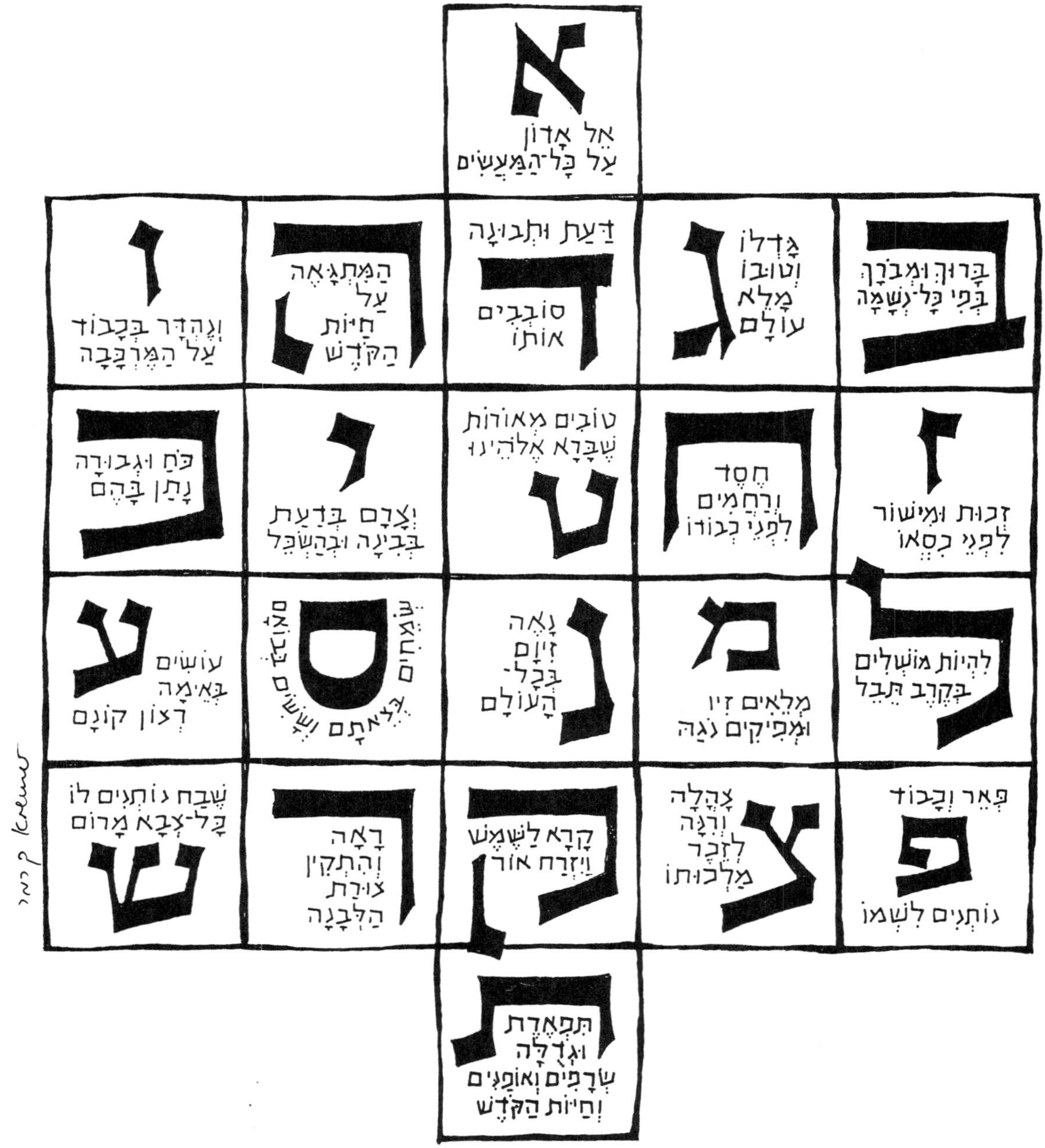

***S**habbat* rest is a state of peace between humanity and nature.

On *Shabbat*, we don't catch a butterfly, pick flowers, or pull out a blade of grass. We leave them alone to just enjoy and we thank God for creating them.

***S**habbat* is a time when we can appreciate what we're often too busy to notice during the other days of the week.

On weekdays only we say:

הַמֵּאִיר לָאָרֶץ וְלַדָּרִים עָלֶיהָ בְּרַחֲמִים וּבְטוּבוֹ מְחַדֵּשׁ בְּכָל־יוֹם תָּמִיד מַעֲשֵׂה בְרֵאשִׁית. מָה רַבּוּ מַעֲשֶׂיךָ יְיָ, כֻּלָּם בְּחָכְמָה עָשִׂיתָ, מָלְאָה הָאָרֶץ קִנְיָנֶךָ. הַמֶּלֶךְ הַמְרוֹמָם לְבַדּוֹ מֵאָז, הַמְשֻׁבָּח וְהַמְפֹאָר וְהַמִּתְנַשֵּׂא מִימוֹת עוֹלָם, אֱלֹהֵי עוֹלָם, בְּרַחֲמֶיךָ הָרַבִּים רַחֵם עָלֵינוּ, אֲדוֹן עֻזֵּנוּ, צוּר מִשְׂגַּבֵּנוּ, מָגֵן יִשְׁעֵנוּ, מִשְׂגָּב בַּעֲדֵנוּ.

In Your mercy, You give light to the earth and all its inhabitants. In Your goodness, You renew each day the work of creation. You are firm like a rock and protecting like a shield. We have depended on You since the world began and have praised You from the beginning of time. Now, today, view us with kindness.

One of the words associated with *Shabbat* is "*menuḥah*" which means "rest." Most of all, in connection with *Shabbat*, it means to relax and be in harmony with the rest of creation. Some *Shabbat menuḥah* activities, are:

- Find a pleasant route to take a walk.
- Sit in a garden; observe and smell.
- Spend time talking to a close friend.
- Play scrabble with a parent. (Play for fun without keeping score, or keep track of your points by placing a bookmark in a paperback.)
- Look at family albums with a brother or sister.
- Ask a grandparent to tell you stories about when he/she was your age.
- Take a little snooze.

לָאֵל בָּרוּךְ, נְעִימוֹת יִתֵּנוּ. לַמֶּלֶךְ אֵל חַי וְקַיָּם, זְמִירוֹת
יֹאמֵרוּ וְתִשְׁבָּחוֹת יַשְׁמִיעוּ, כִּי הוּא לְבַדּוֹ פּוֹעֵל גְּבוּרוֹת, עֹשֶׂה
חֲדָשׁוֹת, בַּעַל מִלְחָמוֹת, זוֹרֵעַ צְדָקוֹת, מַצְמִיחַ יְשׁוּעוֹת, בּוֹרֵא
רְפוּאוֹת, נוֹרָא תְהִלּוֹת, אֲדוֹן הַנִּפְלָאוֹת, הַמְחַדֵּשׁ בְּטוּבוֹ
בְּכָל־יוֹם תָּמִיד מַעֲשֵׂה בְרֵאשִׁית, כָּאָמוּר: לְעֹשֵׂה אוֹרִים
גְּדֹלִים, כִּי לְעוֹלָם חַסְדּוֹ. אוֹר חָדָשׁ עַל צִיּוֹן תָּאִיר, וְנִזְכֶּה
כֻלָּנוּ מְהֵרָה לְאוֹרוֹ. בָּרוּךְ אַתָּה יְיָ יוֹצֵר הַמְּאוֹרוֹת.

To the Source of blessing, they sweetly sing: to the living and eternal God, they utter hymns and praises; for God is unique doing mighty deeds, creating new life, championing justice, producing triumphs, and giving healing. As the psalmist sings: “Praise the One Who makes great lights for the loving-kindness of God endures forever.” Cause a new light to shine on Zion and may we all enjoy its splendor. Praised are You, *Adonai*, Creator of lights.

אַהֲבָה רַבָּה אֲהַבְתָּנוּ, יְיָ אֱלֹהֵינוּ, חֶמְלָה גְדוֹלָה וִיתֵרָה חָמַלְתָּ
עָלֵינוּ. אָבִינוּ מַלְכֵּנוּ, בַּעֲבוּר אֲבוֹתֵינוּ שֶׁבָּטְחוּ בְךָ וַתְּלַמְּדֵם חֻקֵּי
חַיִּים, כֵּן תְּחָנֵּנוּ וּתְלַמְּדֵנוּ. אָבִינוּ הָאָב הָרַחֲמָן, הַמְרַחֵם, רַחֵם
עָלֵינוּ וְתֵן בְּלִבֵּנוּ לְהָבִין וּלְהַשְׂכִּיל, לִשְׁמֹעַ, לִלְמֹד וּלְלַמֵּד,
לִשְׁמֹר וְלַעֲשׂוֹת וּלְקַיֵּם אֶת־כָּל־דִּבְרֵי תַלְמוּד תּוֹרָתֶךָ בְּאַהֲבָה.
וְהָאֵר עֵינֵינוּ בְּתוֹרָתֶךָ, וְדַבֵּק לִבֵּנוּ בְּמִצְוֹתֶיךָ וְיַחֵד לְבָבֵנוּ
לְאַהֲבָה וּלְיִרְאָה אֶת־שְׁמֶךָ, וְלֹא נֵבוֹשׁ לְעוֹלָם וָעֶד. כִּי בְשֵׁם
קָדְשְׁךָ הַגָּדוֹל וְהַנּוֹרָא בָּטָחְנוּ, נָגִילָה וְנִשְׂמְחָה בִּישׁוּעָתֶךָ.

וַהֲבִיאֵנוּ לְשָׁלוֹם מֵאַרְבַּע כַּנְפוֹת הָאָרֶץ, וְתוֹלִיכֵנוּ קוֹמְמִיּוּת
לְאַרְצֵנוּ, כִּי אֵל פּוֹעֵל יְשׁוּעוֹת אָתָּה, וּבָנוּ בָחַרְתָּ מִכָּל־עַם
וְלָשׁוֹן, וְקֵרַבְתָּנוּ לְשִׁמְךָ הַגָּדוֹל סֶלָה בֶּאֱמֶת, לְהוֹדוֹת לְךָ
וּלְיַחֶדְךָ בְּאַהֲבָה. בָּרוּךְ אַתָּה יְיָ הַבּוֹחֵר בְּעַמּוֹ יִשְׂרָאֵל בְּאַהֲבָה.

You have loved us with a great love and shown us much compassion. Holy parent, Who taught our ancestors life-giving laws, for their sake be gracious to us and teach us, too.

Merciful One, give us the ability to understand so that we may in love study Your Torah, follow its instructions, and pass on its teachings. Open our eyes to Your Torah and attach our hearts to your *mitzvot*. Unite our hearts to love and feel awe for You, so that we may never feel shame or humiliation. We trust in Your awesome holiness knowing that we will sing in joy because of your saving help. Safely gather our people from the four corners of the earth and bring us back to our ancient homeland. Draw us close to You so we can feel united as we proclaim Your oneness. Praised are You, *Adonai*, Who has lovingly chosen a closeness with Your people, Israel.

Since the State of Israel was established in 1948, people from all over the world have returned to our ancient homeland. Do you know from what countries the most recent waves of immigration have come? What encouraged them to make *aliyah*?

Ask your rabbi, principal or teacher about organizations that are helping new immigrants in Israel.

THOUGHTS ON *SHEMA YISRAEL*

When the time comes to recite *Shema Yisrael,* we don't need a formal gathering. In fact, we are instructed to stop whatever we are doing to say these important words.

Who do you think is saying *Shema Yisrael* and to whom is it being said?

How is the *Shema* like the Pledge of Allegiance to the flag?

It is customary that when we recite the *Shema*, we say each letter clearly and distinctly.

***A**yin* (ע), the last letter of the word *Shema* and *dalet* (ד), the last letter of the word *eḥad*, are larger than the other letters in the Torah and form the word *ed* (עֵד), or witness. Each time we say the *Shema*, we are like witnesses in court, testifying that God is One.

When you say the *Shema*, think of all the Jews who came before you who have proudly said this prayer!

How can you make sure this prayer will be said in the future?

וְאָהַבְתָּ and וְהָיָה אִם-שָׁמֹעַ

The sections of the *Shema* are all from the Torah.

The commands in the *"V'ahavta"* section are addressed to each individual person. The *"V'ahavta"* is the first example of a person or group being commanded to love God. Do you think it is possible to command someone to love? Why do you think the Torah does this?

Imagine that you were given an important message that must be protected and preserved forever. What would you do? See how your answer compares to the "plan" given to the Jewish people in the *V'ahavta* prayer.

"Bind them as a sign upon your arm" is the origin of *tefillin* (small prayer boxes strapped to the forehead and arm during the morning service on weekdays). They contain the *Shema* and *V'ahavta* and the following section together with other selections from the Torah. They are worn to remind us of the teachings of the Torah.

"On the doorposts": this is the origin of the *mezuzah*, a small case, which is attached to the doorpost, with the *Shema*, *V'ahavta* and *V'haya Im Shamoa* enclosed. It, too, reminds us to love God and follow the commandments.

A *mezuzah* also announces to everyone that this is a Jewish home. A Jewish home is not just a place to keep us warm and fed. It is a holy place where we follow *mitzvot*. It is the place where we enjoy our *Shabbat* meals. It is the place where we light the *Ḥanukkah menorah*. It is the place for a *seder*. It is a place where each day we can say blessings and prayers.

The second section after the *Shema* encourages us to become partners with God in caring for the earth. Today, people are beginning to realize that if we are not more careful, our planet could be destroyed. There are projects now to clear the air and waters, protect the ozone layer, and see that various animal species do not become extinct. We realize that our natural resources could become scarce. We must recycle products and learn to save energy. What programs in your community help to preserve the environment?

There are national organizations that are concerned with environmental issues. Ask your parents, rabbi, principal or teacher how to get in touch with them.

שְׁמַע יִשְׂרָאֵל יְיָ אֱלֹהֵינוּ יְיָ אֶחָד

Hear O Israel:
Adonai our God, *Adonai* is ONE.
Shema Yisrael, Adonai Eloheinu, Adonai Eḥad

In a whisper:

בָּרוּךְ שֵׁם כְּבוֹד מַלְכוּתוֹ לְעוֹלָם וָעֶד.

We praise God, Whose glorious presence is with us now and forever.
Baruḥ shem k'vod malḥuto l'olam va'ed.

וְאָהַבְתָּ אֵת יְהוָה אֱלֹהֶיךָ בְּכָל־לְבָבְךָ וּבְכָל־נַפְשְׁךָ
וּבְכָל־מְאֹדֶךָ: וְהָיוּ הַדְּבָרִים הָאֵלֶּה אֲשֶׁר אָנֹכִי מְצַוְּךָ הַיּוֹם
עַל־לְבָבֶךָ: וְשִׁנַּנְתָּם לְבָנֶיךָ וְדִבַּרְתָּ בָּם בְּשִׁבְתְּךָ בְּבֵיתֶךָ
וּבְלֶכְתְּךָ בַדֶּרֶךְ וּבְשָׁכְבְּךָ וּבְקוּמֶךָ: וּקְשַׁרְתָּם לְאוֹת
עַל־יָדֶךָ וְהָיוּ לְטֹטָפֹת בֵּין עֵינֶיךָ: וּכְתַבְתָּם עַל־מְזֻזוֹת
בֵּיתֶךָ וּבִשְׁעָרֶיךָ:

You shall love *Adonai*, your God, with all your heart, with all your soul and with all your might. And these words which I command you today, shall always be in your heart. Teach them to your children. Speak of them when you are at home and when you are away. Repeat them when you lie down at night and when you rise up in the morning. Bind them as a sign upon your arm and place them as a reminder between your eyes. Write them on the doorposts of your houses and on your gates.

וְהָיָ֗ה אִם־שָׁמֹ֤עַ תִּשְׁמְעוּ֙ אֶל־מִצְוֺתַ֔י אֲשֶׁ֧ר אָנֹכִ֛י מְצַוֶּ֥ה אֶתְכֶ֖ם
הַיּ֑וֹם לְאַהֲבָ֞ה אֶת־יְהֹוָ֤ה אֱלֹֽהֵיכֶם֙ וּלְעָבְד֔וֹ בְּכָל־לְבַבְכֶ֖ם
וּבְכָל־נַפְשְׁכֶֽם׃ וְנָתַתִּ֧י מְטַֽר־אַרְצְכֶ֛ם בְּעִתּ֖וֹ יוֹרֶ֣ה וּמַלְק֑וֹשׁ
וְאָסַפְתָּ֣ דְגָנֶ֔ךָ וְתִירֹֽשְׁךָ֖ וְיִצְהָרֶֽךָ׃ וְנָתַתִּ֛י עֵ֥שֶׂב בְּשָׂדְךָ֖ לִבְהֶמְתֶּ֑ךָ
וְאָכַלְתָּ֖ וְשָׂבָֽעְתָּ׃ הִשָּׁמְר֣וּ לָכֶ֔ם פֶּ֥ן יִפְתֶּ֖ה לְבַבְכֶ֑ם וְסַרְתֶּ֗ם
וַעֲבַדְתֶּם֙ אֱלֹהִ֣ים אֲחֵרִ֔ים וְהִשְׁתַּחֲוִיתֶ֖ם לָהֶֽם׃ וְחָרָ֨ה אַף־יְהֹוָ֜ה
בָּכֶ֗ם וְעָצַ֤ר אֶת־הַשָּׁמַ֙יִם֙ וְלֹא־יִהְיֶ֣ה מָטָ֔ר וְהָ֣אֲדָמָ֔ה לֹ֥א תִתֵּ֖ן
אֶת־יְבוּלָ֑הּ וַאֲבַדְתֶּ֣ם מְהֵרָ֗ה מֵעַל֙ הָאָ֣רֶץ הַטֹּבָ֔ה אֲשֶׁ֥ר יְהֹוָ֖ה
נֹתֵ֥ן לָכֶֽם׃ וְשַׂמְתֶּם֙ אֶת־דְּבָרַ֣י אֵ֔לֶּה עַל־לְבַבְכֶ֖ם וְעַל־נַפְשְׁכֶ֑ם
וּקְשַׁרְתֶּ֨ם אֹתָ֤ם לְאוֹת֙ עַל־יֶדְכֶ֔ם וְהָי֥וּ לְטוֹטָפֹ֖ת בֵּ֥ין עֵינֵיכֶֽם׃
וְלִמַּדְתֶּ֥ם אֹתָ֛ם אֶת־בְּנֵיכֶ֖ם לְדַבֵּ֣ר בָּ֑ם בְּשִׁבְתְּךָ֤ בְּבֵיתֶ֙ךָ֙
וּבְלֶכְתְּךָ֣ בַדֶּ֔רֶךְ וּבְשָׁכְבְּךָ֖ וּבְקוּמֶֽךָ׃ וּכְתַבְתָּ֛ם עַל־מְזוּז֥וֹת
בֵּיתֶ֖ךָ וּבִשְׁעָרֶֽיךָ׃ לְמַ֨עַן יִרְבּ֤וּ יְמֵיכֶם֙ וִימֵ֣י בְנֵיכֶ֔ם עַ֚ל הָֽאֲדָמָ֔ה
אֲשֶׁ֨ר נִשְׁבַּ֧ע יְהֹוָ֛ה לַאֲבֹתֵיכֶ֖ם לָתֵ֣ת לָהֶ֑ם כִּימֵ֥י הַשָּׁמַ֖יִם
עַל־הָאָֽרֶץ׃

If you sincerely follow My commandments, then I will favor your land
with rain at the proper season. Then you will have a full harvest of
grain, wine and oil and there will be grass in the fields for your cattle. You will eat and be satisfied. But if you turn from God's ways,
there will be no rain and the earth will not bring forth its produce.
In the end, you will even disappear from the good land which *Adonai*
has given you. Therefore, place these words of Mine in your heart
and in your soul. Bind them as a sign upon your arm and as a
reminder between your eyes. Teach them to your children. Speak
of them when you are at home and when you are away. Repeat
them when you lie down at night and when your rise up in the morning. Write them on the doorposts of your houses and on your gates.
They will make your days and the days of your descendants fuller
when you live in the land that God promised your ancestors.

וַיֹּאמֶר

The third section of the *Shema* instructs us to wear *tzitzit* (fringes on our *tallit*) to remind us to do the *mitzvot*, commandments.

Why do we need "reminders" to be good Jews?

Many parents or grandparents present students with a *tallit* on the occasion of their becoming *B'nei* or *B'not Mitzvah*. Why is this most appropriate?

If we just read the teachings of the Torah, this will do little good. It is only when we keep them in our minds and hearts — so they can remind us how we should act that these teachings make a difference.

The Rabbis point out that the Hebrew word *emet* (אֱמֶת) has three letters in it, *Aleph* (א), *Mem* (מ), and *Tav* (ת). These letters are found at the beginning, middle and end of the Hebrew alphabet. This is to teach us that there should be truthfulness at the start, during, and at the end of all we do. What else might this teach us about truth?

When we recite the *Va'yomer* section, it is customary to kiss the *tzitzit* (fringes)
each time we mention them.

וַיֹּאמֶר יְהֹוָה אֶל־מֹשֶׁה לֵּאמֹר: דַּבֵּר אֶל־בְּנֵי יִשְׂרָאֵל

וְאָמַרְתָּ אֲלֵהֶם וְעָשׂוּ לָהֶם צִיצִת עַל־כַּנְפֵי בִגְדֵיהֶם

לְדֹרֹתָם וְנָתְנוּ עַל־צִיצִת הַכָּנָף פְּתִיל תְּכֵלֶת: וְהָיָה לָכֶם

לְצִיצִת וּרְאִיתֶם אֹתוֹ וּזְכַרְתֶּם אֶת־כָּל־מִצְוֹת יְהֹוָה וַעֲשִׂיתֶם

אֹתָם וְלֹא תָתוּרוּ אַחֲרֵי לְבַבְכֶם וְאַחֲרֵי עֵינֵיכֶם אֲשֶׁר־אַתֶּם

זֹנִים אַחֲרֵיהֶם: לְמַעַן תִּזְכְּרוּ וַעֲשִׂיתֶם אֶת־כָּל־מִצְוֹתָי

וִהְיִיתֶם קְדֹשִׁים לֵאלֹהֵיכֶם: אֲנִי יְהֹוָה אֱלֹהֵיכֶם אֲשֶׁר

הוֹצֵאתִי אֶתְכֶם מֵאֶרֶץ מִצְרַיִם לִהְיוֹת לָכֶם לֵאלֹהִים

אֲנִי יְהֹוָה אֱלֹהֵיכֶם:

And *Adonai* spoke to Moses: Speak to the Israelites and tell them to
put fringes on the corners of their garments and bind a thread of
blue in the fringe of each corner. When you look at these fringes
you will be reminded of all the commandments of God and you will
do them and not be tempted to go in other directions. Then you
will be dedicated and do all my *mitzvot* and you will be holy to your
God. I am *Adonai*, your God, who brought you out of *Mitzrayim* to
be your God. I, *Adonai,* am your God.

Leader:

יְהֹוָה אֱלֹהֵיכֶם אֱמֶת.

Adonai, your God, is truth.

The *Mi ḥamoḥah* is from the Song of Moses *(Exodus* 15:1-15:18) sung after the crossing of the Re(e)d Sea. It reminds us of both God's uniqueness and rule in the world. It praises God for helping us become a free people. Why do you think our prayers include events that happened a long time ago?

The *"Mi ḥamoḥah"* prayer was first said at a time when the Israelites felt very close to God. Think of a time when you felt especially close to God.

When the Israelites approached the Re(e)d Sea, they were too terrified to enter into the water. There is a *midrash* that finally, Naḥshon Ben Aminadav, from the tribe of Judah took that first step. That's when the waters parted and the Israelites were able to cross. This teaches that we are partners with God in making our prayers come true and in achieving our goals. This often requires courage and trust.

Imagine how difficult it was for the Israelites to cross the Re(e)d Sea. Imagine how much courage it took and how thankful they were to have crossed over safely. Recite the *Mi ḥamoḥah* as if you yourself were there and experienced this great moment.

The initials of the verse, *"Mi ḥamoḥah ba'elim Adonai"* (מכבי) form the word "Maccabee." It is thought that Judah, the hero of the *Ḥanukkah* story, used this verse to rally the people to battle the Syrian Greek tyrants. How does this verse fit the *Ḥanukkah* story?

Did someone ever inspire you to do something difficult or courageous?

Did you ever do a brave act that helped you or others succeed?

Are there people now that you wish were free? Say your own prayer on their behalf. Also, think about any way you and others in the community can help them.

מֹשֶׁה וּבְנֵי יִשְׂרָאֵל לְךָ עָנוּ שִׁירָה בְּשִׂמְחָה רַבָּה, וְאָמְרוּ כֻלָּם:

מִי־כָמֹכָה בָּאֵלִם יְיָ,
מִי כָּמֹכָה נֶאְדָּר בַּקֹּדֶשׁ,
נוֹרָא תְהִלֹּת, עֹשֵׂה פֶלֶא.

שִׁירָה חֲדָשָׁה שִׁבְּחוּ גְאוּלִים לְשִׁמְךָ עַל שְׂפַת הַיָּם. יַחַד
כֻּלָּם הוֹדוּ וְהִמְלִיכוּ וְאָמְרוּ:

יְיָ יִמְלֹךְ לְעֹלָם וָעֶד.

צוּר יִשְׂרָאֵל, קוּמָה בְּעֶזְרַת יִשְׂרָאֵל וּפְדֵה כִנְאֻמֶךָ יְהוּדָה וְיִשְׂרָאֵל.
גֹּאֲלֵנוּ יְיָ צְבָאוֹת שְׁמוֹ קְדוֹשׁ יִשְׂרָאֵל. בָּרוּךְ אַתָּה יְיָ גָּאַל יִשְׂרָאֵל.

At the shores of the Re(e)d Sea, Moses and all the people of Israel burst into joyous song and all said as one:

"Who is like You, *Adonai*,
among the mighty?
Who is like You, *Adonai*,
glorious in holiness,
awesome in splendor,
the Maker of miracles?"

The Israelites saw Your majesty when You split the waters and they crossed in safety. Then, led by Moses and Miriam, they sang a new song of rejoicing.

Together they shouted: "*ADONAI*, YOU WILL RULE FOREVER."

Rock of Israel, arise to help Your people.

Blessed are You, *Adonai*, Who helped the people Israel.

Reuven and Shimon

The Rabbis tell a story about two Israelites, *Reuven* and *Shimon*, who were there and crossed through the Re(e)d Sea.

It seems that the bottom of the Re(e)d Sea, though possible to walk on, was not completely dry. It was muddy, like a beach at low tide. *Reuven* stepped into it, looked down and said, "What is this mud?"

Shimon, his buddy, took a step and scowled, "Ech! There's mud all over the place."

And so it went, with each couple of steps they took.

"This is just like the slime pits of Egypt!" said *Reuven*. "When we were making bricks, we had mud up to our knees."

"What difference does it make?" complained *Shimon*. "Mud here, mud there back in Egypt; its all the same."

And so they went, the two of them, *Reuven* and *Shimon*, across the bottom of the Sea, grumbling the entire way. They never once looked up and they never understood why, when they got to the other shore, everyone else was singing songs of praise.

They were there, but for *Reuven* and *Shimon*, the miracle never happened.

Reuven and *Shimon* did not see the miracle.

DIRECTIONS FOR THE *AMIDAH*

The *Amidah* means the "standing prayer" and we do, in fact, stand for the *Amidah*. As a sign of respect, we recite the *Amidah* with our feet together and at attention. It is also customary to bow when we say the opening blessing formula of the first blessing (*Baruḥ atah Adonai*) and its closing blessing (*Baruḥ atah*) formula. We bow again when we say "*Modim anaḥnu laḥ*" and its closing blessing formula.

The *Amidah* for *Shabbat* with the version of the first blessing which speaks of our forefathers is found on p.110. The version which includes both the forefathers and mothers is found on p.113.

The *Amidah* for festivals with the version of the first blessing which speaks of our forefathers begins on p.129. The version which includes both the forefathers and mothers is found on p.131.

The book of *Samuel* includes the story of *Ḥannah*, a childless woman, who desperately wanted to become pregnant. At the shrine at *Shilo*, she wept and silently prayed to God: "Now *Ḥannah* spoke her heart, only her lips moved but her voice was not heard." God was moved by *Ḥannah's* prayer and answered it. Soon after, she and her husband *Elkanah* returned home, *Ḥannah* became pregnant and nine months later, a son was born. He was Samuel, a great prophet and leader in Israel. *(I Samuel* 1:13*)*

In most adult congregations, some of the *Amidah* is recited in a whisper like *Ḥannah's* prayer. Speaking quietly can encourage us to speak from our hearts.

THOUGHTS ON THE *AMIDAH*

We approach God not as individuals but as part of a community that started long ago with the forefathers and foremothers.

Each person has different preferences and ideas. The *Avot* prayer does not just say, "God of our ancestors," but lists them separately. The prayer points out to us that each human being experiences and understands God in his or her own way.

The *Amidah* gives us the opportunity to have private time with God. As we recite the blessings, we can think about their meaning. The words may be the same but each of us says them with our own special thoughts and feelings.

Is God the only one to whom we speak in the *Avot* prayer? How is the *Avot* prayer a reminder to us?

The word *Baruḥ* begins the *Amidah* and occurs in it many times. Complete these sentence stems:

> When I say the word *Baruḥ*, I think about...
> When I say the word *Baruḥ*, I feel....

Some people believe that we have God's power within us. When we pray, we reach for the part of us that is God-like and we remember to do our best in the world.

How can praising God for being mighty or great, help us use our own inner strength to do a difficult task or something especially worthwhile?

AMIDAH FOR *SHABBAT* MORNING

Adonai, open my lips that my mouth may declare Your praise.

אֲדֹנָי, שְׂפָתַי תִּפְתָּח וּפִי יַגִּיד תְּהִלָּתֶךָ.

בָּרוּךְ אַתָּה יְיָ אֱלֹהֵינוּ וֵאלֹהֵי אֲבוֹתֵינוּ, אֱלֹהֵי אַבְרָהָם
אֱלֹהֵי יִצְחָק וֵאלֹהֵי יַעֲקֹב, הָאֵל הַגָּדוֹל הַגִּבּוֹר וְהַנּוֹרָא,
אֵל עֶלְיוֹן, גּוֹמֵל חֲסָדִים טוֹבִים וְקוֹנֵה הַכֹּל, וְזוֹכֵר חַסְדֵי
אָבוֹת וּמֵבִיא גוֹאֵל לִבְנֵי בְנֵיהֶם לְמַעַן שְׁמוֹ בְּאַהֲבָה.

On *Shabbat* before *Yom Kippur* we say:

זָכְרֵנוּ לְחַיִּים, מֶלֶךְ חָפֵץ בַּחַיִּים,
וְכָתְבֵנוּ בְּסֵפֶר הַחַיִּים לְמַעַנְךָ אֱלֹהִים חַיִּים.

מֶלֶךְ עוֹזֵר וּמוֹשִׁיעַ וּמָגֵן. בָּרוּךְ אַתָּה יְיָ מָגֵן אַבְרָהָם.

אַתָּה גִּבּוֹר לְעוֹלָם אֲדֹנָי, מְחַיֵּה מֵתִים אַתָּה רַב לְהוֹשִׁיעַ.

From *Sh'mini Atzeret* to *Pesaḥ* we say:

מַשִּׁיב הָרוּחַ וּמוֹרִיד הַגֶּשֶׁם.

מְכַלְכֵּל חַיִּים בְּחֶסֶד, מְחַיֵּה מֵתִים בְּרַחֲמִים רַבִּים, סוֹמֵךְ
נוֹפְלִים וְרוֹפֵא חוֹלִים וּמַתִּיר אֲסוּרִים, וּמְקַיֵּם אֱמוּנָתוֹ
לִישֵׁנֵי עָפָר. מִי כָמוֹךָ בַּעַל גְּבוּרוֹת וּמִי דוֹמֶה לָּךְ, מֶלֶךְ
מֵמִית וּמְחַיֶּה וּמַצְמִיחַ יְשׁוּעָה.

On *Shabbat* before *Yom Kippur* we say:

מִי כָמוֹךָ אַב הָרַחֲמִים, זוֹכֵר יְצוּרָיו לְחַיִּים בְּרַחֲמִים.

וְנֶאֱמָן אַתָּה לְהַחֲיוֹת מֵתִים. בָּרוּךְ אַתָּה יְיָ מְחַיֵּה הַמֵּתִים.

Adonai, open my lips that my mouth may declare Your praise.

Blessed are You, *Adonai*, our God and God of our ancestors,
God of Abraham, God of Isaac and God of Jacob.
Supreme God Who responds with kindness,
You remember the good deeds of our ancestors and
lovingly bring help to us.

On the *Shabbat* before *Yom Kippur* add:

Remember us for life, Ruler, Who desires life, and write us in Your book of life, for Your sake, ever-living God.

Ruler, Supporter, Helper and Shield, praised are You, *Adonai*,
Who protects Abraham.

You are powerful, Almighty One.
You renew life with Your saving acts.

From *Sh'mini Atzeret* to *Pesaḥ* we say:

You cause the wind to blow and the rain to fall.

You sustain the living with loving-kindness and with mercy, renew life. You support the falling, heal the sick, free the captives and remember those who have passed on. Who can compare to You, Almighty God? Who resembles You, the Source of life and death, the Source of blossoming hope?

On the *Shabbat* before *Yom Kippur* add:

Who is like You, merciful Parent?
You remember with mercy all creatures for life.

You are faithful in giving life to all. Praised are You, Who renews life.

THE *GEVUROT* PRAYER - GOD'S POWER

When we acknowledge God's power to heal and save lives, we recognize that we can be partners with God to help ourselves and others. We can exercise and eat nutritious meals. We can contribute to the charities that bring food to the poor or infirm. We can study and become doctors or dentists as well as medical researchers, or donate money to establish hospitals and clinics.

What do you think...

1. Can someone refuse medicine and also pray for healing?
2. Are life-support machines healing?
3. Has a mother on drugs, who gives birth to an addicted baby, committed a crime?
4. What rights do smokers and non-smokers have?
5. Who in our society is entitled to medical care?

AMIDAH FOR *SHABBAT* MORNING

Adonai, open my lips that my mouth may declare Your praise.

אֲדֹנָי, שְׂפָתַי תִּפְתָּח וּפִי יַגִּיד תְּהִלָּתֶךָ.

בָּרוּךְ אַתָּה יְיָ אֱלֹהֵינוּ וֵאלֹהֵי אֲבוֹתֵינוּ, אֱלֹהֵי אַבְרָהָם אֱלֹהֵי יִצְחָק וֵאלֹהֵי יַעֲקֹב, אֱלֹהֵי שָׂרָה אֱלֹהֵי רִבְקָה אֱלֹהֵי רָחֵל וֵאלֹהֵי לֵאָה, הָאֵל הַגָּדוֹל הַגִּבּוֹר וְהַנּוֹרָא, אֵל עֶלְיוֹן, גּוֹמֵל חֲסָדִים טוֹבִים וְקוֹנֵה הַכֹּל, וְזוֹכֵר חַסְדֵי אָבוֹת וּמֵבִיא גוֹאֵל לִבְנֵי בְנֵיהֶם לְמַעַן שְׁמוֹ בְּאַהֲבָה.

On *Shabbat* before *Yom Kippur* we say:

זָכְרֵנוּ לְחַיִּים, מֶלֶךְ חָפֵץ בַּחַיִּים,
וְכָתְבֵנוּ בְּסֵפֶר הַחַיִּים לְמַעַנְךָ אֱלֹהִים חַיִּים.

מֶלֶךְ עוֹזֵר וּפֹקֵד וּמוֹשִׁיעַ וּמָגֵן. בָּרוּךְ אַתָּה יְיָ מָגֵן אַבְרָהָם וּפֹקֵד שָׂרָה.

אַתָּה גִּבּוֹר לְעוֹלָם אֲדֹנָי, מְחַיֵּה מֵתִים אַתָּה רַב לְהוֹשִׁיעַ.

From *Sh'mini Atzeret* to *Pesaḥ* we say:

מַשִּׁיב הָרוּחַ וּמוֹרִיד הַגָּשֶׁם.

מְכַלְכֵּל חַיִּים בְּחֶסֶד, מְחַיֵּה מֵתִים בְּרַחֲמִים רַבִּים, סוֹמֵךְ נוֹפְלִים וְרוֹפֵא חוֹלִים וּמַתִּיר אֲסוּרִים, וּמְקַיֵּם אֱמוּנָתוֹ לִישֵׁנֵי עָפָר. מִי כָמוֹךָ בַּעַל גְּבוּרוֹת וּמִי דּוֹמֶה לָּךְ, מֶלֶךְ מֵמִית וּמְחַיֶּה וּמַצְמִיחַ יְשׁוּעָה.

On *Shabbat* before *Yom Kippur* we say:

מִי כָמוֹךָ אַב הָרַחֲמִים, זוֹכֵר יְצוּרָיו לְחַיִּים בְּרַחֲמִים.

וְנֶאֱמָן אַתָּה לְהַחֲיוֹת מֵתִים. בָּרוּךְ אַתָּה יְיָ מְחַיֵּה הַמֵּתִים.

Adonai, open my lips that my mouth may declare Your praise.

Blessed are You, *Adonai*, our God and God of our ancestors,
God of Abraham, God of Isaac and God of Jacob,
God of Sarah, God of Rebecca, God of Leah and God of Rachel.
Supreme God Who responds with kindness,
You remember the good deeds of our ancestors and
lovingly bring help to us.

On the *Shabbat* before *Yom Kippur* add:

> Remember us for life, Ruler, Who desires life, and write us in Your book of life, for Your sake, ever-living God.

Ruler, Supporter, Helper and Shield, praised are You, *Adonai*,
Who protects Abraham and remembers Sarah.

You are powerful, Almighty One.
You renew life with Your saving acts.

From *Sh'mini Atzeret* to *Pesaḥ* we say:

> You cause the wind to blow and the rain to fall.

You sustain the living with loving-kindness, and with mercy, renew life. You support the falling, heal the sick, free the captives and remember those who have passed on. Who can compare to You, Almighty God? Who resembles You, the Source of life and death, the Source of blossoming hope?

On the *Shabbat* before *Yom Kippur* add:

> Who is like You, merciful Parent?
> You remember with mercy all creatures for life.

You are faithful in giving life to all. Praised are You, Who renews life.

THE *GEVUROT* PRAYER - GOD'S POWER

When we acknowledge God's power to heal and save lives, we recognize that we can be partners with God to help ourselves and others. We can exercise and eat nutritious meals. We can contribute to the charities that bring food to the poor or infirm. We can study and become doctors or dentists as well as medical researchers, or donate money to establish hospitals and clinics.

What do you think...

1. Can someone refuse medicine and also pray for healing?
2. Are life-support machines healing?
3. Has a mother on drugs, who gives birth to an addicted baby, committed a crime?
4. What rights do smokers and non-smokers have?
5. Who in our society is entitled to medical care?

THOUGHTS ON THE *KEDUSHAH*

We say the *Kedushah* only when there is a *minyan*. It is as members of the Jewish community, and not just as individuals, that we must sanctify God. We must act with fairness and kindness to others to sanctify God's name. When Jews act in a good way, it makes a statement not only about ourselves but our religion as well. It says that our God is a God of justice and compassion and that this is the behavior God requests of all believers.

We sanctify God with words but, even more, by what we do.

Rabbi Simon And The Pearl

To make a living, Rabbi Simon was a peddler who walked from town to town with a pack of linen on his back. His students, who wanted to ease his burden, bought a donkey for him from a non-Jew. After the purchase, they happened to find a valuable pearl hidden in the lining of the saddle.

Excited about their discovery, the students rushed to tell Rabbi Simon. He immediately asked them if the owner knew about the pearl when he sold them the donkey. "No," they answered gleefully, "he has no knowledge of this."

"You bought the donkey, not the pearl. You must return the pearl at once."

When the students explained their mission to the former owner of the donkey, he said to them, "Praised be the God of Rabbi Simon. Praised be the God of the Jews."

How did what Rabbi Simon had his students do reflect on him? on the Jewish religion? on God?

קְדוּשָּׁה

ON *KEDUSHAH* – BEING HOLY

There is a story in the Torah about how Abraham made God's name holy in the world: Abraham and his allies once had to defend themselves against five powerful kings who had captured Abraham's nephew, Lot. Abraham was victorious and was able to free his nephew. Although according to custom, Abraham could have taken all of their captured wealth, he refused to do this. One king was so impressed with Abraham's kindness that he not only blessed Abraham, but his God as well. *(Genesis* 14:20*)*

"If you make yourselves holy, it is as though you make Me holy and if you do not make yourselves holy, you do not make Me holy."

If God is holy and we are created in God's image, then we are holy! But to remain holy we have to work at it.

If each person, including those different from us, is holy in God's eyes, how should each be treated?

Mitzvot are the Jewish way of sanctifying God in the world. One set of *mitzvot* is doing good deeds. In doing good deeds, we show that we and others are sacred for we are created in God's image. Such deeds can bring us closer to God and other humans.

Another set of *mitzvot* are ways we relate to God, such as prayer. These, too, can bring us closer to God.

Brainstorm a list of *mitzvot* you can do in the coming week.

We recite the *Kedushah* which proclaims God's holiness.
(The Congregation chants the indented lines aloud.)

נְקַדֵּשׁ אֶת־שִׁמְךָ בָּעוֹלָם, כְּשֵׁם שֶׁמַּקְדִּישִׁים אוֹתוֹ בִּשְׁמֵי מָרוֹם, כַּכָּתוּב עַל יַד נְבִיאֶךָ, וְקָרָא זֶה אֶל זֶה וְאָמַר:

קָדוֹשׁ קָדוֹשׁ קָדוֹשׁ יְיָ צְבָאוֹת, מְלֹא כָל־הָאָרֶץ כְּבוֹדוֹ.

אָז בְּקוֹל רַעַשׁ גָּדוֹל אַדִּיר וְחָזָק מַשְׁמִיעִים קוֹל, מִתְנַשְּׂאִים לְעֻמַּת שְׂרָפִים, לְעֻמָּתָם בָּרוּךְ יֹאמֵרוּ:

בָּרוּךְ כְּבוֹד יְיָ מִמְּקוֹמוֹ.

מִמְּקוֹמְךָ מַלְכֵּנוּ תוֹפִיעַ וְתִמְלֹךְ עָלֵינוּ כִּי מְחַכִּים אֲנַחְנוּ לָךְ. מָתַי תִּמְלֹךְ בְּצִיּוֹן, בְּקָרוֹב בְּיָמֵינוּ לְעוֹלָם וָעֶד תִּשְׁכּוֹן. תִּתְגַּדַּל וְתִתְקַדַּשׁ בְּתוֹךְ יְרוּשָׁלַיִם עִירְךָ לְדוֹר וָדוֹר וּלְנֵצַח נְצָחִים. וְעֵינֵינוּ תִרְאֶינָה מַלְכוּתֶךָ, כַּדָּבָר הָאָמוּר בְּשִׁירֵי עֻזֶּךָ, עַל יְדֵי דָוִד מְשִׁיחַ צִדְקֶךָ:

יִמְלֹךְ יְיָ לְעוֹלָם אֱלֹהַיִךְ צִיּוֹן לְדֹר וָדֹר, הַלְלוּיָהּ.

Leader:

לְדוֹר וָדוֹר נַגִּיד גָּדְלֶךָ וּלְנֵצַח נְצָחִים קְדֻשָּׁתְךָ נַקְדִּישׁ. וְשִׁבְחֲךָ אֱלֹהֵינוּ מִפִּינוּ לֹא יָמוּשׁ לְעוֹלָם וָעֶד, כִּי אֵל מֶלֶךְ גָּדוֹל וְקָדוֹשׁ אָתָּה.

Each congregant while or after leader says above:

אַתָּה קָדוֹשׁ וְשִׁמְךָ קָדוֹשׁ וּקְדוֹשִׁים בְּכָל־יוֹם יְהַלְלוּךָ סֶּלָה.

On *Shabbat* before *Yom Kippur* we say the words below and not the line which follows:

בָּרוּךְ אַתָּה יְיָ הַמֶּלֶךְ הַקָּדוֹשׁ.

בָּרוּךְ אַתָּה יְיָ הָאֵל הַקָּדוֹשׁ.

We will declare God's holiness here on earth as we imagine heavenly angels do above:

Holy, holy, holy — the whole world is filled with God's glory.

The angels, in a thundering chorus, lift up their majestic voices and answer:

Praised is the glory of *Adonai* throughout the Universe.

Our Ruler, reveal Yourself to us, for we wait for You. When will You rule in Zion? Soon, please, soon, establish Yourself in Zion forever. May You be praised within Your city, Jerusalem, for generation after generation, now and always. May we see Your rule with our own eyes.

May You rule throughout time, *Halleluyah*!

Leader:

From generation to generation, we will tell of Your greatness and we will declare Your holiness forever. Your praise will never leave our mouths, for You are our Holy One.

Each congregant:

You are holy and Your name is holy and those who strive to be holy praise you each day,

On *Shabbat* before *Yom Kippur* we say the words below and not the line which follows:

Praised are You, holy Ruler.

Praised are You, holy God.

REACHING OUT

Reb Nahman taught that we reach out in three directions — up to God, out to other people and into our own hearts. The secret is that all three directions are truly the same. When I reach out to another person, I find myself and God. When I find God, I find others and the true me. When I find myself, I reach God and other people.

Why is the *Kedushah* a "reaching out" prayer?

יִשְׂמַח מֹשֶׁה בְּמַתְּנַת חֶלְקוֹ, כִּי עֶבֶד נֶאֱמָן קָרָאתָ לוֹ. כְּלִיל תִּפְאֶרֶת בְּרֹאשׁוֹ נָתַתָּ, בְּעָמְדוֹ לְפָנֶיךָ עַל הַר סִינָי. וּשְׁנֵי לוּחוֹת אֲבָנִים הוֹרִיד בְּיָדוֹ, וְכָתוּב בָּהֶם שְׁמִירַת שַׁבָּת, וְכֵן כָּתוּב בְּתוֹרָתֶךָ:

To Moses, being called a faithful servant by You
was a gift.
You placed a crown of glory on his head,
as he stood before You on Mount Sinai.
In his arms, he carried the two tablets of stone
on which the commandment of *Shabbat* was written.

אֱלֹהֵינוּ וֵאלֹהֵי אֲבוֹתֵינוּ, רְצֵה בִמְנוּחָתֵנוּ: קַדְּשֵׁנוּ בְּמִצְוֹתֶיךָ וְתֵן חֶלְקֵנוּ בְּתוֹרָתֶךָ, שַׂבְּעֵנוּ מִטּוּבֶךָ וְשַׂמְּחֵנוּ בִּישׁוּעָתֶךָ וְטַהֵר לִבֵּנוּ לְעָבְדְּךָ בֶּאֱמֶת. וְהַנְחִילֵנוּ יְיָ אֱלֹהֵינוּ בְּאַהֲבָה וּבְרָצוֹן שַׁבַּת קָדְשֶׁךָ, וְיָנוּחוּ בָהּ יִשְׂרָאֵל מְקַדְּשֵׁי שְׁמֶךָ. בָּרוּךְ אַתָּה יְיָ מְקַדֵּשׁ הַשַּׁבָּת.

רְצֵה יְיָ אֱלֹהֵינוּ בְּעַמְּךָ יִשְׂרָאֵל וּבִתְפִלָּתָם, וְהָשֵׁב אֶת־הָעֲבוֹדָה לִדְבִיר בֵּיתֶךָ, וּתְפִלָּתָם בְּאַהֲבָה תְקַבֵּל בְּרָצוֹן, וּתְהִי לְרָצוֹן תָּמִיד עֲבוֹדַת יִשְׂרָאֵל עַמֶּךָ.

Our God and God of our ancestors, be pleased with our rest. Let Your *mitzvot* lead us to holy deeds and the study of Torah. Let us find happiness in Your blessings and joy in Your supporting power. Let our hearts be pure to serve You with sincerity. With Your gracious love, let us continue our holy tradition of keeping the *Shabbat*. Let the people Israel rest on *Shabbat* and honor Your name. We praise You *Adonai*, Who makes *Shabbat* holy.

Be pleased, *Adonai*, our God, with Your people Israel and their prayers. May our worship always be acceptable to You.

מְנוּחָה

On *Shabbat*, the middle *braḥah* of the *Amidah* differs from the week-day blessings. On weekdays, there are thirteen middle *braḥot* which request things from God. On *Shabbat*, there is one middle *brahah* and it does not contain requests. The Rabbis felt that requests were not appropriate on *Shabbat*. *Braḥot* of requests focus on our needs — what we lack — rather than our well-being.

The single middle blessing gives praise and thanks to God for creation and for *menuḥah*, rest, on *Shabbat*.

By taking a break from our normal routines, we don't have to worry about whether we are rich or poor; about our grades in school or our standing on the softball team. We can just be ourselves and celebrate who we are.

We do not rest on *Shabbat* just so we can do more work during the week. *Menuḥah* itself is good. A day of *menuḥah* means that we can take more time to be with family or friends. *Shabbat* is a wonderful time to share what has happened in the week that has passed or anything that has been on our minds.

On *Shabbat*, we can play a board game or curl up with a good book — preferably one that has not been assigned for homework. Weather permitting, we can take a walk and enjoy nature or play outdoor games.

How can *Shabbat* help us to be more in harmony with nature? Picture a beautiful flower growing outside. Our first impulse is to pick it and take it home. However, on *Shabbat,* we may admire its beauty and smell its fragrance but we leave the flower alone. *Shabbat* is a time to enjoy nature, not change it. That's why we don't plant a garden on *Shabbat* or prune our trees. We don't mow our lawns or pick fruit from the trees. It is a time to be at one with nature. It is a time to just be.

During the week, we're always rushing. On *Shabbat,* we can notice buds that have blossomed or observe an ant colony. We can listen to the song of a bird or watch a squirrel scurry up a tree. Enjoying nature in a relaxed way, we often begin to feel more in harmony with the world.

We try to please God by resting on *Shabbat*. Why does God care about what we do on *Shabbat?*

On *Rosh Ḥodesh* and *Ḥol Hamo'ed* we say:

אֱלֹהֵינוּ וֵאלֹהֵי אֲבוֹתֵינוּ, יַעֲלֶה וְיָבֹא וְיַגִּיעַ, וְיֵרָאֶה וְיֵרָצֶה וְיִשָּׁמַע, וְיִפָּקֵד וְיִזָּכֵר זִכְרוֹנֵנוּ וּפִקְדוֹנֵנוּ, וְזִכְרוֹן אֲבוֹתֵינוּ, וְזִכְרוֹן מָשִׁיחַ בֶּן־דָּוִד עַבְדֶּךָ, וְזִכְרוֹן יְרוּשָׁלַיִם עִיר קָדְשֶׁךָ, לְחֵן וּלְחֶסֶד וּלְרַחֲמִים, לְחַיִּים וּלְשָׁלוֹם בְּיוֹם

On Rosh Ḥodesh: רֹאשׁ הַחֹדֶשׁ

On Pesaḥ: חַג הַמַּצּוֹת

On Sukkot: חַג הַסֻּכּוֹת

הַזֶּה. זָכְרֵנוּ יְיָ אֱלֹהֵינוּ בּוֹ לְטוֹבָה, וּפָקְדֵנוּ בוֹ לִבְרָכָה, וְהוֹשִׁיעֵנוּ בוֹ לְחַיִּים.

Our God and God of our ancestors, may Your remembering us, our ancestors, Jerusalem the holy city, and Your promises for our future allow You to grant us happiness, peace and life on this day of

Rosh Ḥodesh:	*Pesaḥ*:	*Sukkot*:
New Moon	The Feast of *Matzah*	The Festival of *Sukkot*

וְתֶחֱזֶינָה עֵינֵינוּ בְּשׁוּבְךָ לְצִיּוֹן בְּרַחֲמִים. בָּרוּךְ אַתָּה יְיָ הַמַּחֲזִיר שְׁכִינָתוֹ לְצִיּוֹן.

May we witness your merciful return to Zion. Praised are You, *Adonai*, Who seeks closeness to us. May we feel Your closeness in Zion.

The "*Modim*" prayer lists four things for which we thank *Adonai*. Can you add to this prayer by listing other reasons to express our thanks?

מוֹדִים אֲנַחְנוּ לָךְ שָׁאַתָּה הוּא יְיָ אֱלֹהֵינוּ וֵאלֹהֵי אֲבוֹתֵינוּ לְעוֹלָם
וָעֶד, צוּר חַיֵּינוּ מָגֵן יִשְׁעֵנוּ אַתָּה הוּא לְדוֹר וָדוֹר. נוֹדֶה לְּךָ
וּנְסַפֵּר תְּהִלָּתֶךָ, עַל חַיֵּינוּ הַמְּסוּרִים בְּיָדֶךָ וְעַל נִשְׁמוֹתֵינוּ
הַפְּקוּדוֹת לָךְ וְעַל נִסֶּיךָ שֶׁבְּכָל־יוֹם עִמָּנוּ וְעַל נִפְלְאוֹתֶיךָ
וְטוֹבוֹתֶיךָ שֶׁבְּכָל־עֵת, עֶרֶב וָבֹקֶר וְצָהֳרָיִם. הַטּוֹב כִּי לֹא כָלוּ
רַחֲמֶיךָ, וְהַמְרַחֵם כִּי לֹא תַמּוּ חֲסָדֶיךָ, מֵעוֹלָם קִוִּינוּ לָךְ.

How grateful we are to You, God of our ancestors, the Eternal One. You are the Source of our strength, just as You have been the protecting Shield of each generation.

We thank You for our lives which are in Your hand, and our souls which are in Your care. We thank You for Your miracles which surround us all the time and the wondrous acts of Your kindness that we experience each morning, noon and night.

וְעַל נִסֶּיךָ שֶׁבְּכָל יוֹם עִמָּנוּ.

On *Ḥanukkah*:

עַל הַנִּסִּים וְעַל הַפֻּרְקָן, וְעַל הַגְּבוּרוֹת, וְעַל הַתְּשׁוּעוֹת, וְעַל הַמִּלְחָמוֹת שֶׁעָשִׂיתָ לַאֲבוֹתֵינוּ בַּיָּמִים הָהֵם וּבַזְּמַן הַזֶּה.

בִּימֵי מַתִּתְיָהוּ בֶּן־יוֹחָנָן כֹּהֵן גָּדוֹל, חַשְׁמוֹנַי וּבָנָיו, כְּשֶׁעָמְדָה מַלְכוּת יָוָן הָרְשָׁעָה עַל עַמְּךָ יִשְׂרָאֵל לְהַשְׁכִּיחָם תּוֹרָתֶךָ וּלְהַעֲבִירָם מֵחֻקֵּי רְצוֹנֶךָ, וְאַתָּה בְּרַחֲמֶיךָ הָרַבִּים עָמַדְתָּ לָהֶם בְּעֵת צָרָתָם, רַבְתָּ אֶת־רִיבָם, דַּנְתָּ אֶת־דִּינָם, נָקַמְתָּ אֶת־נִקְמָתָם, מָסַרְתָּ גִבּוֹרִים בְּיַד חַלָּשִׁים, וְרַבִּים בְּיַד מְעַטִּים, וּטְמֵאִים בְּיַד טְהוֹרִים, וּרְשָׁעִים בְּיַד צַדִּיקִים, וְזֵדִים בְּיַד עוֹסְקֵי תוֹרָתֶךָ. וּלְךָ עָשִׂיתָ שֵׁם גָּדוֹל וְקָדוֹשׁ בְּעוֹלָמֶךָ, וּלְעַמְּךָ יִשְׂרָאֵל עָשִׂיתָ תְּשׁוּעָה גְדוֹלָה וּפֻרְקָן כְּהַיּוֹם הַזֶּה. וְאַחַר כֵּן בָּאוּ בָנֶיךָ לִדְבִיר בֵּיתֶךָ וּפִנּוּ אֶת־הֵיכָלֶךָ, וְטִהֲרוּ אֶת־מִקְדָּשֶׁךָ, וְהִדְלִיקוּ נֵרוֹת בְּחַצְרוֹת קָדְשֶׁךָ, וְקָבְעוּ שְׁמוֹנַת יְמֵי חֲנֻכָּה אֵלּוּ לְהוֹדוֹת וּלְהַלֵּל לְשִׁמְךָ הַגָּדוֹל.

וְעַל כֻּלָּם יִתְבָּרַךְ וְיִתְרוֹמַם שִׁמְךָ מַלְכֵּנוּ תָּמִיד לְעוֹלָם וָעֶד.

On *Shabbat* before *Yom Kippur* we say:

וּכְתֹב לְחַיִּים טוֹבִים כָּל־בְּנֵי בְרִיתֶךָ.

וְכֹל הַחַיִּים יוֹדוּךָ סֶּלָה וִיהַלְלוּ אֶת־שִׁמְךָ בֶּאֱמֶת, הָאֵל יְשׁוּעָתֵנוּ וְעֶזְרָתֵנוּ סֶלָה. בָּרוּךְ אַתָּה יְיָ הַטּוֹב שִׁמְךָ וּלְךָ נָאֶה לְהוֹדוֹת.

On *Ḥanukkah* we say:

We thank You for the miracles, the triumphs, the heroism, the help You gave to our ancestors in days past and in our own time.

In the days of the High Priest, Mattathias, and his sons (known as the Maccabees), a cruel government, the Syrian Greeks, rose up against Israel, demanding that they abandon the Torah and *mitzvot*. You, with great mercy, stood by Your people in their time of trouble. You championed their cause, defended their rights and punished their enemies. You delivered the strong into the hands of the weak, the many into the hands of the few, the corrupt into the hands of the pure, the wicked into the hands of the righteous, and the arrogant into the hands of students of Torah. You have made great victories for Your people Israel to this day, showing Your glory and holiness to the world. Then Your children came to Your shrine, cleaned Your temple, made Your sanctuary pure and lit candles in Your sacred courts. They set aside these eight days to give thanks and praise to Your holy name.

For all these blessings, may Your name be praised and exalted forever.

You are the Source of never-ending loving-kindness. You are our hope forever.

On *Shabbat Shuvah* before *Yom Kippur*

May we all look forward to a good year of life.

Praised are You, *Adonai*, Who deserves our praise.

The leader adds:

אֱלֹהֵינוּ וֵאלֹהֵי אֲבוֹתֵינוּ, בָּרְכֵנוּ בַבְּרָכָה הַמְשֻׁלֶּשֶׁת, בַּתּוֹרָה
הַכְּתוּבָה עַל יְדֵי מֹשֶׁה עַבְדֶּךָ, הָאֲמוּרָה מִפִּי אַהֲרֹן וּבָנָיו,
כֹּהֲנִים, עַם קְדוֹשֶׁךָ, כָּאָמוּר:

יְבָרֶכְךָ יְיָ וְיִשְׁמְרֶךָ.	כֵּן יְהִי רָצוֹן.
יָאֵר יְיָ פָּנָיו אֵלֶיךָ וִיחֻנֶּךָּ.	כֵּן יְהִי רָצוֹן.
יִשָּׂא יְיָ פָּנָיו אֵלֶיךָ וְיָשֵׂם לְךָ שָׁלוֹם.	כֵּן יְהִי רָצוֹן.

May *Adonai* bless and protect you.
May *Adonai* shine upon you with graciousness.
May *Adonai* look upon you with favor and grant you peace.

Albert Einstein said, “Peace cannot be kept by force. It can only be achieved by understanding.”

Simcha Bunim once said, “You cannot find peace anywhere except in your own heart.”

What is your idea about achieving peace? Peace can come when....

שִׂים שָׁלוֹם בָּעוֹלָם, טוֹבָה וּבְרָכָה, חֵן וָחֶסֶד וְרַחֲמִים עָלֵינוּ
וְעַל כָּל־יִשְׂרָאֵל עַמֶּךָ. בָּרְכֵנוּ אָבִינוּ כֻּלָּנוּ כְּאֶחָד בְּאוֹר
פָּנֶיךָ, כִּי בְאוֹר פָּנֶיךָ נָתַתָּ לָנוּ, יְיָ אֱלֹהֵינוּ, תּוֹרַת חַיִּים
וְאַהֲבַת חֶסֶד, וּצְדָקָה וּבְרָכָה וְרַחֲמִים וְחַיִּים וְשָׁלוֹם. וְטוֹב
בְּעֵינֶיךָ לְבָרֵךְ אֶת־עַמְּךָ יִשְׂרָאֵל בְּכָל־עֵת וּבְכָל־שָׁעָה
בִּשְׁלוֹמֶךָ.

On *Shabbat Shuvah* before *Yom Kippur* we say the following lines instead of the line below:

בְּסֵפֶר חַיִּים, בְּרָכָה וְשָׁלוֹם, וּפַרְנָסָה טוֹבָה, נִזָּכֵר וְנִכָּתֵב לְפָנֶיךָ,
אֲנַחְנוּ וְכָל־עַמְּךָ בֵּית יִשְׂרָאֵל, לְחַיִּים טוֹבִים וּלְשָׁלוֹם.
בָּרוּךְ אַתָּה יְיָ עֹשֵׂה הַשָּׁלוֹם.

בָּרוּךְ אַתָּה יְיָ הַמְבָרֵךְ אֶת־עַמּוֹ יִשְׂרָאֵל בַּשָּׁלוֹם.

Let peace, happiness and love come to the world, to us and to all the Jewish people. Bless us all, Holy One, with Your light, for by that light You have given the Torah to guide us. May it please You to bless the Jewish people in every season and at all times with goodness and peace.

On *Shabbat Shuvah* before *Yom Kippur* we say the following lines instead of the line below:

May we and all the Jewish people be remembered and recorded in Your book for a good and peaceful life. Praised are You, *Adonai*, Source of Peace.

Praised are You, *Adonai*, Who blesses the people Israel with peace.

שָׁלוֹם בָּעוֹלָם

שָׁ לוֹם בָּעוֹלָם

לְ עוֹלָם וָעֶד,

וְ שֶׁלֹּא יִהְיֶה רַע בְּכָל הַתֵּבֵל.

מִ י הַמְבַקֵּשׁ מִשְׁאָלָה זוֹ? אֲנִי!

בְּ כָל הָעוֹלָם,

עִ ם כָּל הָאֲרָצוֹת,

וּ לְתָמִיד, אֲנִי רוֹצֶה שָׁלוֹם!

לָ מָה, אַתָּה שׁוֹאֵל?

מִ לְמָחָה לֹא פּוֹתֶרֶת כְּלוּם!

בנימין יעקב רוזינה
כיתה ו׳

Amidah for *Yom Tov*

Adonai, open my lips that my mouth may declare Your praise.

אֲדֹנָי, שְׂפָתַי תִּפְתָּח וּפִי יַגִּיד תְּהִלָּתֶךָ.

בָּרוּךְ אַתָּה יְיָ אֱלֹהֵינוּ וֵאלֹהֵי אֲבוֹתֵינוּ, אֱלֹהֵי אַבְרָהָם אֱלֹהֵי יִצְחָק וֵאלֹהֵי יַעֲקֹב, הָאֵל הַגָּדוֹל הַגִּבּוֹר וְהַנּוֹרָא, אֵל עֶלְיוֹן, גּוֹמֵל חֲסָדִים טוֹבִים וְקוֹנֵה הַכֹּל, וְזוֹכֵר חַסְדֵי אָבוֹת וּמֵבִיא גוֹאֵל לִבְנֵי בְנֵיהֶם לְמַעַן שְׁמוֹ בְּאַהֲבָה. מֶלֶךְ עוֹזֵר וּמוֹשִׁיעַ וּמָגֵן. בָּרוּךְ אַתָּה יְיָ מָגֵן אַבְרָהָם.

אַתָּה גִּבּוֹר לְעוֹלָם אֲדֹנָי, מְחַיֵּה מֵתִים אַתָּה רַב לְהוֹשִׁיעַ.

On *Simḥat Torah* and on the first day of *Pesaḥ* we say:

מַשִּׁיב הָרוּחַ וּמוֹרִיד הַגָּשֶׁם.

מְכַלְכֵּל חַיִּים בְּחֶסֶד, מְחַיֵּה מֵתִים בְּרַחֲמִים רַבִּים, סוֹמֵךְ נוֹפְלִים וְרוֹפֵא חוֹלִים וּמַתִּיר אֲסוּרִים, וּמְקַיֵּם אֱמוּנָתוֹ לִישֵׁנֵי עָפָר. מִי כָמוֹךָ בַּעַל גְּבוּרוֹת וּמִי דּוֹמֶה לָּךְ, מֶלֶךְ מֵמִית וּמְחַיֶּה וּמַצְמִיחַ יְשׁוּעָה. וְנֶאֱמָן אַתָּה לְהַחֲיוֹת מֵתִים. בָּרוּךְ אַתָּה יְיָ מְחַיֵּה הַמֵּתִים.

Amidah for *Yom Tov*

Adonai, open my lips that my mouth may declare Your praise.

Blessed are You, *Adonai*, our God and God of our ancestors,
God of Abraham, God of Isaac and God of Jacob.
Supreme God Who responds with kindness,
You remember the good deeds of our ancestors and
lovingly bring help to us. Ruler, Supporter, Helper and Shield,
praised are You, *Adonai*, Who protects Abraham.

You are powerful, Almighty One.
You renew life with Your saving acts.

On *Simḥat Torah* and on the first day of *Pesaḥ* we say:

You cause the wind to blow and the rain to fall.

You sustain the living with loving-kindness, and with mercy, renew life. You support the falling, heal the sick, free the captives and remember those who have passed on. Who can compare to You, Almighty God? Who resembles You, the Source of life and death, the Source of blossoming hope?

You are faithful in giving life to all. Praised are You, Who renews life.

Amidah for *Yom Tov*

Adonai, open my lips that my mouth may declare Your praise.

אֲדֹנָי, שְׂפָתַי תִּפְתָּח וּפִי יַגִּיד תְּהִלָּתֶךָ.

בָּרוּךְ אַתָּה יְיָ אֱלֹהֵינוּ וֵאלֹהֵי אֲבוֹתֵינוּ, אֱלֹהֵי אַבְרָהָם אֱלֹהֵי יִצְחָק וֵאלֹהֵי יַעֲקֹב, אֱלֹהֵי שָׂרָה אֱלֹהֵי רִבְקָה אֱלֹהֵי רָחֵל וֵאלֹהֵי לֵאָה, הָאֵל הַגָּדוֹל הַגִּבּוֹר וְהַנּוֹרָא, אֵל עֶלְיוֹן, גּוֹמֵל חֲסָדִים טוֹבִים וְקוֹנֵה הַכֹּל, וְזוֹכֵר חַסְדֵי אָבוֹת וּמֵבִיא גוֹאֵל לִבְנֵי בְנֵיהֶם לְמַעַן שְׁמוֹ בְּאַהֲבָה. מֶלֶךְ עוֹזֵר וּפוֹקֵד וּמוֹשִׁיעַ וּמָגֵן. בָּרוּךְ אַתָּה יְיָ מָגֵן אַבְרָהָם וּפוֹקֵד שָׂרָה.

אַתָּה גִּבּוֹר לְעוֹלָם אֲדֹנָי, מְחַיֵּה מֵתִים אַתָּה רַב לְהוֹשִׁיעַ.

On *Simḥat Toraḥ* and on the first day of *Pesaḥ* we say:

מַשִּׁיב הָרוּחַ וּמוֹרִיד הַגָּשֶׁם.

מְכַלְכֵּל חַיִּים בְּחֶסֶד, מְחַיֵּה מֵתִים בְּרַחֲמִים רַבִּים, סוֹמֵךְ נוֹפְלִים וְרוֹפֵא חוֹלִים וּמַתִּיר אֲסוּרִים, וּמְקַיֵּם אֱמוּנָתוֹ לִישֵׁנֵי עָפָר. מִי כָמוֹךָ בַּעַל גְּבוּרוֹת וּמִי דּוֹמֶה לָּךְ, מֶלֶךְ מֵמִית וּמְחַיֶּה וּמַצְמִיחַ יְשׁוּעָה. וְנֶאֱמָן אַתָּה לְהַחֲיוֹת מֵתִים. בָּרוּךְ אַתָּה יְיָ מְחַיֵּה הַמֵּתִים.

Amidah for *Yom Tov*

Adonai, open my lips that my mouth may declare Your praise.

Blessed are You, *Adonai*, our God and God of our ancestors,
God of Abraham, God of Isaac and God of Jacob,
God of Sarah, God of Rebecca, God of Leah and God of Rachel.
Supreme God Who responds with kindness,
You remember the good deeds of our ancestors and
lovingly bring help to us. Ruler, Supporter, Helper and Shield, praised are You, *Adonai*, Who protects Abraham and remembers Sarah.

You are powerful, Almighty One.
You renew life with Your saving acts.

On *Simḥat Torah* and on the first day of *Pesaḥ* we say:

You cause the wind to blow and the rain to fall.

You sustain the living with loving kindness, and with mercy, renew life. You support the falling, heal the sick, free the captives and remember those who have passed on. Who can compare to You, Almighty God? Who resembles You, the Source of life and death, the Source of blossoming hope?

You are faithful in giving life to all. Praised are You, Who renews life.

We recite the *Kedushah* which proclaims God's holiness.

(The Congregation chants the indented lines aloud.)

נְקַדֵּשׁ אֶת־שִׁמְךָ בָּעוֹלָם, כְּשֵׁם שֶׁמַּקְדִּישִׁים אוֹתוֹ בִּשְׁמֵי מָרוֹם,
כַּכָּתוּב עַל יַד נְבִיאֶךָ, וְקָרָא זֶה אֶל זֶה וְאָמַר:

קָדוֹשׁ קָדוֹשׁ קָדוֹשׁ יְיָ צְבָאוֹת, מְלֹא כָל־הָאָרֶץ כְּבוֹדוֹ.

אָז בְּקוֹל רַעַשׁ גָּדוֹל אַדִּיר וְחָזָק מַשְׁמִיעִים קוֹל, מִתְנַשְּׂאִים
לְעֻמַּת שְׂרָפִים, לְעֻמָּתָם בָּרוּךְ יֹאמֵרוּ:

בָּרוּךְ כְּבוֹד יְיָ מִמְּקוֹמוֹ.

מִמְּקוֹמְךָ מַלְכֵּנוּ תוֹפִיעַ וְתִמְלֹךְ עָלֵינוּ כִּי מְחַכִּים אֲנַחְנוּ לָךְ.
מָתַי תִּמְלֹךְ בְּצִיּוֹן, בְּקָרוֹב בְּיָמֵינוּ לְעוֹלָם וָעֶד תִּשְׁכּוֹן. תִּתְגַּדַּל
וְתִתְקַדַּשׁ בְּתוֹךְ יְרוּשָׁלַיִם עִירְךָ לְדוֹר וָדוֹר וּלְנֵצַח נְצָחִים.
וְעֵינֵינוּ תִרְאֶינָה מַלְכוּתֶךָ, כַּדָּבָר הָאָמוּר בְּשִׁירֵי עֻזֶּךָ, עַל יְדֵי
דָוִד מְשִׁיחַ צִדְקֶךָ:

יִמְלֹךְ יְיָ לְעוֹלָם אֱלֹהַיִךְ צִיּוֹן לְדֹר וָדֹר, הַלְלוּיָהּ.

Leader:

לְדוֹר וָדוֹר נַגִּיד גָּדְלֶךָ וּלְנֵצַח נְצָחִים קְדֻשָּׁתְךָ נַקְדִּישׁ. וְשִׁבְחֲךָ אֱלֹהֵינוּ
מִפִּינוּ לֹא יָמוּשׁ לְעוֹלָם וָעֶד, כִּי אֵל מֶלֶךְ גָּדוֹל וְקָדוֹשׁ אָתָּה.

Each congregant while or after leader says above.

אַתָּה קָדוֹשׁ וְשִׁמְךָ קָדוֹשׁ וּקְדוֹשִׁים בְּכָל־יוֹם יְהַלְלוּךָ סֶּלָה.

בָּרוּךְ אַתָּה יְיָ הָאֵל הַקָּדוֹשׁ.

We will declare God's holiness here on earth as we imagine heavenly angels do above:

Holy, holy, holy — the whole world is filled with God's glory.

The angels in a thundering chorus lift up their majestic voices and answer:

Praised is the glory of *Adonai* throughout the Universe.

Our Ruler, reveal Yourself to us, for we wait for You. When will you rule in Zion? Soon, please, soon, establish Yourself in Zion forever. May You be praised within Your city, Jerusalem, for generation after generation, now and always. May we see Your rule with our own eyes.

May You rule throughout time, *Halleluyah*!

Leader:

From generation to generation, we will tell of Your greatness and we will declare Your holiness forever. Your praise will never leave our mouths, for You are our Holy One.

Each congregant:

You are holy and Your name is holy and those who strive to be holy praise you each day,

Praised are You, holy God.

אַתָּה בְחַרְתָּנוּ מִכָּל־הָעַמִּים, אָהַבְתָּ אוֹתָנוּ וְרָצִיתָ בָּנוּ, וְרוֹמַמְתָּנוּ מִכָּל־הַלְּשׁוֹנוֹת, וְקִדַּשְׁתָּנוּ בְּמִצְוֹתֶיךָ, וְקֵרַבְתָּנוּ מַלְכֵּנוּ לַעֲבוֹדָתֶךָ, וְשִׁמְךָ הַגָּדוֹל וְהַקָּדוֹשׁ עָלֵינוּ קָרָאתָ.

וַתִּתֶּן לָנוּ יְיָ אֱלֹהֵינוּ בְּאַהֲבָה (שַׁבָּתוֹת לִמְנוּחָה וּ)מוֹעֲדִים לְשִׂמְחָה, חַגִּים וּזְמַנִּים לְשָׂשׂוֹן, אֶת־יוֹם (הַשַּׁבָּת הַזֶּה וְאֶת־יוֹם)

:On *Pesaḥ* חַג הַמַּצּוֹת הַזֶּה, זְמַן חֵרוּתֵנוּ,

:On *Shavuot* חַג הַשָּׁבוּעוֹת הַזֶּה, זְמַן מַתַּן תּוֹרָתֵנוּ,

:On *Sukkot* חַג הַסֻּכּוֹת הַזֶּה, זְמַן שִׂמְחָתֵנוּ,

:On *Sh'mini Atzeret* and on *Simḥat Torah*

הַשְּׁמִינִי, חַג הָעֲצֶרֶת הַזֶּה, זְמַן שִׂמְחָתֵנוּ,

(בְּאַהֲבָה) מִקְרָא קֹדֶשׁ, זֵכֶר לִיצִיאַת מִצְרָיִם.

You have cherished us as a people by giving us Your *mitzvot* and bringing us closer to Your service. Lovingly, You have given us (*Shabbat* for rest), festivals for gladness and seasons for joy, such as (this *Shabbat* and) this

On *Pesaḥ*:

Festival of *Matzot*, the time of our becoming free,

On *Shavuot*:

Festival of *Shavuot*, the time of our receiving the Torah,

On *Sukkot*:

Festival of *Sukkot*, the time of our rejoicing,

On *Sh'mini Atzeret* and on *Simḥat Torah*:

Festival of *Sh'mini Atzeret*, this time of our rejoicing,

a day for assembly, recalling the Exodus from Egypt.

אֱלֹהֵֽינוּ וֵאלֹהֵי אֲבוֹתֵֽינוּ, יַעֲלֶה וְיָבֹא וְיַגִּֽיעַ, וְיֵרָאֶה וְיֵרָצֶה

וְיִשָּׁמַע, וְיִפָּקֵד וְיִזָּכֵר זִכְרוֹנֵֽנוּ וּפִקְדוֹנֵֽנוּ, וְזִכְרוֹן אֲבוֹתֵֽינוּ,

וְזִכְרוֹן מָשִֽׁיחַ בֶּן־דָּוִד עַבְדֶּֽךָ, וְזִכְרוֹן יְרוּשָׁלַֽיִם עִיר קָדְשֶֽׁךָ,

לְחֵן וּלְחֶֽסֶד וּלְרַחֲמִים, לְחַיִּים וּלְשָׁלוֹם בְּיוֹם

On *Pesah*:　חַג הַמַּצּוֹת הַזֶּה.

On *Shavuot*:　חַג הַשָּׁבֻעוֹת הַזֶּה.

On *Sukkot*:　חַג הַסֻּכּוֹת הַזֶּה.

On *Sh'mini Atzeret* and on *Simhat Torah*:

הַשְּׁמִינִי, חַג הָעֲצֶֽרֶת הַזֶּה.

זָכְרֵֽנוּ יְיָ אֱלֹהֵֽינוּ בּוֹ לְטוֹבָה, וּפָקְדֵֽנוּ בוֹ לִבְרָכָה, וְהוֹשִׁיעֵֽנוּ בוֹ

לְחַיִּים.

Our God and God of our ancestors, may Your remembering us, our
ancestors, Jerusalem the holy city, and Your promises for our future
allow You to grant us happiness, peace and life on this day of

Pesah:	*Shavuot*	*Sukkot:*	*Sh'mini Atzeret* and *Simhat Torah*
The Feast of *Matzah*	The Festival of *Shavuot*	The Festival of *Sukkot*	This Festival of *Sh'mini Atzeret*

וְהַשִּׂיאֵנוּ יְיָ אֱלֹהֵינוּ אֶת־בִּרְכַּת מוֹעֲדֶיךָ לְחַיִּים וּלְשָׁלוֹם,
לְשִׂמְחָה וּלְשָׂשׂוֹן, כַּאֲשֶׁר רָצִיתָ וְאָמַרְתָּ לְבָרְכֵנוּ. אֱלֹהֵינוּ
וֵאלֹהֵי אֲבוֹתֵינוּ, (רְצֵה בִמְנוּחָתֵנוּ,) קַדְּשֵׁנוּ בְּמִצְוֹתֶיךָ וְתֵן
חֶלְקֵנוּ בְּתוֹרָתֶךָ, שַׂבְּעֵנוּ מִטּוּבֶךָ וְשַׂמְּחֵנוּ בִּישׁוּעָתֶךָ, וְטַהֵר
לִבֵּנוּ לְעָבְדְּךָ בֶּאֱמֶת. וְהַנְחִילֵנוּ יְיָ אֱלֹהֵינוּ (בְּאַהֲבָה וּבְרָצוֹן)
בְּשִׂמְחָה וּבְשָׂשׂוֹן (שַׁבָּת וּ)מוֹעֲדֵי קָדְשֶׁךָ, וְיִשְׂמְחוּ בְךָ יִשְׂרָאֵל
מְקַדְּשֵׁי שְׁמֶךָ. בָּרוּךְ אַתָּה יְיָ מְקַדֵּשׁ (הַשַּׁבָּת וְ)יִשְׂרָאֵל
וְהַזְּמַנִּים.

Grant us the blessing of Your festivals for life and peace, joy and gladness. May our hearts be devoted to You. Praised are You, *Adonai*, Who makes holy (the *Shabbat*), Israel and the festivals.

רְצֵה יְיָ אֱלֹהֵינוּ בְּעַמְּךָ יִשְׂרָאֵל וּבִתְפִלָּתָם, וְהָשֵׁב
אֶת־הָעֲבוֹדָה לִדְבִיר בֵּיתֶךָ, וּתְפִלָּתָם בְּאַהֲבָה תְקַבֵּל
בְּרָצוֹן, וּתְהִי לְרָצוֹן תָּמִיד עֲבוֹדַת יִשְׂרָאֵל עַמֶּךָ. וְתֶחֱזֶינָה
עֵינֵינוּ בְּשׁוּבְךָ לְצִיּוֹן בְּרַחֲמִים. בָּרוּךְ אַתָּה יְיָ הַמַּחֲזִיר
שְׁכִינָתוֹ לְצִיּוֹן.

Be pleased, *Adonai*, our God, with Your people Israel and their prayers. May our worship always be acceptable to You. May we witness your merciful return to Zion. Praised are You, *Adonai*, Who returns to Zion.

מוֹדִים אֲנַחְנוּ לָךְ שָׁאַתָּה הוּא יְיָ אֱלֹהֵינוּ וֵאלֹהֵי אֲבוֹתֵינוּ לְעוֹלָם וָעֶד, צוּר חַיֵּינוּ מָגֵן יִשְׁעֵנוּ אַתָּה הוּא לְדוֹר וָדוֹר. נוֹדֶה לְּךָ וּנְסַפֵּר תְּהִלָּתֶךָ, עַל חַיֵּינוּ הַמְּסוּרִים בְּיָדֶךָ וְעַל נִשְׁמוֹתֵינוּ הַפְּקוּדוֹת לָךְ וְעַל נִסֶּיךָ שֶׁבְּכָל־יוֹם עִמָּנוּ וְעַל נִפְלְאוֹתֶיךָ וְטוֹבוֹתֶיךָ שֶׁבְּכָל־עֵת, עֶרֶב וָבֹקֶר וְצָהֳרָיִם. הַטּוֹב כִּי לֹא כָלוּ רַחֲמֶיךָ, וְהַמְרַחֵם כִּי לֹא תַמּוּ חֲסָדֶיךָ, מֵעוֹלָם קִוִּינוּ לָךְ.

וְעַל כֻּלָּם יִתְבָּרַךְ וְיִתְרוֹמַם שִׁמְךָ מַלְכֵּנוּ תָּמִיד לְעוֹלָם וָעֶד. וְכֹל הַחַיִּים יוֹדוּךָ סֶּלָה, וִיהַלְלוּ אֶת־שִׁמְךָ בֶּאֱמֶת, הָאֵל יְשׁוּעָתֵנוּ וְעֶזְרָתֵנוּ סֶלָה. בָּרוּךְ אַתָּה יְיָ הַטּוֹב שִׁמְךָ וּלְךָ נָאֶה לְהוֹדוֹת.

How grateful we are to You, God of our ancestors, the Eternal One. You are the source of our strength, just as You have been the protecting shield of each generation.

We thank You for our lives which are in Your hand and our souls which are in Your care. We thank You for Your miracles which surround us all the time and the wondrous acts of Your kindness that we experience each morning, noon and night.

You are the source of never-ending loving-kindness. You are our hope forever.

Praised are You, *Adonai*, who deserves praise.

The leader adds:

אֱלֹהֵינוּ וֵאלֹהֵי אֲבוֹתֵינוּ, בָּרְכֵנוּ בַבְּרָכָה הַמְשֻׁלֶּשֶׁת, בַּתּוֹרָה
הַכְּתוּבָה עַל יְדֵי מֹשֶׁה עַבְדֶּךָ, הָאֲמוּרָה מִפִּי אַהֲרֹן וּבָנָיו,
כֹּהֲנִים, עַם קְדוֹשֶׁךָ, כָּאָמוּר:

יְבָרֶכְךָ יְיָ וְיִשְׁמְרֶךָ. כֵּן יְהִי רָצוֹן.
יָאֵר יְיָ פָּנָיו אֵלֶיךָ וִיחֻנֶּךָּ. כֵּן יְהִי רָצוֹן.
יִשָּׂא יְיָ פָּנָיו אֵלֶיךָ וְיָשֵׂם לְךָ שָׁלוֹם. כֵּן יְהִי רָצוֹן.

God of our ancestors, bless us with the threefold blessing recited by the priests of old:

May *Adonai* bless and protect you;

May *Adonai* shine upon you with graciousness;

May *Adonai* look upon you with favor and grant you peace.

שִׂים שָׁלוֹם בָּעוֹלָם, טוֹבָה וּבְרָכָה, חֵן וָחֶסֶד וְרַחֲמִים עָלֵינוּ
וְעַל כָּל־יִשְׂרָאֵל עַמֶּךָ. בָּרְכֵנוּ אָבִינוּ כֻּלָּנוּ כְּאֶחָד בְּאוֹר
פָּנֶיךָ, כִּי בְאוֹר פָּנֶיךָ נָתַתָּ לָּנוּ, יְיָ אֱלֹהֵינוּ, תּוֹרַת חַיִּים
וְאַהֲבַת חֶסֶד, וּצְדָקָה וּבְרָכָה וְרַחֲמִים וְחַיִּים וְשָׁלוֹם. וְטוֹב
בְּעֵינֶיךָ לְבָרֵךְ אֶת־עַמְּךָ יִשְׂרָאֵל בְּכָל־עֵת וּבְכָל־שָׁעָה
בִּשְׁלוֹמֶךָ.

בָּרוּךְ אַתָּה יְיָ הַמְבָרֵךְ אֶת־עַמּוֹ יִשְׂרָאֵל בַּשָּׁלוֹם.

Let peace, happiness and love come to the world, to us and to all the Jewish people. Bless us all, Holy One, with Your light, for by that light You have given the Torah to guide us. May it please You to bless the Jewish people in every season and at all times with goodness and peace.

Praised are You, *Adonai*, Who blesses the people Israel with peace.

Taking the *Lulav* and *Etrog* on *Sukkot*

On *Sukkot*, hold your *lulav* in your right hand, the *etrog* in your left hand, and hold your hands close together. Before and while you recite the blessing over the *lulav*, hold the *etrog* with the *pitam* (the thumb-like stem) facing down. After the blessing, hold the *etrog* with the *pitam* facing up. Recite the blessings while standing.

Before

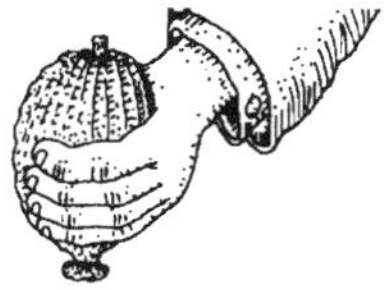

After

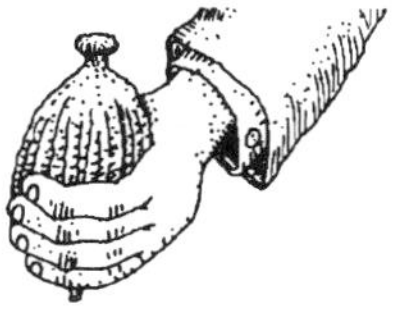

Blessing over the *lulav*:

בָּרוּךְ אַתָּה יְיָ אֱלֹהֵינוּ מֶלֶךְ הָעוֹלָם, אֲשֶׁר קִדְּשָׁנוּ בְּמִצְוֹתָיו
וְצִוָּנוּ עַל נְטִילַת לוּלָב.

We praise You, *Adonai*, Ruler of the Universe, Who has made us holy by Your *mitzvot* and commanded us to take up the *lulav*.

Baruḥ atah Adonai Eloheinu Meleḥ ha'olam, asher kid'deshanu b'mitzvotav v'tzivanu al n'tilat lulav.

Each year, we say the following blessing when we take the *lulav* for the very first time:

בָּרוּךְ אַתָּה יְיָ אֱלֹהֵינוּ מֶלֶךְ הָעוֹלָם, שֶׁהֶחֱיָנוּ וְקִיְּמָנוּ
וְהִגִּיעָנוּ לַזְּמַן הַזֶּה.

We praise You, *Adonai*, our God, Ruler of the Universe, Who has kept us alive and well so that we can celebrate this special time.

Baruḥ atah Adonai Eloheinu Meleḥ ha'olam, sheheḥeyanu, v'ki'yi'manu, v'higi'anu la'zman hazeh.

The *lulav* is shaken three times in each direction, successively, in the following order: Pointed in front of you, to your right, pointed behind you (over your right shoulder), to your left, and while holding the *lulav* in front of you, point upward and shake three times, and downward and shake three times.

HALLEL

Hallel is said on the new moon, *Rosh Ḥodesh*, and on festivals, *Yom Tov*, as an extra expression of our gratefulness to God. We recite a shorter version of *Hallel* on the last six days of *Pesah* as a reminder that our celebration should be diminished because the Egyptians drowned in the Re(e)d Sea as they attempted to cross it. We should not rejoice at anyone's sorrows, not even our enemies'.

בָּרוּךְ אַתָּה יְיָ אֱלֹהֵינוּ מֶלֶךְ הָעוֹלָם, אֲשֶׁר קִדְּשָׁנוּ בְּמִצְוֹתָיו וְצִוָּנוּ לִקְרֹא אֶת־הַהַלֵּל.

Baruḥ atah Adonai Eloheinu Meleḥ ha'olam, asher kid'deshanu b'mitzvotav, v'tzivanu li'kro et haHallel.

Praised are You, *Adonai*, our God, Ruler of the universe, Who has made us holy with Your *mitzvot*, and gave us the *mitzvah* of saying the *Hallel*.

בְּצֵאת יִשְׂרָאֵל מִמִּצְרָיִם, בֵּית יַעֲקֹב מֵעַם לֹעֵז.
הָיְתָה יְהוּדָה לְקָדְשׁוֹ, יִשְׂרָאֵל מַמְשְׁלוֹתָיו.
הַיָּם רָאָה וַיָּנֹס, הַיַּרְדֵּן יִסֹּב לְאָחוֹר.
הֶהָרִים רָקְדוּ כְאֵילִים, גְּבָעוֹת כִּבְנֵי צֹאן.
מַה לְּךָ הַיָּם כִּי תָנוּס, הַיַּרְדֵּן תִּסֹּב לְאָחוֹר.
הֶהָרִים תִּרְקְדוּ כְאֵילִים, גְּבָעוֹת כִּבְנֵי־צֹאן.
מִלִּפְנֵי אָדוֹן חוּלִי אָרֶץ, מִלִּפְנֵי אֱלוֹהַּ יַעֲקֹב,
הַהֹפְכִי הַצּוּר אֲגַם מָיִם, חַלָּמִישׁ לְמַעְיְנוֹ מָיִם.

When Israel left the land of Egypt and when Jacob's household left a foreign people, Judah became God's sanctuary; Israel became God's own.

The Sea saw and fled; the Jordan flowed backwards. Mountains skipped like frightened lambs, the hills like young sheep.

Even the earth trembled at *Adonai's* presence – the presence of the God of Jacob – who turns rock into pools of water, stone into a flowing fountain.
Psalm 114

We recall a momentous time in our history — the exodus from Egypt and imagine all of nature expressing amazement. Can you add to these verses by completing these sentence stems?

The sun...
and the moon...
The plants...
and the stars...

Can you add verses with animals, trees or plants?

יְיָ זְכָרָנוּ יְבָרֵךְ,
יְבָרֵךְ אֶת־בֵּית יִשְׂרָאֵל,
יְבָרֵךְ אֶת־בֵּית אַהֲרוֹן,
יְבָרֵךְ יִרְאֵי יְיָ, הַקְּטַנִּים עִם הַגְּדֹלִים.
יֹסֵף יְיָ עֲלֵיכֶם, עֲלֵיכֶם וְעַל בְּנֵיכֶם.
בְּרוּכִים אַתֶּם לַייָ , עֹשֵׂה שָׁמַיִם וָאָרֶץ.
הַשָּׁמַיִם שָׁמַיִם לַייָ,
וְהָאָרֶץ נָתַן לִבְנֵי אָדָם.
לֹא הַמֵּתִים יְהַלְלוּ יָהּ
וְלֹא כָּל־יֹרְדֵי דוּמָה.
וַאֲנַחְנוּ נְבָרֵךְ יָהּ מֵעַתָּה וְעַד עוֹלָם.
הַלְלוּיָהּ.

Adonai remembers us – God is the Source of blessing.
Bless the House of Israel. Bless the House of Aaron.
Those who recognize God will be blessed, the young and old alike.
May *Adonai* make us and future generations fruitful.
May you be blessed by *Adonai,* who made heaven and earth.
Heaven belongs to *Adonai*, but the earth is given in trust to us.
The dead cannot praise God for they are now silent.
But we shall praise *Adonai,* now and forever.
Halleluyah!

Why is the blessing of having children so important?

When we say the verse that the dead cannot praise God, some people think it means that only people who are alive and open to God can sing praises. Those who are shut off to experiencing God cannot. God is not real or alive to them.

Have you ever closed yourself off to an experience that you later decided to try? How did you feel when you closed yourself off; after you had the experience? Are there experiences not worth trying?

הַלְלוּ אֶת־יְיָ כָּל־גּוֹיִם, שַׁבְּחוּהוּ כָּל־הָאֻמִּים.
כִּי גָבַר עָלֵינוּ חַסְדּוֹ, וֶאֱמֶת יְיָ לְעוֹלָם.
הַלְלוּיָהּ.

Praise *Adonai*, all nations.
Celebrate the Holy One, all peoples.
We are overwhelmed with God's kindness
and unending faithfulness. *Halleluyah*!
Psalm 117

Although we praise God as Jews, we recognize that God is universal. God belongs to all peoples. They, too, express their love and gratitude.

הוֹדוּ לַייָ כִּי טוֹב, כִּי לְעוֹלָם חַסְדּוֹ.
יֹאמַר נָא יִשְׂרָאֵל, כִּי לְעוֹלָם חַסְדּוֹ.
יֹאמְרוּ נָא בֵית אַהֲרֹן, כִּי לְעוֹלָם חַסְדּוֹ.
יֹאמְרוּ נָא יִרְאֵי יְיָ, כִּי לְעוֹלָם חַסְדּוֹ.

Leader:	Congregation:
Give thanks to *Adonai* for God is good.	God's love is forever.
Let Israel say:	*Ki l'olam ḥasdo.*
Let the house of Aaron say:	*Ki l'olam ḥasdo.*
Let all who recognize God say:	*Ki l'olam ḥasdo.*

Psalm 118:1-4

Hodu l'Adonai ki tov.	*Ki l'olam ḥasdo.*
Yomar na Yisrael:	*Ki l'olam ḥasdo.*
Yomru na beit Aharon:	*Ki l'olam ḥasdo.*
Yomru na yirei Adonai:	*Ki l'olam ḥasdo.*

Each of the following verses is said twice:

אוֹדְךָ כִּי עֲנִיתָנִי וַתְּהִי לִי לִישׁוּעָה.
אֶבֶן מָאֲסוּ הַבּוֹנִים הָיְתָה לְרֹאשׁ פִּנָּה.
מֵאֵת יְיָ הָיְתָה זֹּאת, הִיא נִפְלָאת בְּעֵינֵינוּ.
זֶה הַיּוֹם עָשָׂה יְיָ, נָגִילָה וְנִשְׂמְחָה בוֹ.

I praise You, for You have answered me.
It was You Who saved me.
The stone the builders rejected
has become the cornerstone.
This is all *Adonai's* doing; it is a miracle for us to see.
This is the day *Adonai* has made.
Let us be happy and rejoice on it.

Psalm 118: 21-24

Who are the builders in this verse? Who or what is the stone the builders rejected? What does it mean that this stone became the cornerstone? Why does this act make us rejoice?

Can you think of a day when you wanted or will want to say, "This is the day *Adonai* has made, let us be happy and rejoice on it?"

The leader says each phrase and then the congregation repeats it.

אָנָּא יְיָ הוֹשִׁיעָה נָּא. אָנָּא יְיָ הוֹשִׁיעָה נָּא.
אָנָּא יְיָ הַצְלִיחָה נָּא. אָנָּא יְיָ הַצְלִיחָה נָּא.

We ask You, *Adona*i, please save us.
We ask You, *Adona*i, please save us.
We ask You, *Adona*i, please help us succeed.
We ask You, *Adona*i, please help us succeed.
Psalm 118:25

Ana Adonai hoshi'ah na.
Ana Adonai hoshi'ah na.
Ana Adonai hatzliḥah na.
Ana Adonai hatzliḥah na.

From what do we want to be saved or protected?
In what do we want to succeed?

Many beautiful and joyful melodies have been composed for the words of the *Hallel*. Do you have a favorite?

כִּי לְךָ טוֹב לְהוֹדוֹת וּלְשִׁמְךָ נָאֶה לְזַמֵּר, כִּי מֵעוֹלָם עַד עוֹלָם
אַתָּה אֵל. בָּרוּךְ אַתָּה יְיָ , מֶלֶךְ מְהֻלָּל בַּתִּשְׁבָּחוֹת.

It is good to give thanks to You and fitting to sing Your praise.
For You are God through all time.
Praised are You, Whose praise we announce.

Reflections V

In the First Century of the Common Era, a certain Queen Helena and her son, Monobaz, converted to Judaism. The kingdom was called Adiabene, in what is now modern-day Iraq. Monobaz (or Munbaz, as he is known in the ancient Jewish texts) eventually succeeded his father, Monobaz I, to the throne and a number of wonderful stories about the royal mother and son are related in the *Talmud*. One such story about Munbaz II is a Grand Tale of *Tzedakah*:

At a certain point in his life, King Munbaz gave away all of his wealth to the poor. His relatives complained to him, saying, "The generation before you accumulated even greater treasures than their ancestors. Now see what you have done! You have wasted both your own wealth and that of your ancestors!"

King Munbaz replied, "I have outdone them all.

My ancestors accumulated earthly things; I have gathered things for Heaven....

My ancestors saved money that did not pay dividends; my money is paying dividends....

My ancestors stored things that could be stolen; mine can't be stolen....

My ancestors amassed money; I have collected souls....

My ancestors hoarded things that wound up in the possession of other people; what I have done will always be mine...."

Jerusalem *Talmud*, *Pe'ah* 1:1

KADDISH SHALEM

קַדִּישׁ שָׁלֵם

Leader:

יִתְגַּדַּל וְיִתְקַדַּשׁ שְׁמֵהּ רַבָּא בְּעָלְמָא דִּי בְרָא כִרְעוּתֵהּ,
וְיַמְלִיךְ מַלְכוּתֵהּ בְּחַיֵּיכוֹן וּבְיוֹמֵיכוֹן וּבְחַיֵּי דְכָל־בֵּית יִשְׂרָאֵל,
בַּעֲגָלָא וּבִזְמַן קָרִיב, וְאִמְרוּ אָמֵן.

Congregation and Leader answer:

יְהֵא שְׁמֵהּ רַבָּא מְבָרַךְ לְעָלַם וּלְעָלְמֵי עָלְמַיָּא.

Y'hei shmei rabba m'voraḥ l'olam u'l'olmei almay'ya.

Leader:

יִתְבָּרַךְ וְיִשְׁתַּבַּח וְיִתְפָּאַר וְיִתְרוֹמַם וְיִתְנַשֵּׂא, וְיִתְהַדַּר וְיִתְעַלֶּה
וְיִתְהַלַּל שְׁמֵהּ דְּקֻדְשָׁא,

Congregation and Leader answer:

בְּרִיךְ הוּא.

Briḥ hu.

Leader:

לְעֵלָּא [לְעֵלָּא מִכָּל־] מִן כָּל־בִּרְכָתָא וְשִׁירָתָא תֻּשְׁבְּחָתָא
וְנֶחֱמָתָא דַּאֲמִירָן בְּעָלְמָא, וְאִמְרוּ אָמֵן.

תִּתְקַבַּל צְלוֹתְהוֹן וּבָעוּתְהוֹן דְּכָל־יִשְׂרָאֵל קֳדָם אֲבוּהוֹן דִּי
בִשְׁמַיָּא, וְאִמְרוּ אָמֵן.

יְהֵא שְׁלָמָא רַבָּא מִן שְׁמַיָּא וְחַיִּים עָלֵינוּ וְעַל כָּל־יִשְׂרָאֵל,
וְאִמְרוּ אָמֵן.

עוֹשֶׂה שָׁלוֹם בִּמְרוֹמָיו, הוּא יַעֲשֶׂה שָׁלוֹם עָלֵינוּ וְעַל
כָּל־יִשְׂרָאֵל, וְאִמְרוּ אָמֵן.

The Challenge

Once a rabbi and a soapmaker went for a stroll. As they walked along, the soapmaker challenged the rabbi. "What good is the Torah? After thousands of years of teaching about honesty, truth, loving-kindness, justice and peace the world is still full of misery and trouble."

The rabbi was quiet. They came upon a young child playing. The child was covered with dirt and grime. The rabbi turned to the soapmaker and said, "What use is soap? With all the soap that exists, this child is still filthy."

"But rabbi, soap can't do any good unless we use it!"

"So it is with Torah," the rabbi replied. "We must apply its words to our lives."

TORAH AND THE ARK

Imagine that you own something very precious. You'd want to keep it in a box or container to preserve it. This is how Jews feel about the Torah. That's why we build arks — to keep our Torah scrolls safe. Besides being sturdy, they are often beautifully decorated. Can you describe the ark in your synagogue?

When the ancient Israelites lived in the desert, they were instructed to build a *Mishkan* (Tabernacle). In it they placed the ark and inside the ark were the Ten Commandments. Keeping the *luḥot* (two tablets of the law) safe was very important because the Israelites carried the ark with them whenever they traveled.

We are told that as they marched through the desert, the twelve tribes of Israel surrounded the ark. This, too, was a way of protecting the *luḥot*. It also gave the Israelites an orderly way to proceed.

The verse "*Kuma Adonai v'yafutzu oyveḥa v'yanusu m'saneḥa mipaneḥa*. Rise up, *Adonai*, let your enemies be scattered and let those who hate You be put to flight" (*Numbers* 10:35) was said by Moses when the ark moved, leading the Israelites. Hearing this gave them courage.

Close your eyes and imagine that you were there when the ark moved forward. How would having the ark guide you on your journey make you feel?

אֵין כָּמְוֹךָ בָאֱלֹהִים אֲדֹנָי,
Ein ka'moḥa va'Elohim Adonai

וְאֵין כְּמַעֲשֶֽׂיךָ.
v'ein k'ma'aseḥa.

מַלְכוּתְךָ מַלְכוּת כָּל־עוֹלָמִים,
Malḥut'ḥa malḥut kol olamim,

וּמֶמְשַׁלְתְּךָ בְּכָל־דּוֹר וָדוֹר.
umem'shalt'ḥa b'ḥol dor va'dor.

יְיָ מֶלֶךְ, יְיָ מָלָךְ,
Adonai Meleḥ, Adonai malaḥ,

יְיָ יִמְלֹךְ לְעוֹלָם וָעֶד.
Adonai yimloḥ l'olam va'ed.

יְיָ עֹז לְעַמּוֹ יִתֵּן,
Adonai oz l'amo yiten,

יְיָ יְבָרֵךְ אֶת־עַמּוֹ בַשָּׁלוֹם.
Adonai y'vareḥ et amo va'shalom.

There is no God like You, *Adonai*, and no deeds like Yours.
Your majesty is everlasting and Your rule continues for all generations.

Adonai rules, *Adonai* ruled. *Adonai* will rule forever and ever.
May You give strength to Your people and bless them with peace.

אַב הָרַחֲמִים, הֵיטִֽיבָה בִרְצוֹנְךָ אֶת־צִיּוֹן, תִּבְנֶה חוֹמוֹת יְרוּשָׁלָֽיִם.

כִּי בְךָ לְבַד בָּטָֽחְנוּ, מֶלֶךְ אֵל רָם וְנִשָּׂא, אֲדוֹן עוֹלָמִים.

Source of mercy, favor the people Israel with Your goodness and strengthen Jerusalem, for in You alone do we put our trust.

We rise as the ark is opened:

Vay'hi binso'a ha'aron,	וַיְהִי בִּנְסֹעַ הָאָרֹן
vay'yomer Mosheh:	וַיֹּאמֶר מֹשֶׁה:
Kuma Adonai v'yafutzu oyveḥa,	קוּמָה יְיָ וְיָפֻצוּ אֹיְבֶיךָ,
v'yanusu m'saneḥa mipaneḥa.	וְיָנֻסוּ מְשַׂנְאֶיךָ מִפָּנֶיךָ.
Ki mitziyon tetzei Torah,	כִּי מִצִּיּוֹן תֵּצֵא תוֹרָה,
u'd'var Adonai mirushalayim.	וּדְבַר יְיָ מִירוּשָׁלָיִם.
Baruḥ shenatan Torah l'amo	בָּרוּךְ שֶׁנָּתַן תּוֹרָה לְעַמּוֹ
Yisrael bik'dushato.	יִשְׂרָאֵל בִּקְדֻשָּׁתוֹ.

And it happened that when the ark was carried forward, Moses would say, "Rise up, *Adonai*, let Your enemies be scattered and let those who hate You be put to flight." Torah shall come out of Zion and the word of God from Jerusalem. Praised is God who gave the Torah to the people Israel.

We omit on *Shabbat*.
On festivals, the leader recites this three times before the opened ark:

יְיָ יְיָ אֵל רַחוּם וְחַנּוּן, אֶרֶךְ אַפַּיִם וְרַב חֶסֶד וֶאֱמֶת,
נֹצֵר חֶסֶד לָאֲלָפִים, נֹשֵׂא עָוֹן וָפֶשַׁע וְחַטָּאָה, וְנַקֵּה.

וַאֲנִי תְפִלָּתִי לְךָ יְיָ עֵת רָצוֹן, אֱלֹהִים בְּרָב־חַסְדֶּךָ, עֲנֵנִי
בֶּאֱמֶת יִשְׁעֶךָ.

Adonai, Adonai, merciful and patient God,
You remember our kind acts for a thousand generations.
You accept our shortcomings and pardon our sins.

May the words I say today be acceptable to You, *Adonai.*
Show me kindness and answer the prayers of my heart.

Adonai, Adonai, El raḥum v'ḥanun,
ereḥ apayim v'rav ḥesed ve'emet.

Notzer ḥesed la'alafim,
nosei avon vafesha v'ḥata'ah v'nakeh.

Va'ani t'filati l'ḥa Adonai et ratzon.
Elohim b'rov ḥasdeḥa aneini be'emet yish'eḥa.

The Torah is taken and held.
Leader and then congregation say:

שְׁמַע יִשְׂרָאֵל יְיָ אֱלֹהֵינוּ יְיָ אֶחָד.

Hear O Israel: *Adonai* our God, *Adonai* is One.
Shema Yisrael Adonai Eloheinu Adonai eḥad.

Leader and then congregation say:

אֶחָד אֱלֹהֵינוּ, גָּדוֹל אֲדוֹנֵינוּ, קָדוֹשׁ שְׁמוֹ.

Our God is One, Great and Holy.
Eḥad Eloheinu, gadol Adoneinu, kadosh sh'mo.

Leader bows and says:

גַּדְּלוּ לַייָ אִתִּי, וּנְרוֹמְמָה שְׁמוֹ יַחְדָּו.

Join me in proclaiming God's greatness. Together, let us praise God.

As the Torah is carried around the congregation,
we kiss the Torah and all sing:

לְךָ יְיָ הַגְּדֻלָּה וְהַגְּבוּרָה וְהַתִּפְאֶרֶת וְהַנֵּצַח וְהַהוֹד, כִּי כֹל
בַּשָּׁמַיִם וּבָאָרֶץ, לְךָ יְיָ הַמַּמְלָכָה וְהַמִּתְנַשֵּׂא לְכֹל לְרֹאשׁ.

רוֹמְמוּ יְיָ אֱלֹהֵינוּ וְהִשְׁתַּחֲווּ לַהֲדֹם רַגְלָיו, קָדוֹשׁ הוּא.
רוֹמְמוּ יְיָ אֱלֹהֵינוּ וְהִשְׁתַּחֲווּ לְהַר קָדְשׁוֹ, כִּי קָדוֹשׁ יְיָ אֱלֹהֵינוּ.

Yours, *Adonai*, is the greatness, power and splendor.
Yours is the triumph and the majesty.
For all in heaven and on earth is Yours.
You rule over all.
Praise *Adonai*, the Holy One. Worship at God's holy mountain,
for there is none like *Adonai*, our God.

L'ḥa Adonai hag'dulah v'hag'vurah v'hatiferet v'hanetzaḥ v'hahod.
Ki ḥol bashamayim u'va'aretz,
l'ḥa Adonai hamamlaḥa v'hamitnasei l'ḥol l'rosh.
Romemu Adonai Eloheinu v'hishtaḥavu lahadom raglav, kadosh hu.
Romemu Adonai Eloheinu v'hishtaḥavu l'har kod'sho,
Ki kadosh Adonai Eloheinu.

Here are some additional songs for everyone to sing:

Yisrael v'orayta v'kudsha	יִשְׂרָאֵל וְאוֹרַיְתָא וְקוּדְשָׁא
briḥ hu ḥad hu	בְּרִיךְ הוּא חַד הוּא
Torah Orah halleluyah.	תּוֹרָה אוֹרָה הַלְלוּיָה.

V'ha'er eineinu b'Torateḥa	וְהָאֵר עֵינֵינוּ בְּתוֹרָתֶךָ,
v'dabek libeinu b'mitzvoteḥa	וְדַבֵּק לִבֵּנוּ בְּמִצְוֹתֶיךָ
v'yaḥed l'vaveinu l'ahavah	וְיַחֵד לְבָבֵנוּ לְאַהֲבָה
u'l'yir'ah et sh'meḥa	וּלְיִרְאָה אֶת שְׁמֶךָ,
v'lo neivosh l'olam va'ed.	וְלֹא נֵבוֹשׁ לְעוֹלָם וָעֶד.
Ki v'shem kodsh'ḥa hagadol	כִּי בְשֵׁם קָדְשְׁךָ הַגָּדוֹל
v'hanora bataḥnu	וְהַנּוֹרָא בָּטָחְנוּ,
nagilah v'nis'm'ḥa bishu'ateḥa.	נָגִילָה וְנִשְׂמְחָה בִּישׁוּעָתֶךָ.

Torah tzivah lanu Mosheh	תּוֹרָה צִוָּה לָנוּ מֹשֶׁה
morashah k'hilat Ya'akov.	מוֹרָשָׁה קְהִלַּת יַעֲקֹב.

READING THE TORAH

We do not know exactly when Jews began to read the Torah in public as part of the prayer service. The Rabbis of the second century believed that it had begun a long time before. The *Mishnah* and *Talmud* already take for granted that the Torah reading is part of the service. A source after the *Talmud* tells us that Moses introduced the practice of reading the Torah on *Shabbat* and holidays. Ezra the Scribe is credited with having introduced the practice of reading on Mondays, Thursdays, and *Shabbat* afternoons. Telling us that Moses and Ezra introduced the practice is a way of indicating its importance and that it began a long time before.

Scholars believe it is very possible that the prayer service developed around the reading of the Torah and not the other way around. When the Jews were allowed to return from Babylonian Exile, their leader, Ezra the Scribe, gathered them together in the public square of Jerusalem and read and explained the Torah to them.

It, perhaps, became natural for Jews to gather to listen to the reading of the Torah — to listen to what God said to them. It would be natural to also pray to God at such times.

We do know that several hundred years after Ezra's public reading of the Torah, its reading became a regular part of the service. This developed after the destruction of the Temple (70 C.E.).

At first, the leader selected what section of the Torah would be read. Around the second century B.C.E., a rule was established to read consecutive *parshiot* (portions).

In Israel, the reading took three years. In Babylonia, where many Jews remained, the reading took one year and was completed at the end of *Sukkot*. Most congregations follow this custom, though there are many which read a third of the *parashah* each week.

Imagine, wherever you go in the world, the same Torah portion is being read on a particular *Shabbat*!

Every Jew is required to study Torah, no matter how old or young, no matter how rich or poor. Studying Torah gives us a feeling of who we are and how we are connected to the Jewish people and God. It gives us rules and guidelines so that we can lead a good life.

ALIYOT

The Torah is so special that we say a *braḥah* both before and after we read from it.

List the special ways we treat the Torah to show it honor and love.

It is a great honor for a congregant to receive an *"aliyah"* to recite the blessing before and the blessing after the Torah is read. The word *aliyah* means "going up," for we go up to the *bimah* (platform) for this honor.

There are seven *aliyot* on *Shabbat*, plus *Maftir* (an additional *aliyah* for the one chanting the *Haftarah*). The *Maftir* is often a young person celebrating becoming a *Bar* or *Bat Mitzvah*. For each *aliyah* at least three verses should be read.

Torah Blessings

The one(s) being honored say(s):

בָּרְכוּ אֶת־יְיָ הַמְבֹרָךְ.

Praise *Adonai*, Source of all blessing.

Barḥu et Adonai hamvoraḥ

The congregation answers:

בָּרוּךְ יְיָ הַמְבֹרָךְ לְעוֹלָם וָעֶד.

Praise *Adonai*, Source of all blessing, forever and ever.

Baruḥ Adonai hamvoraḥ l'olam va'ed.

The one(s) being honored repeats the above line and continue(s):

בָּרוּךְ אַתָּה יְיָ אֱלֹהֵינוּ מֶלֶךְ הָעוֹלָם אֲשֶׁר בָּחַר בָּנוּ מִכָּל־הָעַמִּים
וְנָתַן לָנוּ אֶת־תּוֹרָתוֹ. בָּרוּךְ אַתָּה יְיָ נוֹתֵן הַתּוֹרָה.

Praised are You, *Adonai*, Ruler of the universe, Who has chosen us with the gift of the Torah. Praised are You, *Adonai*, Giver of the Torah.

Baruḥ atah Adonai Eloheinu Meleḥ ha'olam asher baḥar banu mikol ha'amim v'natan lanu et Torato. Baruḥ atah Adonai, noten haTorah.

After the Torah is read, the one(s) being honored say(s):

בָּרוּךְ אַתָּה יְיָ אֱלֹהֵינוּ מֶלֶךְ הָעוֹלָם אֲשֶׁר נָתַן לָנוּ תּוֹרַת אֱמֶת וְחַיֵּי עוֹלָם נָטַע בְּתוֹכֵנוּ. בָּרוּךְ אַתָּה יְיָ נוֹתֵן הַתּוֹרָה.

Praised are You, *Adonai*, Ruler of the universe, Who has given us a Torah of truth, a guide forever. Praised are You, *Adonai,* Giver of the Torah.
Baruḥ atah Adonai Eloheinu Meleḥ ha'olam asher natan lanu Torat emet, v'ḥayay olam nata b'toḥeinu. Baruḥ atah Adonai, noten haTorah.

> "...Although we have but one God, God has more than one nation."
> What do you think this means?
> From *Emet Ve-Emunah, The Principles of Conservative Judaism.*

This blessing is said, usually after an *aliyah*, by anyone who has recovered from a serious illness, returned safely from a long trip, or escaped danger of any kind.

בָּרוּךְ אַתָּה יְיָ אֱלֹהֵינוּ מֶלֶךְ הָעוֹלָם, הַגּוֹמֵל לְחַיָּבִים טוֹבוֹת, שֶׁגְּמָלַנִי כָּל־טוֹב.

Praised are You, *Adonai* our God, Ruler of the Universe, Who has graciously favored me.

The congregation answers:

מִי שֶׁגְּמָלְךָ (שֶׁגְּמָלֵךְ) כָּל־טוֹב הוּא יִגְמָלְךָ (יִגְמְלֵךְ) כָּל־טוֹב סֶלָה.

May the One Who has been gracious to you continue to favor you with all that is good.

Prayer for Someone Who is Ill:

מִי שֶׁבֵּרַךְ אֲבוֹתֵינוּ, אַבְרָהָם יִצְחָק וְיַעֲקֹב, שָׂרָה רִבְקָה
רָחֵל וְלֵאָה, הוּא יְבָרֵךְ וִירַפֵּא אֶת־הַחוֹלֶה ______ בֶּן
______ . הַקָּדוֹשׁ בָּרוּךְ הוּא יִמָּלֵא רַחֲמִים עָלָיו,
לְהַחֲזִיקוֹ וּלְרַפְּאוֹתוֹ, וְיִשְׁלַח לוֹ מְהֵרָה רְפוּאָה שְׁלֵמָה
לְכָל־אֵבָרָיו וְגִידָיו בְּתוֹךְ שְׁאָר חוֹלֵי יִשְׂרָאֵל, הַשְׁתָּא
בַּעֲגָלָא וּבִזְמַן קָרִיב, וְנֹאמַר אָמֵן.

מִי שֶׁבֵּרַךְ אֲבוֹתֵינוּ, אַבְרָהָם יִצְחָק וְיַעֲקֹב, שָׂרָה רִבְקָה
רָחֵל וְלֵאָה, הוּא יְבָרֵךְ וִירַפֵּא אֶת־הַחוֹלָה ______ בַּת
______ . הַקָּדוֹשׁ בָּרוּךְ הוּא יִמָּלֵא רַחֲמִים עָלֶיהָ,
לְהַחֲזִיקָהּ, וּלְרַפְּאוֹתָהּ, וְיִשְׁלַח לָהּ מְהֵרָה רְפוּאָה שְׁלֵמָה
לְכָל־אֵבָרֶיהָ וְגִידֶיהָ בְּתוֹךְ שְׁאָר חוֹלֵי יִשְׂרָאֵל, הַשְׁתָּא
בַּעֲגָלָא וּבִזְמַן קָרִיב, וְנֹאמַר אָמֵן.

May the One Who blessed our ancestors, Abraham, Isaac and Jacob, Sarah, Rebecca, Rachel and Leah, bless ______________________
son/daughter of ______________________ and ______________________
who is sick. name of mother name of father
May the Holy One quickly restore him/her to good health, together with others who are ill.

Prayer for those who had *aliyot*:

מִי שֶׁבֵּרַךְ אֲבוֹתֵֽינוּ, אַבְרָהָם יִצְחָק וְיַֽעֲקֹב, שָׂרָה רִבְקָה
רָחֵל וְלֵאָה, הוּא יְבָרֵךְ אֶת־כָּל־הַקְּרוּאִים אֲשֶׁר עָלוּ הַיּוֹם
לִכְבוֹד הַמָּקוֹם, לִכְבוֹד הַתּוֹרָה וְלִכְבוֹד הַשַּׁבָּת [וְלִכְבוֹד
הָרֶֽגֶל]. הַקָּדוֹשׁ בָּרוּךְ הוּא יְבָרֵךְ אוֹתָם וְאֶת־מִשְׁפְּחוֹתָם
וְיִשְׁלַח בְּרָכָה וְהַצְלָחָה בְּכָל־מַעֲשֵׂה יְדֵיהֶם עִם כָּל־יִשְׂרָאֵל
אֲחֵיהֶם, וְנֹאמַר אָמֵן.

May the One who blessed our ancestors, Abraham, Isaac and Jacob, Sarah, Rebecca, Rachel and Leah, bless all who have come forward to honor God, the Torah and the Sabbath (and this festival). May the Holy One, the Source of Blessing, bless them and their families. May the Holy One send blessing and success on all they do (and grant them the privilege of going up to Jerusalem for the festivals) together with all Israel with whom they are united. And let us say, "Amen."

חֲצִי קַדִּישׁ

Ḥatzi Kaddish

Leader:

יִתְגַּדַּל וְיִתְקַדַּשׁ שְׁמֵהּ רַבָּא בְּעָלְמָא דִּי בְרָא כִרְעוּתֵהּ,
וְיַמְלִיךְ מַלְכוּתֵהּ בְּחַיֵּיכוֹן וּבְיוֹמֵיכוֹן וּבְחַיֵּי דְכָל־בֵּית
יִשְׂרָאֵל, בַּעֲגָלָא וּבִזְמַן קָרִיב, וְאִמְרוּ אָמֵן.

Congregation and Leader answer:

יְהֵא שְׁמֵהּ רַבָּא מְבָרַךְ לְעָלַם וּלְעָלְמֵי עָלְמַיָּא.

Y'hei shmei rabba m'voraḥ l'olam u'l'olmei almay'ya.

Leader:

יִתְבָּרַךְ וְיִשְׁתַּבַּח וְיִתְפָּאַר וְיִתְרוֹמַם וְיִתְנַשֵּׂא, וְיִתְהַדַּר
וְיִתְעַלֶּה וְיִתְהַלָּל שְׁמֵהּ דְּקֻדְשָׁא,

Congregation and Leader answer:

בְּרִיךְ הוּא.

Briḥ hu.

Leader:

לְעֵלָּא (לְעֵלָּא מִכָּל־) מִן כָּל־בִּרְכָתָא וְשִׁירָתָא תֻּשְׁבְּחָתָא
וְנֶחֱמָתָא דַּאֲמִירָן בְּעָלְמָא, וְאִמְרוּ אָמֵן.

We stand as the Torah is raised and we say:

וְזֹאת הַתּוֹרָה אֲשֶׁר שָׂם מֹשֶׁה לִפְנֵי בְּנֵי יִשְׂרָאֵל עַל פִּי יְיָ בְּיַד מֹשֶׁה.

This is the Torah of God, given through Moses who presented it to the people of Israel.

V'zot haTorah asher sam Mosheh lifnei b'nei Yisrael al pi Adonai b'yad Mosheh.

The word "*Haftarah*" means conclusion or dismissal. It may have been that in ancient times the worship service ended with a reading from the Prophets and then the congregation was dismissed.

Each letter in the Hebrew word ***TaNaKH*** stands for a section of the Bible. The ***T**av* ת stands for **T**orah תּוֹרָה, the ***N**un* נ stands for ***N**evi'im* נְבִיאִים (Prophets), and the ***K**af* כ stands for ***K**etuvim* כְּתוּבִים (Scrolls).

The *Haftarot* are taken from the second section of the Bible — *Nevi'im* (Prophets).

Blessings before the *Haftarah*:

בָּרוּךְ אַתָּה יְיָ אֱלֹהֵינוּ מֶלֶךְ הָעוֹלָם אֲשֶׁר בָּחַר בִּנְבִיאִים טוֹבִים וְרָצָה בְדִבְרֵיהֶם הַנֶּאֱמָרִים בֶּאֱמֶת. בָּרוּךְ אַתָּה יְיָ הַבּוֹחֵר בַּתּוֹרָה וּבְמשֶׁה עַבְדּוֹ וּבְיִשְׂרָאֵל עַמּוֹ וּבִנְבִיאֵי הָאֱמֶת וָצֶדֶק.

Blessings after the *Haftarah*:

בָּרוּךְ אַתָּה יְיָ אֱלֹהֵינוּ מֶלֶךְ הָעוֹלָם, צוּר כָּל־הָעוֹלָמִים, צַדִּיק בְּכָל־הַדּוֹרוֹת, הָאֵל הַנֶּאֱמָן הָאוֹמֵר וְעוֹשֶׂה הַמְדַבֵּר וּמְקַיֵּם, שֶׁכָּל־דְּבָרָיו אֱמֶת וָצֶדֶק. נֶאֱמָן אַתָּה הוּא יְיָ אֱלֹהֵינוּ וְנֶאֱמָנִים דְּבָרֶיךָ, וְדָבָר אֶחָד מִדְּבָרֶיךָ אָחוֹר לֹא יָשׁוּב רֵיקָם, כִּי אֵל מֶלֶךְ נֶאֱמָן וְרַחֲמָן אָתָּה. בָּרוּךְ אַתָּה יְיָ הָאֵל הַנֶּאֱמָן בְּכָל־דְּבָרָיו.

רַחֵם עַל צִיּוֹן כִּי הִיא בֵּית חַיֵּינוּ. וְלַעֲלוּבַת נֶפֶשׁ תּוֹשִׁיעַ בִּמְהֵרָה בְיָמֵינוּ. בָּרוּךְ אַתָּה יְיָ מְשַׂמֵּחַ צִיּוֹן בְּבָנֶיהָ.

שַׂמְּחֵנוּ יְיָ אֱלֹהֵינוּ בְּאֵלִיָּהוּ הַנָּבִיא עַבְדֶּךָ וּבְמַלְכוּת בֵּית דָּוִד מְשִׁיחֶךָ. בִּמְהֵרָה יָבוֹא וְיָגֵל לִבֵּנוּ, עַל כִּסְאוֹ לֹא יֵשֵׁב זָר וְלֹא יִנְחֲלוּ עוֹד אֲחֵרִים אֶת־כְּבוֹדוֹ, כִּי בְשֵׁם קָדְשְׁךָ נִשְׁבַּעְתָּ לּוֹ שֶׁלֹּא יִכְבֶּה נֵרוֹ לְעוֹלָם וָעֶד. בָּרוּךְ אַתָּה יְיָ מָגֵן דָּוִד.

On *Shabbat*, including the *Shabbat* of *Ḥol haMo'ed Pesaḥ* we conclude saying:

עַל הַתּוֹרָה וְעַל הָעֲבוֹדָה וְעַל הַנְּבִיאִים וְעַל יוֹם הַשַּׁבָּת הַזֶּה שֶׁנָּתַתָּ לָּנוּ יְיָ אֱלֹהֵינוּ לִקְדֻשָּׁה וְלִמְנוּחָה לְכָבוֹד וּלְתִפְאָרֶת. עַל הַכֹּל יְיָ אֱלֹהֵינוּ אֲנַחְנוּ מוֹדִים לָךְ, וּמְבָרְכִים אוֹתָךְ. יִתְבָּרַךְ שִׁמְךָ בְּפִי כָּל־חַי תָּמִיד לְעוֹלָם וָעֶד. בָּרוּךְ אַתָּה יְיָ מְקַדֵּשׁ הַשַּׁבָּת.

On Festivals, *Yom Tov*, including the *Shabbat* of *Ḥol haMo'ed Sukkot* we say:

עַל הַתּוֹרָה וְעַל הָעֲבוֹדָה וְעַל הַנְּבִיאִים (וְעַל יוֹם הַשַּׁבָּת הַזֶּה) וְעַל יוֹם

On *Pesaḥ*: חַג הַמַּצּוֹת הַזֶּה

On *Shavuot*: חַג הַשָּׁבוּעוֹת הַזֶּה

On *Sukkot*: חַג הַסֻּכּוֹת הַזֶּה

On *Sh'mini Atzeret* and on *Simḥat Torah*:

הַשְּׁמִינִי, חַג הָעֲצֶרֶת הַזֶּה

שֶׁנָּתַתָּ לָּנוּ יְיָ אֱלֹהֵינוּ (לִקְדֻשָּׁה וְלִמְנוּחָה) לְשָׂשׂוֹן וּלְשִׂמְחָה, לְכָבוֹד וּלְתִפְאָרֶת. עַל הַכֹּל יְיָ אֱלֹהֵינוּ אֲנַחְנוּ מוֹדִים לָךְ, וּמְבָרְכִים אוֹתָךְ. יִתְבָּרַךְ שִׁמְךָ בְּפִי כָּל־חַי תָּמִיד לְעוֹלָם וָעֶד. בָּרוּךְ אַתָּה יְיָ מְקַדֵּשׁ (הַשַּׁבָּת וְ)יִשְׂרָאֵל וְהַזְּמַנִּים.

A PRAYER FOR ISRAEL

For over two thousand years, our people dreamed a dream. It was our deepest hope to be a free nation in our own land. That dream has now been fulfilled.

We pray to God, the Rock of Ages and the Source of courage and strength, that the State of Israel may be safe and secure, ever seeking and finding peace. May Israel's leaders make wise decisions for the welfare of all her inhabitants.

May Israel continue to be a refuge for those in need. May she welcome with open arms all who return and help them rebuild their lives.

May our ties to Israel be strong, giving us inspiration and determination. May we find ways to help sustain the State of Israel and may the holy land be filled with justice and peace.

A PRAYER FOR OUR COUNTRY

"Proclaim liberty throughout the land (*Leviticus* 25:10)." May our country continue to be based on this biblical verse. May equal rights be granted to all and may each citizen assume the responsibility of preserving our democracy.

May our nation be free of hunger, poverty and prejudice. May all its people always be full of goodness, graciousness, respect and reverence, recognizing that each is created in the image of God. May we live healthy and prosperous lives, growing individually while contributing to the common good.

May the Creator teach us to live in harmony with our land and may the Author of peace teach us to live peacefully with each other and other nations. And let us say, "Amen."

BIRKAT HAḤODESH

We recite this on the *Shabbat* before *Rosh Ḥodesh*.

יְהִי רָצוֹן מִלְּפָנֶיךָ יְיָ אֱלֹהֵינוּ וֵאלֹהֵי אֲבוֹתֵינוּ, שֶׁתְּחַדֵּשׁ עָלֵינוּ אֶת־הַחֹדֶשׁ הַבָּא לְטוֹבָה וְלִבְרָכָה. וְתִתֶּן לָנוּ חַיִּים אֲרֻכִּים, חַיִּים שֶׁל שָׁלוֹם, חַיִּים שֶׁל טוֹבָה, חַיִּים שֶׁל בְּרָכָה, חַיִּים שֶׁל פַּרְנָסָה, חַיִּים שֶׁל חִלּוּץ עֲצָמוֹת, חַיִּים שֶׁיֵּשׁ בָּהֶם יִרְאַת שָׁמַיִם וְיִרְאַת חֵטְא, חַיִּים שֶׁתְּהֵא בָנוּ אַהֲבַת תּוֹרָה וְיִרְאַת שָׁמַיִם, חַיִּים שֶׁיִּמָּלְאוּ מִשְׁאֲלוֹת לִבֵּנוּ לְטוֹבָה, אָמֵן סֶלָה.

The leader holds the *Sefer Torah* and continues:

מִי שֶׁעָשָׂה נִסִּים לַאֲבוֹתֵינוּ וְגָאַל אוֹתָם מֵעַבְדוּת לְחֵרוּת, הוּא יִגְאַל אוֹתָנוּ בְּקָרוֹב וִיקַבֵּץ נִדָּחֵינוּ מֵאַרְבַּע כַּנְפוֹת הָאָרֶץ, חֲבֵרִים כָּל־יִשְׂרָאֵל, וְנֹאמַר אָמֵן.

רֹאשׁ חֹדֶשׁ _____ יִהְיֶה בְּיוֹם _____ הַבָּא עָלֵינוּ וְעַל כָּל־יִשְׂרָאֵל לְטוֹבָה.

The congregation repeats the above two lines and then continues below.
It is repeated by the leader:

יְחַדְּשֵׁהוּ הַקָּדוֹשׁ בָּרוּךְ הוּא עָלֵינוּ וְעַל כָּל־עַמּוֹ בֵּית יִשְׂרָאֵל לְחַיִּים וּלְשָׁלוֹם, לְשָׂשׂוֹן וּלְשִׂמְחָה, לִישׁוּעָה וּלְנֶחָמָה, וְנֹאמַר אָמֵן.

ANNOUNCING THE NEW MONTH

This blessing is said on the *Shabbat* before *Rosh Ḥodesh*:

May it be Your will, *Adonai*, our God and God of our ancestors to renew our lives in the coming month for every blessing. Grant us a long and peaceful life, a life with a healthy body and mind, a life free from shame and disgrace, a life of abundance and honor, a life filled with love of Torah and awe of God, and a life in which the wishes of our hearts will be fulfilled.

The leader holds the *Sefer Torah* and continues:

May the One Who did miracles for our ancestors, bringing them from slavery to freedom, save us soon and gather those spread out to the ends of the earth. May all Jews know the closeness and friendship of other Jews, and let us say, "Amen."

The new month _______________ will begin on _______________ .
May it bring with it goodness for us and all the people Israel.

The congregation repeats the above two lines and continues below. It is repeated by the leader:

May the Holy One bless the new month for us and all the people Israel, with life and peace, joy and gladness, help and comfort. And let us say, "Amen."

אַשְׁרֵי יוֹשְׁבֵי בֵיתֶךָ, עוֹד יְהַלְלוּךָ סֶּלָה.
אַשְׁרֵי הָעָם שֶׁכָּכָה לּוֹ, אַשְׁרֵי הָעָם שֶׁיְיָ אֱלֹהָיו.

תְּהִלָּה לְדָוִד.
אֲרוֹמִמְךָ אֱלוֹהַי הַמֶּלֶךְ, וַאֲבָרְכָה שִׁמְךָ לְעוֹלָם וָעֶד.
בְּכָל־יוֹם אֲבָרְכֶךָּ, וַאֲהַלְלָה שִׁמְךָ לְעוֹלָם וָעֶד.
גָּדוֹל יְיָ וּמְהֻלָּל מְאֹד, וְלִגְדֻלָּתוֹ אֵין חֵקֶר.
דּוֹר לְדוֹר יְשַׁבַּח מַעֲשֶׂיךָ, וּגְבוּרֹתֶיךָ יַגִּידוּ.
הֲדַר כְּבוֹד הוֹדֶךָ, וְדִבְרֵי נִפְלְאֹתֶיךָ אָשִׂיחָה.
וֶעֱזוּז נוֹרְאֹתֶיךָ יֹאמֵרוּ, וּגְדוּלָּתְךָ אֲסַפְּרֶנָּה.
זֵכֶר רַב טוּבְךָ יַבִּיעוּ, וְצִדְקָתְךָ יְרַנֵּנוּ.
חַנּוּן וְרַחוּם יְיָ, אֶרֶךְ אַפַּיִם וּגְדָל־חָסֶד.
טוֹב יְיָ לַכֹּל, וְרַחֲמָיו עַל כָּל־מַעֲשָׂיו.
יוֹדוּךָ יְיָ כָּל־מַעֲשֶׂיךָ, וַחֲסִידֶיךָ יְבָרְכוּכָה.
כְּבוֹד מַלְכוּתְךָ יֹאמֵרוּ, וּגְבוּרָתְךָ יְדַבֵּרוּ.
לְהוֹדִיעַ לִבְנֵי הָאָדָם גְּבוּרֹתָיו, וּכְבוֹד הֲדַר מַלְכוּתוֹ.
מַלְכוּתְךָ מַלְכוּת כָּל־עֹלָמִים, וּמֶמְשַׁלְתְּךָ בְּכָל־דּוֹר וָדֹר.
סוֹמֵךְ יְיָ לְכָל־הַנֹּפְלִים, וְזוֹקֵף לְכָל־הַכְּפוּפִים.
עֵינֵי כֹל אֵלֶיךָ יְשַׂבֵּרוּ, וְאַתָּה נוֹתֵן לָהֶם אֶת־אָכְלָם בְּעִתּוֹ.
פּוֹתֵחַ אֶת־יָדֶךָ, וּמַשְׂבִּיעַ לְכָל־חַי רָצוֹן.
צַדִּיק יְיָ בְּכָל־דְּרָכָיו, וְחָסִיד בְּכָל־מַעֲשָׂיו.
קָרוֹב יְיָ לְכָל־קֹרְאָיו, לְכֹל אֲשֶׁר יִקְרָאֻהוּ בֶאֱמֶת.
רְצוֹן יְרֵאָיו יַעֲשֶׂה, וְאֶת־שַׁוְעָתָם יִשְׁמַע וְיוֹשִׁיעֵם.
שׁוֹמֵר יְיָ אֶת־כָּל־אֹהֲבָיו, וְאֵת כָּל־הָרְשָׁעִים יַשְׁמִיד.
תְּהִלַּת יְיָ יְדַבֶּר־פִּי, וִיבָרֵךְ כָּל־בָּשָׂר שֵׁם קָדְשׁוֹ לְעוֹלָם וָעֶד.
וַאֲנַחְנוּ נְבָרֵךְ יָהּ, מֵעַתָּה וְעַד עוֹלָם. הַלְלוּיָהּ.

Portions

Happy are they
for whom Life is divine.

Happy are they
whose home is God.

Happy are they
whose portion is this:
the everyday wonders
of a divine
and
simple world.

Happy are the people who dwell in Your house. They will always praise You.
Happy are the people who are so favored and know You are God.

Psalm 84:5; 144:15

I will praise You my God, my Guide, and bless You every day.
Each generation will praise Your deeds, telling of Your wondrous powers.
They speak of Your goodness and rejoice in Your justice for You are gracious and merciful, slow to anger and full of love.
You support those who fall and lift up those who are low.
We speak to You with hope, for Your hand satisfies our every need.
You are near to all who call, to all who call You sincerely.
May my lips declare God's praise and all bless God's name forever.

Selections from Psalm 145

And as for us, we will praise God, from now until the end of time, *Halleluyah*.

Psalm 115:18

Everyone stands as the Torah is lifted up, carried through the congregation and then returned to the Ark. As the Torah is carried around the congregation, the leader sings:

יְהַלְלוּ אֶת־שֵׁם יְיָ כִּי נִשְׂגָּב שְׁמוֹ לְבַדּוֹ.

Let them praise *Adonai* Whose name alone is exalted.

The congregation sings:

הוֹדוֹ עַל אֶרֶץ וְשָׁמָיִם, וַיָּרֶם קֶרֶן לְעַמּוֹ
תְּהִלָּה לְכָל־חֲסִידָיו, לִבְנֵי יִשְׂרָאֵל עַם קְרֹבוֹ. הַלְלוּיָהּ.

God's majesty is above heaven and earth. God raises the honor of the people, the glory of the faithful ones.

Hodo al eretz v'shamayim. Va'yarem keren l'amo,
t'hilah l'ḥol ḥasidav, livnei Yisrael am k'rovo, halleluyah.

We sing this on *Shabbat*:

מִזְמוֹר לְדָוִד. הָבוּ לַייָ, בְּנֵי אֵלִים, הָבוּ לַייָ כָּבוֹד וָעֹז.
הָבוּ לַייָ כְּבוֹד שְׁמוֹ, הִשְׁתַּחֲווּ לַייָ בְּהַדְרַת קֹדֶשׁ.
קוֹל יְיָ עַל הַמָּיִם, אֵל הַכָּבוֹד הִרְעִים, יְיָ עַל מַיִם רַבִּים.
קוֹל יְיָ בַּכֹּחַ, קוֹל יְיָ בֶּהָדָר.
קוֹל יְיָ שֹׁבֵר אֲרָזִים, וַיְשַׁבֵּר יְיָ אֶת־אַרְזֵי הַלְּבָנוֹן.
וַיַּרְקִידֵם כְּמוֹ עֵגֶל, לְבָנוֹן וְשִׂרְיוֹן כְּמוֹ בֶן־רְאֵמִים.
קוֹל יְיָ חֹצֵב לַהֲבוֹת אֵשׁ, קוֹל יְיָ יָחִיל מִדְבָּר, יָחִיל יְיָ
מִדְבַּר קָדֵשׁ. קוֹל יְיָ יְחוֹלֵל אַיָּלוֹת וַיֶּחֱשֹׂף יְעָרוֹת,
וּבְהֵיכָלוֹ כֻּלּוֹ אֹמֵר כָּבוֹד. יְיָ לַמַּבּוּל יָשָׁב, וַיֵּשֶׁב יְיָ מֶלֶךְ
לְעוֹלָם. יְיָ עֹז לְעַמּוֹ יִתֵּן, יְיָ יְבָרֵךְ אֶת־עַמּוֹ בַשָּׁלוֹם.

Mizmor L'David
A Psalm of David

Give to *Adonai*, you mighty ones, give to *Adonai*, glory and strength. Honor God's name, bowing before the holy presence.

The voice of *Adonai* is above the waters, thundering across the oceans with strength and majesty.
The voice of *Adonai* shatters the cedars of Lebanon, making the hills skip like rams and mountains leap like lambs.
The voice of *Adonai* creates fiery lightening. It stirs the desert sands and makes the wilderness of Kadesh tremble.
The voice of *Adonai* whirls the oaks and strips the forests bare; while in God's sanctuary, all chant: "Glory."

At the great Flood, *Adonai* ruled. *Adonai* will remain our ruler forever, giving strength to our people and blessing us with peace.

Psalm 29

We sing this on Festivals occurring on weekdays:

לְדָוִד מִזְמוֹר. לַייָ הָאָרֶץ וּמְלוֹאָהּ, תֵּבֵל וְיֹשְׁבֵי בָהּ. כִּי
הוּא עַל יַמִּים יְסָדָהּ, וְעַל נְהָרוֹת יְכוֹנְנֶהָ. מִי יַעֲלֶה בְהַר
יְיָ, וּמִי יָקוּם בִּמְקוֹם קָדְשׁוֹ. נְקִי כַפַּיִם וּבַר לֵבָב,
אֲשֶׁר לֹא נָשָׂא לַשָּׁוְא נַפְשִׁי, וְלֹא נִשְׁבַּע לְמִרְמָה.

The earth is *Adonai's* and all that it contains: The land and all who dwell in it.
For God founded it upon the seas and set it firm upon the flood waters.

Who may go up to *Adonai's* mountain? Who may stand in God's holy space?
The one with clean hands and a pure heart, who does not swear falsely nor tells lies to deceive others.
This person shall receive a blessing from *Adonai* and justice from the helping God.

Such are those who seek the presence of the God of Jacob.
Lift the gates high and open the doors wide, for the Sovereign of glory to enter.
Who is this sovereign ruler?
Adonai, strong and mighty; *Adonai*, the triumphant one, is our ruler!

Psalm 24

The Torah is placed in the ark:

וּבְנֻחֹה יֹאמַר: שׁוּבָה יְיָ, רִבְבוֹת אַלְפֵי יִשְׂרָאֵל. קוּמָה יְיָ
לִמְנוּחָתֶךָ, אַתָּה וַאֲרוֹן עֻזֶּךָ. כֹּהֲנֶיךָ יִלְבְּשׁוּ־צֶדֶק, וַחֲסִידֶיךָ
יְרַנֵּנוּ. בַּעֲבוּר דָּוִד עַבְדֶּךָ, אַל תָּשֵׁב פְּנֵי מְשִׁיחֶךָ. כִּי לֶקַח
טוֹב נָתַתִּי לָכֶם, תּוֹרָתִי אַל תַּעֲזֹבוּ.

עֵץ חַיִּים הִיא לַמַּחֲזִיקִים בָּהּ, וְתֹמְכֶיהָ מְאֻשָּׁר.
דְּרָכֶיהָ דַרְכֵי־נֹעַם, וְכָל־נְתִיבוֹתֶיהָ שָׁלוֹם.
הֲשִׁיבֵנוּ יְיָ אֵלֶיךָ וְנָשׁוּבָה, חַדֵּשׁ יָמֵינוּ כְּקֶדֶם.

The Torah is a tree of life to those who live by its teachings.
Its ways are ways of pleasantness and its paths are paths of peace.
Guide us back to You, *Adonai*.
Renew our glory as in days of old.

Eitz ḥayim hi lamaḥazikim bah,
v'tomḥeha m'ushar.
D'raḥeha darḥei no'am v'ḥol n'tivoteha shalom.
Hashiveinu Adonai eleḥa v'nashuvah,
ḥadesh yameinu k'kedem.

The Torah is like a tree because...

Can you think of other comparisons?

The name for a Torah handle in Hebrew is *eitz ḥaim*, a tree of life. Why is this a perfect name?

Musaf is found on p.184.

KADDISH SHALEM

קַדִּישׁ שָׁלֵם

Leader:

יִתְגַּדַּל וְיִתְקַדַּשׁ שְׁמֵהּ רַבָּא בְּעָלְמָא דִּי בְרָא כִרְעוּתֵהּ,
וְיַמְלִיךְ מַלְכוּתֵהּ בְּחַיֵּיכוֹן וּבְיוֹמֵיכוֹן וּבְחַיֵּי דְכָל־בֵּית יִשְׂרָאֵל,
בַּעֲגָלָא וּבִזְמַן קָרִיב, וְאִמְרוּ אָמֵן.

Congregation and Leader answer:

יְהֵא שְׁמֵהּ רַבָּא מְבָרַךְ לְעָלַם וּלְעָלְמֵי עָלְמַיָּא.

Y'hei shmei rabba m'voraḥ l'olam u'l'olmei almay'ya.

Leader:

יִתְבָּרַךְ וְיִשְׁתַּבַּח וְיִתְפָּאַר וְיִתְרוֹמַם וְיִתְנַשֵּׂא, וְיִתְהַדַּר וְיִתְעַלֶּה
וְיִתְהַלַּל שְׁמֵהּ דְּקֻדְשָׁא,

Congregation and Leader answer:

בְּרִיךְ הוּא.

Briḥ hu.

Leader:

לְעֵלָּא [לְעֵלָּא מִכָּל־] מִן כָּל־בִּרְכָתָא וְשִׁירָתָא, תֻּשְׁבְּחָתָא
וְנֶחֱמָתָא דַּאֲמִירָן בְּעָלְמָא, וְאִמְרוּ אָמֵן.

תִּתְקַבַּל צְלוֹתְהוֹן וּבָעוּתְהוֹן דְּכָל־יִשְׂרָאֵל קֳדָם אֲבוּהוֹן דִּי
בִשְׁמַיָּא, וְאִמְרוּ אָמֵן.

יְהֵא שְׁלָמָא רַבָּא מִן שְׁמַיָּא וְחַיִּים עָלֵינוּ וְעַל כָּל־יִשְׂרָאֵל,
וְאִמְרוּ אָמֵן.

עוֹשֶׂה שָׁלוֹם בִּמְרוֹמָיו, הוּא יַעֲשֶׂה שָׁלוֹם עָלֵינוּ וְעַל
כָּל־יִשְׂרָאֵל, וְאִמְרוּ אָמֵן.

אֵין כֵּאלֹהֵינוּ, אֵין כַּאדוֹנֵינוּ, אֵין כְּמַלְכֵּנוּ, אֵין כְּמוֹשִׁיעֵנוּ.

מִי כֵאלֹהֵינוּ, מִי כַאדוֹנֵינוּ, מִי כְמַלְכֵּנוּ, מִי כְמוֹשִׁיעֵנוּ.

נוֹדֶה לֵאלֹהֵינוּ, נוֹדֶה לַאדוֹנֵינוּ, נוֹדֶה לְמַלְכֵּנוּ, נוֹדֶה לְמוֹשִׁיעֵנוּ.

בָּרוּךְ אֱלֹהֵינוּ, בָּרוּךְ אֲדוֹנֵינוּ, בָּרוּךְ מַלְכֵּנוּ, בָּרוּךְ מוֹשִׁיעֵנוּ.

אַתָּה הוּא אֱלֹהֵינוּ, אַתָּה הוּא אֲדוֹנֵינוּ, אַתָּה הוּא מַלְכֵּנוּ, אַתָּה הוּא מוֹשִׁיעֵנוּ.

None compares to You
Our God
Our Lord
Ruler
and Deliverer.

Let us praise You for You are
Our God
Our Lord
Ruler
and Deliverer.

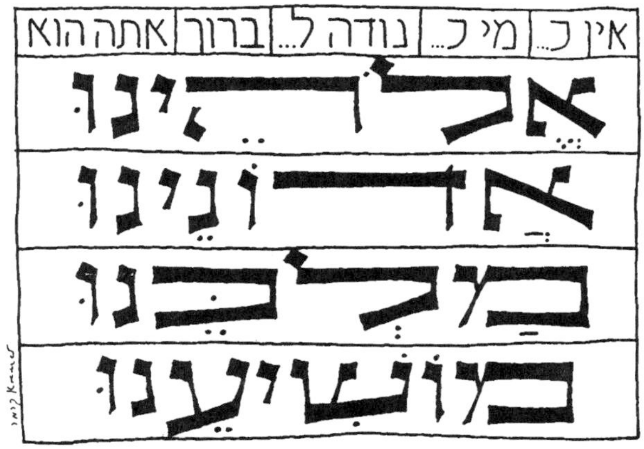

Ein k'Eloheinu, Ein k'Adoneinu, Ein k'Malkeinu, Ein k'Moshi'einu.
Mi ḥ'Eloheinu, Mi ḥ'Adoneinu, Mi ḥ'Malkeinu, Mi ḥ'Moshi'einu.
Nodeh l'Eloheinu, Nodeh l'Adoneinu, Nodeh l'Malkeinu, Nodeh l'Moshi'einu.
Baruḥ Eloheinu, Baruḥ Adoneinu, Baruḥ Malkeinu, Baruḥ Moshi'einu.
Atah hu Eloheinu, Atah hu Adoneinu, Atah hu Malkeinu, Atah hu Moshi'einu.
Atah hu she'hiktiru lavoteinu lifaneḥa et k'toret hasamim.

In the *Aleinu* prayer, we acknowledge that God is the Source of creation as well as order and unity in the world.

We rise.

עָלֵינוּ לְשַׁבֵּחַ לַאֲדוֹן הַכֹּל, לָתֵת גְּדֻלָּה לְיוֹצֵר בְּרֵאשִׁית,
שֶׁלֹּא עָשָׂנוּ כְּגוֹיֵי הָאֲרָצוֹת וְלֹא שָׂמָנוּ כְּמִשְׁפְּחוֹת הָאֲדָמָה,
שֶׁלֹּא שָׂם חֶלְקֵנוּ כָּהֶם וְגוֹרָלֵנוּ כְּכָל־הֲמוֹנָם. וַאֲנַחְנוּ
כּוֹרְעִים וּמִשְׁתַּחֲוִים וּמוֹדִים לִפְנֵי מֶלֶךְ מַלְכֵי הַמְּלָכִים
הַקָּדוֹשׁ בָּרוּךְ הוּא, שֶׁהוּא נוֹטֶה שָׁמַיִם וְיוֹסֵד אָרֶץ וּמוֹשַׁב
יְקָרוֹ בַּשָּׁמַיִם מִמַּעַל וּשְׁכִינַת עֻזּוֹ בְּגָבְהֵי מְרוֹמִים. הוּא
אֱלֹהֵינוּ אֵין עוֹד. אֱמֶת מַלְכֵּנוּ אֶפֶס זוּלָתוֹ, כַּכָּתוּב
בְּתוֹרָתוֹ: וְיָדַעְתָּ הַיּוֹם וַהֲשֵׁבֹתָ אֶל לְבָבֶךָ כִּי יְיָ הוּא
הָאֱלֹהִים בַּשָּׁמַיִם מִמַּעַל וְעַל הָאָרֶץ מִתָּחַת, אֵין עוֹד.

עַל כֵּן נְקַוֶּה לְּךָ יְיָ אֱלֹהֵינוּ לִרְאוֹת מְהֵרָה בְּתִפְאֶרֶת עֻזֶּךָ,
לְהַעֲבִיר גִּלּוּלִים מִן הָאָרֶץ וְהָאֱלִילִים כָּרוֹת יִכָּרֵתוּן,
לְתַקֵּן עוֹלָם בְּמַלְכוּת שַׁדַּי וְכָל־בְּנֵי בָשָׂר יִקְרְאוּ בִשְׁמֶךָ,
לְהַפְנוֹת אֵלֶיךָ כָּל רִשְׁעֵי אָרֶץ. יַכִּירוּ וְיֵדְעוּ כָּל־יוֹשְׁבֵי
תֵבֵל כִּי לְךָ תִּכְרַע כָּל־בֶּרֶךְ תִּשָּׁבַע כָּל־לָשׁוֹן. לְפָנֶיךָ יְיָ
אֱלֹהֵינוּ יִכְרְעוּ וְיִפֹּלוּ וְלִכְבוֹד שִׁמְךָ יְקָר יִתֵּנוּ, וִיקַבְּלוּ
כֻלָּם אֶת־עֹל מַלְכוּתֶךָ וְתִמְלֹךְ עֲלֵיהֶם מְהֵרָה לְעוֹלָם וָעֶד,
כִּי הַמַּלְכוּת שֶׁלְּךָ הִיא וּלְעוֹלְמֵי עַד תִּמְלוֹךְ בְּכָבוֹד,
כַּכָּתוּב בְּתוֹרָתֶךָ: יְיָ יִמְלֹךְ לְעֹלָם וָעֶד.

וְנֶאֱמַר: וְהָיָה יְיָ לְמֶלֶךְ עַל כָּל־הָאָרֶץ, בַּיּוֹם הַהוּא יִהְיֶה יְיָ
אֶחָד וּשְׁמוֹ אֶחָד.

It is for us to praise the Ruler of all and to glorify the Creator of the world for giving us a special heritage and a unique destiny.

Before our supreme Ruler we bend the knee and bow in devotion.

As it is written in the Torah, "Accept this day with both mind and heart. Know that God's presence fills creation."

Because we believe in You, we hope for the day when Your majesty will triumph and all will work to mend the world and live according to Your ways. For it is written in the Torah, "*Adonai* shall rule for ever and ever."

Aleinu l'shabei'aḥ la'adon hakol,
latet g'dulah l'yotzer b'reshit.
Shelo asanu k'goyei ha'aratzot,
v'lo samanu k'mishp'ḥot ha'adamah.
Shelo sam ḥelkeinu kahem,
v'goraleinu k'ḥol hamonam.

Va'anaḥnu korim umishtaḥavim umodim,
lifnei Meleḥ malḥei ham'laḥim,
hakadosh baruḥ hu.

V'ne'emar, v'hayah Adonai l'Meleḥ al kol ḥa'aretz.
Bayom hahu yih'yeh Adonai eḥad ush'mo eḥad.

We **R**ise to **P**raise and **W**eave the **D**ream
Merger Poem

And then all that has divided us will merge.
And then compassion will be wedded to power.
And then softness will come to a world that is harsh and unkind.
And then both men and women will be gentle.
And then both men and women will be strong.
And then no person will be subject to another's will.
And then all will be rich and free and varied.
And then all will share equally in the earth's abundance.
And then all will care for the sick and the weak and the old.
And then all will nourish life's creatures.
And then all will live in harmony with each-other and the earth.
And then everywhere will be called Eden once again.

MOURNER'S KADDISH

Mourners and those observing a memorial day rise and say:

יִתְגַּדַּל וְיִתְקַדַּשׁ שְׁמֵהּ רַבָּא בְּעָלְמָא דִּי בְרָא כִרְעוּתֵהּ,
וְיַמְלִיךְ מַלְכוּתֵהּ בְּחַיֵּיכוֹן וּבְיוֹמֵיכוֹן וּבְחַיֵּי דְכָל־בֵּית
יִשְׂרָאֵל בַּעֲגָלָא וּבִזְמַן קָרִיב, וְאִמְרוּ אָמֵן.

The congregation says together with the mourners:

יְהֵא שְׁמֵהּ רַבָּא מְבָרַךְ לְעָלַם וּלְעָלְמֵי עָלְמַיָּא.

Y'hei shmei rabba m'voraḥ l'olam u'l'olmei almay'ya.

Mourners continue:

יִתְבָּרַךְ וְיִשְׁתַּבַּח וְיִתְפָּאַר וְיִתְרוֹמַם וְיִתְנַשֵּׂא, וְיִתְהַדַּר
וְיִתְעַלֶּה וְיִתְהַלַּל שְׁמֵהּ דְּקֻדְשָׁא,

Congregation together with the mourners:

בְּרִיךְ הוּא.

Briḥ hu.

לְעֵלָּא (לְעֵלָּא מִכָּל־) מִן כָּל־בִּרְכָתָא וְשִׁירָתָא תֻּשְׁבְּחָתָא
וְנֶחֱמָתָא דַּאֲמִירָן בְּעָלְמָא, וְאִמְרוּ אָמֵן.

יְהֵא שְׁלָמָא רַבָּא מִן שְׁמַיָּא וְחַיִּים עָלֵינוּ וְעַל כָּל־יִשְׂרָאֵל,
וְאִמְרוּ אָמֵן.

עוֹשֶׂה שָׁלוֹם בִּמְרוֹמָיו הוּא יַעֲשֶׂה שָׁלוֹם עָלֵינוּ וְעַל
כָּל־יִשְׂרָאֵל, וְאִמְרוּ אָמֵן.

שִׁיר הַכָּבוֹד

The Ark is opened:

אַנְעִים זְמִירוֹת וְשִׁירִים אֶאֱרוֹג, כִּי אֵלֶיךָ נַפְשִׁי תַעֲרוֹג.
נַפְשִׁי חָמְדָה בְּצֵל יָדֶךָ, לָדַעַת כָּל־רָז סוֹדֶךָ.

מִדֵּי דַבְּרִי בִּכְבוֹדֶךָ הוֹמֶה לִבִּי אֶל דּוֹדֶיךָ.
עַל כֵּן אֲדַבֵּר בְּךָ נִכְבָּדוֹת, וְשִׁמְךָ אֲכַבֵּד בְּשִׁירֵי יְדִידוֹת.

אֲסַפְּרָה כְבוֹדְךָ וְלֹא רְאִיתִיךָ, אֲדַמְּךָ אֲכַנְּךָ וְלֹא יְדַעְתִּיךָ.
בְּיַד נְבִיאֶיךָ בְּסוֹד עֲבָדֶיךָ דִּמִּיתָ הֲדַר כְּבוֹד הוֹדֶךָ.

גְּדֻלָּתְךָ וּגְבוּרָתֶךָ, כִּנּוּ לְתֹקֶף פְּעֻלָּתֶךָ.
דִּמּוּ אוֹתְךָ וְלֹא כְּפִי יֶשְׁךָ, וַיְשַׁוּוּךָ לְפִי מַעֲשֶׂיךָ.

הִמְשִׁילוּךָ בְּרוֹב חֶזְיוֹנוֹת, הִנְּךָ אֶחָד בְּכָל־דִּמְיוֹנוֹת.
וַיֶּחֱזוּ בְךָ זִקְנָה וּבַחֲרוּת, וּשְׂעַר רֹאשְׁךָ בְּשֵׂיבָה וְשַׁחֲרוּת.

זִקְנָה בְּיוֹם דִּין וּבַחֲרוּת בְּיוֹם קְרָב, כְּאִישׁ מִלְחָמוֹת יָדָיו לוֹ רָב.
חָבַשׁ כּוֹבַע יְשׁוּעָה בְּרֹאשׁוֹ, הוֹשִׁיעָה לּוֹ יְמִינוֹ וּזְרוֹעַ קָדְשׁוֹ.

טַלְלֵי אוֹרוֹת רֹאשׁוֹ נִמְלָא, קְוֻצּוֹתָיו רְסִיסֵי לָיְלָה.
יִתְפָּאֵר בִּי כִּי חָפֵץ בִּי, וְהוּא יִהְיֶה לִּי לַעֲטֶרֶת צְבִי.

כֶּתֶם טָהוֹר פָּז דְּמוּת רֹאשׁוֹ, וְחַק עַל מֵצַח כְּבוֹד שֵׁם קָדְשׁוֹ.
לְחֵן וּלְכָבוֹד צְבִי תִפְאָרָה, אֻמָּתוֹ לוֹ עִטְּרָה עֲטָרָה.

I offer sweet hymns and chants for my soul longs for You.
To be in the shadow of Your hand and to understand You, too.
You are unseen, yet praised for You fulfill my needs.
I will meditate all my days on the power of Your deeds.

The letters for the Hebrew words for "was," "is" and "will be" — *Hayah, hoveh, yih'yeh* — make up God's name; so God is the One Who was, is and will always remain.

אֲדוֹן עוֹלָם אֲשֶׁר מָלַךְ   בְּטֶרֶם כָּל־יְצִיר נִבְרָא.
לְעֵת נַעֲשָׂה בְחֶפְצוֹ כֹּל   אֲזַי מֶלֶךְ שְׁמוֹ נִקְרָא.
וְאַחֲרֵי כִּכְלוֹת הַכֹּל   לְבַדּוֹ יִמְלֹךְ נוֹרָא.
וְהוּא הָיָה וְהוּא הֹוֶה   וְהוּא יִהְיֶה בְּתִפְאָרָה.
וְהוּא אֶחָד וְאֵין שֵׁנִי   לְהַמְשִׁיל לוֹ לְהַחְבִּירָה.
בְּלִי רֵאשִׁית בְּלִי תַכְלִית   וְלוֹ הָעֹז וְהַמִּשְׂרָה.
וְהוּא אֵלִי וְחַי גּוֹאֲלִי   וְצוּר חֶבְלִי בְּעֵת צָרָה.
וְהוּא נִסִּי וּמָנוֹס לִי   מְנָת כּוֹסִי בְּיוֹם אֶקְרָא.
בְּיָדוֹ אַפְקִיד רוּחִי   בְּעֵת אִישַׁן וְאָעִירָה.
וְעִם רוּחִי גְּוִיָּתִי   יְיָ לִי וְלֹא אִירָא.

God ruled before the world came to be
and will rule at the end of time.
Our days and nights are in God's care.
Because we trust in God, we have no fear.

KIDDUSH FOR *SHABBAT* AND *YOM TOV* MORNINGS

The *Kiddush* for *Shabbat* morning is called *Kiddush Rabba* (the Great *Kiddush*). According to tradition, the Ten Commandments were given on *Shabbat* morning. Thus, *Shabbat* morning was the first opportunity to fulfill the verse, "Remember the Sabbath day to sanctify it." By reciting the *Kiddush* we declare the sanctity of *Shabbat*.

On *Shabbat*, this is said:

וְשָׁמְרוּ בְנֵי־יִשְׂרָאֵל אֶת־הַשַּׁבָּת, לַעֲשׂוֹת אֶת־הַשַּׁבָּת לְדֹרֹתָם, בְּרִית עוֹלָם. בֵּינִי וּבֵין בְּנֵי יִשְׂרָאֵל אוֹת הִיא לְעוֹלָם כִּי־שֵׁשֶׁת יָמִים עָשָׂה יְיָ אֶת־הַשָּׁמַיִם וְאֶת־הָאָרֶץ וּבַיּוֹם הַשְּׁבִיעִי שָׁבַת וַיִּנָּפַשׁ׃

עַל כֵּן בֵּרַךְ יְיָ אֶת־יוֹם הַשַּׁבָּת וַיְקַדְּשֵׁהוּ.

The people of Israel shall bless the *Shabbat*, observing it throughout the generations as an everlasting covenant. It is a sign between Me and the people Israel forever, that in six days *Adonai* made the heavens and the earth and, on the seventh day, *Adonai* rested and was refreshed.

V'shamru v'nei yisrael et ha'Shabbat la'asot et ha'Shabbat le'dorotam b'rit olam. Beini uvein b'nei yisrael ot hi l'olam ki sheishet yamim asah Adonai et hashamayim v'et ha'aretz u'vayom ha'shvi'i shavat va'yi'nafash.

On Festivals, *Yom Tov*, this is said:

וַיְדַבֵּר מֹשֶׁה אֶת־מֹעֲדֵי יְיָ אֶל בְּנֵי יִשְׂרָאֵל׃

And Moses spoke to the people Israel concerning the festivals.

Vay'daber Moshe et mo'adei Adonai el b'nei yisrael.

We continue on *Shabbat* and *Yom Tov*:

סַבְרִי מָרָנָן

בָּרוּךְ אַתָּה יְיָ אֱלֹהֵינוּ מֶלֶךְ הָעוֹלָם, בּוֹרֵא פְּרִי הַגָּפֶן.

We praise You, *Adonai* our God, Ruler of the Universe, Who creates the fruit of the vine.

Savri Maranan
Baruḥ atah Adonai Eloheinu Meleḥ ha'olam borei p'ri hagafen.

In a *sukkah* add:

בָּרוּךְ אַתָּה יְיָ אֱלֹהֵינוּ מֶלֶךְ הָעוֹלָם, אֲשֶׁר קִדְּשָׁנוּ בְּמִצְוֹתָיו
וְצִוָּנוּ לֵישֵׁב בַּסֻּכָּה.

We praise You, *Adonai* our God, Ruler of the universe, Who has made us holy by Your *mitzvot* and commands us to be in the *sukkah*.

Baruḥ atah Adonai Eloheinu Meleḥ ha'olam, asher kid'deshanu b'mitzvotav v'tzvivanu leishev basukkah.

After the ritual washing of hands we say:

בָּרוּךְ אַתָּה יְיָ אֱלֹהֵינוּ מֶלֶךְ הָעוֹלָם, אֲשֶׁר קִדְּשָׁנוּ בְּמִצְוֹתָיו
וְצִוָּנוּ עַל נְטִילַת יָדָיִם.

We praise You, *Adonai* our God, Ruler of the Universe, Who has made us holy by Your *mitzvot* and commands us to wash our hands.

Baruḥ atah Adonai Eloheinu Meleḥ ha'olam asher kid'deshanu b'mitzvotav v'tzivanu al n'tilat yadayim.

The *Motzi* (blessing for bread) is recited over two *ḥallot*:

בָּרוּךְ אַתָּה יְיָ אֱלֹהֵינוּ מֶלֶךְ הָעוֹלָם, הַמּוֹצִיא לֶחֶם מִן הָאָרֶץ.

We praise You, *Adonai* our God, Ruler of the Universe, Who brings forth bread from the earth.

Baruḥ atah Adonai Eloheinu Meleḥ ha'olam hamotzi leḥem min ha'aretz.

חֲצִי קַדִּישׁ

Ḥatzi Kaddish

Leader:

יִתְגַּדַּל וְיִתְקַדַּשׁ שְׁמֵהּ רַבָּא בְּעָלְמָא דִּי בְרָא כִרְעוּתֵהּ,
וְיַמְלִיךְ מַלְכוּתֵהּ בְּחַיֵּיכוֹן וּבְיוֹמֵיכוֹן וּבְחַיֵּי דְכָל־בֵּית
יִשְׂרָאֵל, בַּעֲגָלָא וּבִזְמַן קָרִיב, וְאִמְרוּ אָמֵן.

Congregation and Leader answer:

יְהֵא שְׁמֵהּ רַבָּא מְבָרַךְ לְעָלַם וּלְעָלְמֵי עָלְמַיָּא.

Y'hei shmei rabba m'voraḥ l'olam u'l'olmei almay'ya.

Leader:

יִתְבָּרַךְ וְיִשְׁתַּבַּח וְיִתְפָּאַר וְיִתְרוֹמַם וְיִתְנַשֵּׂא, וְיִתְהַדַּר
וְיִתְעַלֶּה וְיִתְהַלַּל שְׁמֵהּ דְּקֻדְשָׁא,

Congregation and Leader answer:

בְּרִיךְ הוּא.

Briḥ hu.

Leader:

לְעֵלָּא (לְעֵלָּא מִכָּל־) מִן כָּל־בִּרְכָתָא וְשִׁירָתָא תֻּשְׁבְּחָתָא
וְנֶחֱמָתָא דַּאֲמִירָן בְּעָלְמָא, וְאִמְרוּ אָמֵן.

The *Musaf Amidah* for *Shabbat* with the version of the first blessing which speaks of our forefathers is found on p. 185. The version which includes both the forefathers and mothers is found on p.187.

MUSAF AMIDAH FOR *SHABBAT*

Adonai, open my lips that my mouth may declare Your praise.

אֲדֹנָי, שְׂפָתַי תִּפְתָּח וּפִי יַגִּיד תְּהִלָּתֶךָ.

בָּרוּךְ אַתָּה יְיָ אֱלֹהֵינוּ וֵאלֹהֵי אֲבוֹתֵינוּ, אֱלֹהֵי אַבְרָהָם אֱלֹהֵי יִצְחָק וֵאלֹהֵי יַעֲקֹב, הָאֵל הַגָּדוֹל הַגִּבּוֹר וְהַנּוֹרָא, אֵל עֶלְיוֹן, גּוֹמֵל חֲסָדִים טוֹבִים וְקוֹנֵה הַכֹּל, וְזוֹכֵר חַסְדֵי אָבוֹת וּמֵבִיא גוֹאֵל לִבְנֵי בְנֵיהֶם לְמַעַן שְׁמוֹ בְּאַהֲבָה.

On *Shabbat* before *Yom Kippur* we say:

זָכְרֵנוּ לְחַיִּים, מֶלֶךְ חָפֵץ בַּחַיִּים,
וְכָתְבֵנוּ בְּסֵפֶר הַחַיִּים לְמַעַנְךָ אֱלֹהִים חַיִּים.

מֶלֶךְ עוֹזֵר וּמוֹשִׁיעַ וּמָגֵן. בָּרוּךְ אַתָּה יְיָ מָגֵן אַבְרָהָם.

אַתָּה גִּבּוֹר לְעוֹלָם אֲדֹנָי, מְחַיֵּה מֵתִים אַתָּה רַב לְהוֹשִׁיעַ.

From *Sh'mini Atzeret* to *Pesaḥ* we say:

מַשִּׁיב הָרוּחַ וּמוֹרִיד הַגָּשֶׁם.

מְכַלְכֵּל חַיִּים בְּחֶסֶד, מְחַיֵּה מֵתִים בְּרַחֲמִים רַבִּים, סוֹמֵךְ נוֹפְלִים וְרוֹפֵא חוֹלִים וּמַתִּיר אֲסוּרִים, וּמְקַיֵּם אֱמוּנָתוֹ לִישֵׁנֵי עָפָר. מִי כָמוֹךָ בַּעַל גְּבוּרוֹת וּמִי דּוֹמֶה לָּךְ, מֶלֶךְ מֵמִית וּמְחַיֶּה וּמַצְמִיחַ יְשׁוּעָה.

On *Shabbat* before *Yom Kippur* we say:

מִי כָמוֹךָ אַב הָרַחֲמִים, זוֹכֵר יְצוּרָיו לְחַיִּים בְּרַחֲמִים.

וְנֶאֱמָן אַתָּה לְהַחֲיוֹת מֵתִים. בָּרוּךְ אַתָּה יְיָ מְחַיֵּה הַמֵּתִים.

Adonai, open my lips that my mouth may declare Your praise.

Blessed are You, *Adonai*, our God and God of our ancestors,
God of Abraham, God of Isaac and God of Jacob.
Supreme God Who responds with kindness,
You remember the good deeds of our ancestors and
lovingly bring help to us.

On the *Shabbat* before *Yom Kippur* add:

Remember us for life, Ruler, Who desires life, and write us in Your book of life, for Your sake, ever-living God.

Ruler, Supporter, Helper and Shield, praised are You, *Adonai*,
Who protects Abraham.

You are powerful, Almighty One.
You renew life with Your saving acts.

From *Sh'mini Atzeret* to *Pesaḥ* we say:

You cause the wind to blow and the rain to fall.

You sustain the living with loving-kindness, and with mercy, renew life. You support the falling, heal the sick, free the captives and remember those who have passed on. Who can compare to You, Almighty God? Who resembles You, the Source of life and death, the Source of blossoming hope?

On the *Shabbat* before *Yom Kippur* add:

Who is like You, merciful Parent?
You remember with mercy all creatures for life.

You are faithful in giving life to all. Praised are You, Who renews life.

MUSAF AMIDAH FOR *SHABBAT*

Adonai, open my lips that my mouth may declare Your praise.

אֲדֹנָי, שְׂפָתַי תִּפְתָּח וּפִי יַגִּיד תְּהִלָּתֶךָ.

בָּרוּךְ אַתָּה יְיָ אֱלֹהֵינוּ וֵאלֹהֵי אֲבוֹתֵינוּ, אֱלֹהֵי אַבְרָהָם אֱלֹהֵי יִצְחָק וֵאלֹהֵי יַעֲקֹב, אֱלֹהֵי שָׂרָה אֱלֹהֵי רִבְקָה אֱלֹהֵי רָחֵל וֵאלֹהֵי לֵאָה, הָאֵל הַגָּדוֹל הַגִּבּוֹר וְהַנּוֹרָא, אֵל עֶלְיוֹן, גּוֹמֵל חֲסָדִים טוֹבִים וְקוֹנֵה הַכֹּל, וְזוֹכֵר חַסְדֵי אָבוֹת וּמֵבִיא גוֹאֵל לִבְנֵי בְנֵיהֶם לְמַעַן שְׁמוֹ בְּאַהֲבָה.

On *Shabbat* before *Yom Kippur* we say:

זָכְרֵנוּ לְחַיִּים, מֶלֶךְ חָפֵץ בְּחַיִּים,
וְכָתְבֵנוּ בְּסֵפֶר הַחַיִּים לְמַעַנְךָ אֱלֹהִים חַיִּים.

מֶלֶךְ עוֹזֵר וּפוֹקֵד וּמוֹשִׁיעַ וּמָגֵן. בָּרוּךְ אַתָּה יְיָ מָגֵן אַבְרָהָם וּפוֹקֵד שָׂרָה.

אַתָּה גִּבּוֹר לְעוֹלָם אֲדֹנָי, מְחַיֵּה מֵתִים אַתָּה רַב לְהוֹשִׁיעַ.

From *Sh'mini Atzeret* to *Pesaḥ* we say:

מַשִּׁיב הָרוּחַ וּמוֹרִיד הַגָּשֶׁם.

מְכַלְכֵּל חַיִּים בְּחֶסֶד, מְחַיֵּה מֵתִים בְּרַחֲמִים רַבִּים, סוֹמֵךְ נוֹפְלִים וְרוֹפֵא חוֹלִים וּמַתִּיר אֲסוּרִים, וּמְקַיֵּם אֱמוּנָתוֹ לִישֵׁנֵי עָפָר. מִי כָמוֹךָ בַּעַל גְּבוּרוֹת וּמִי דוֹמֶה לָּךְ, מֶלֶךְ מֵמִית וּמְחַיֶּה וּמַצְמִיחַ יְשׁוּעָה.

On *Shabbat* before *Yom Kippur* we say:

מִי כָמוֹךָ אַב הָרַחֲמִים, זוֹכֵר יְצוּרָיו לְחַיִּים בְּרַחֲמִים.

וְנֶאֱמָן אַתָּה לְהַחֲיוֹת מֵתִים. בָּרוּךְ אַתָּה יְיָ מְחַיֵּה הַמֵּתִים.

Adonai, open my lips that my mouth may declare Your praise.

Blessed are You, *Adonai*, our God and God of our ancestors,
God of Abraham, God of Isaac and God of Jacob,
God of Sarah, God of Rebecca, God of Leah and God of Rachel.
Supreme God Who responds with kindness,
You remember the good deeds of our ancestors and
lovingly bring help to us.

On the *Shabbat* before *Yom Kippur* add:

Remember us for life, Ruler, Who desires life, and write us in Your book of life, for Your sake, ever-living God.

Ruler, Supporter, Helper and Shield, praised are You, *Adonai*,
Who protects Abraham and remembers Sarah.

You are powerful, Almighty One.
You renew life with Your saving acts.

From *Sh'mini Atzeret* to *Pesaḥ* we say:

You cause the wind to blow and the rain to fall,

You sustain the living with loving-kindness, and with mercy, renew life. You support the falling, heal the sick, free the captives and remember those who have passed on. Who can compare to You, Almighty God? Who resembles You, the Source of life and death, the Source of blossoming hope?

On the *Shabbat* before *Yom Kippur* add:

Who is like You, merciful Parent?
You remember with mercy all creatures for life.

You are faithful in giving life to all. Praised are You, Who renews life.

נַעֲרִיצְךָ וְנַקְדִּישְׁךָ כְּסוֹד שִׂיחַ שַׂרְפֵי־קֹדֶשׁ הַמַּקְדִּישִׁים שִׁמְךָ בַּקֹּדֶשׁ, כַּכָּתוּב עַל יַד נְבִיאֶךָ, וְקָרָא זֶה אֶל זֶה וְאָמַר:

קָדוֹשׁ קָדוֹשׁ קָדוֹשׁ יְיָ צְבָאוֹת, מְלֹא כָל־הָאָרֶץ כְּבוֹדוֹ.

כְּבוֹדוֹ מָלֵא עוֹלָם, מְשָׁרְתָיו שׁוֹאֲלִים זֶה לָזֶה: אַיֵּה מְקוֹם כְּבוֹדוֹ לְעֻמָּתָם בָּרוּךְ יֹאמֵרוּ:

בָּרוּךְ כְּבוֹד יְיָ מִמְּקוֹמוֹ.

מִמְּקוֹמוֹ הוּא יִפֶן בְּרַחֲמִים וְיָחֹן עַם הַמְיַחֲדִים שְׁמוֹ עֶרֶב וָבֹקֶר בְּכָל־יוֹם תָּמִיד פַּעֲמַיִם בְּאַהֲבָה שְׁמַע אוֹמְרִים:

שְׁמַע יִשְׂרָאֵל יְיָ אֱלֹהֵינוּ יְיָ אֶחָד.

הוּא אֱלֹהֵינוּ, הוּא אָבִינוּ, הוּא מַלְכֵּנוּ, הוּא מוֹשִׁיעֵנוּ, וְהוּא יַשְׁמִיעֵנוּ בְּרַחֲמָיו שֵׁנִית לְעֵינֵי כָּל־חָי, לִהְיוֹת לָכֶם לֵאלֹהִים:

אֲנִי יְיָ אֱלֹהֵיכֶם.

וּבְדִבְרֵי קָדְשְׁךָ כָּתוּב לֵאמֹר:

יִמְלֹךְ יְיָ לְעוֹלָם, אֱלֹהַיִךְ צִיּוֹן לְדֹר וָדֹר, הַלְלוּיָהּ.

Leader:

לְדוֹר וָדוֹר נַגִּיד גָּדְלֶךָ, וּלְנֵצַח נְצָחִים קְדֻשָּׁתְךָ נַקְדִּישׁ. וְשִׁבְחֲךָ אֱלֹהֵינוּ מִפִּינוּ לֹא יָמוּשׁ לְעוֹלָם וָעֶד כִּי אֵל מֶלֶךְ גָּדוֹל וְקָדוֹשׁ אָתָּה.

Each congregant while or after leader says above:

אַתָּה קָדוֹשׁ וְשִׁמְךָ קָדוֹשׁ וּקְדוֹשִׁים בְּכָל־יוֹם יְהַלְלוּךָ סֶּלָה.

On Shabbat before Yom Kippur we say the words below and not the line which follows:

בָּרוּךְ אַתָּה יְיָ הַמֶּלֶךְ הַקָּדוֹשׁ.

בָּרוּךְ אַתָּה יְיָ הָאֵל הַקָּדוֹשׁ.

יִשְׂמְחוּ בְמַלְכוּתְךָ שׁוֹמְרֵי שַׁבָּת וְקוֹרְאֵי עֹנֶג. עַם מְקַדְּשֵׁי שְׁבִיעִי, כֻּלָּם יִשְׂבְּעוּ וְיִתְעַנְּגוּ מִטּוּבֶךָ. וְהַשְּׁבִיעִי רָצִיתָ בּוֹ וְקִדַּשְׁתּוֹ, חֶמְדַּת יָמִים אוֹתוֹ קָרָאתָ, זֵכֶר לְמַעֲשֵׂה בְרֵאשִׁית.

אֱלֹהֵינוּ וֵאלֹהֵי אֲבוֹתֵינוּ, רְצֵה בִמְנוּחָתֵנוּ. קַדְּשֵׁנוּ בְּמִצְוֹתֶיךָ וְתֵן חֶלְקֵנוּ בְּתוֹרָתֶךָ, שַׂבְּעֵנוּ מִטּוּבֶךָ וְשַׂמְּחֵנוּ בִּישׁוּעָתֶךָ, וְטַהֵר לִבֵּנוּ לְעָבְדְּךָ בֶּאֱמֶת. וְהַנְחִילֵנוּ יְיָ אֱלֹהֵינוּ בְּאַהֲבָה וּבְרָצוֹן שַׁבַּת קָדְשֶׁךָ, וְיָנוּחוּ בָהּ יִשְׂרָאֵל מְקַדְּשֵׁי שְׁמֶךָ. בָּרוּךְ אַתָּה יְיָ מְקַדֵּשׁ הַשַּׁבָּת.

רְצֵה יְיָ אֱלֹהֵינוּ בְּעַמְּךָ יִשְׂרָאֵל וּבִתְפִלָּתָם, וְהָשֵׁב אֶת־הָעֲבוֹדָה לִדְבִיר בֵּיתֶךָ, וּתְפִלָּתָם בְּאַהֲבָה תְקַבֵּל בְּרָצוֹן, וּתְהִי לְרָצוֹן תָּמִיד עֲבוֹדַת יִשְׂרָאֵל עַמֶּךָ. וְתֶחֱזֶינָה עֵינֵינוּ בְּשׁוּבְךָ לְצִיּוֹן בְּרַחֲמִים. בָּרוּךְ אַתָּה יְיָ הַמַּחֲזִיר שְׁכִינָתוֹ לְצִיּוֹן.

מוֹדִים אֲנַחְנוּ לָךְ שָׁאַתָּה הוּא יְיָ אֱלֹהֵינוּ וֵאלֹהֵי אֲבוֹתֵינוּ לְעוֹלָם וָעֶד, צוּר חַיֵּינוּ מָגֵן יִשְׁעֵנוּ אַתָּה הוּא לְדוֹר וָדוֹר. נוֹדֶה לְּךָ וּנְסַפֵּר תְּהִלָּתֶךָ, עַל חַיֵּינוּ הַמְּסוּרִים בְּיָדֶךָ וְעַל נִשְׁמוֹתֵינוּ הַפְּקוּדוֹת לָךְ וְעַל נִסֶּיךָ שֶׁבְּכָל־יוֹם עִמָּנוּ וְעַל נִפְלְאוֹתֶיךָ וְטוֹבוֹתֶיךָ שֶׁבְּכָל־עֵת עֶרֶב וָבֹקֶר וְצָהֳרָיִם. הַטּוֹב כִּי לֹא כָלוּ רַחֲמֶיךָ, וְהַמְרַחֵם כִּי לֹא תַמּוּ חֲסָדֶיךָ, מֵעוֹלָם קִוִּינוּ לָךְ.

On *Ḥanukkah* we say:

עַל הַנִּסִּים וְעַל הַפֻּרְקָן, וְעַל הַגְּבוּרוֹת, וְעַל הַתְּשׁוּעוֹת, וְעַל הַמִּלְחָמוֹת שֶׁעָשִׂיתָ לַאֲבוֹתֵינוּ בַּיָּמִים הָהֵם וּבַזְּמַן הַזֶּה.

בִּימֵי מַתִּתְיָהוּ בֶּן־יוֹחָנָן כֹּהֵן גָּדוֹל, חַשְׁמוֹנַי וּבָנָיו, כְּשֶׁעָמְדָה מַלְכוּת יָוָן הָרְשָׁעָה עַל עַמְּךָ יִשְׂרָאֵל לְהַשְׁכִּיחָם תּוֹרָתֶךָ וּלְהַעֲבִירָם מֵחֻקֵּי רְצוֹנֶךָ, וְאַתָּה בְּרַחֲמֶיךָ הָרַבִּים עָמַדְתָּ לָהֶם בְּעֵת צָרָתָם, רַבְתָּ אֶת־רִיבָם, דַּנְתָּ אֶת־דִּינָם, נָקַמְתָּ אֶת־נִקְמָתָם, מָסַרְתָּ גִבּוֹרִים בְּיַד חַלָּשִׁים, וְרַבִּים בְּיַד מְעַטִּים, וּטְמֵאִים בְּיַד טְהוֹרִים, וּרְשָׁעִים בְּיַד צַדִּיקִים, וְזֵדִים בְּיַד עוֹסְקֵי תוֹרָתֶךָ. וּלְךָ עָשִׂיתָ שֵׁם גָּדוֹל וְקָדוֹשׁ בְּעוֹלָמֶךָ, וּלְעַמְּךָ יִשְׂרָאֵל עָשִׂיתָ תְּשׁוּעָה גְדוֹלָה וּפֻרְקָן כְּהַיּוֹם הַזֶּה. וְאַחַר כֵּן בָּאוּ בָנֶיךָ לִדְבִיר בֵּיתֶךָ וּפִנּוּ אֶת־הֵיכָלֶךָ, וְטִהֲרוּ אֶת־מִקְדָּשֶׁךָ, וְהִדְלִיקוּ נֵרוֹת בְּחַצְרוֹת קָדְשֶׁךָ, וְקָבְעוּ שְׁמוֹנַת יְמֵי חֲנֻכָּה אֵלּוּ לְהוֹדוֹת וּלְהַלֵּל לְשִׁמְךָ הַגָּדוֹל.

וְעַל כֻּלָּם יִתְבָּרַךְ וְיִתְרוֹמַם שִׁמְךָ מַלְכֵּנוּ תָּמִיד לְעוֹלָם וָעֶד.

On *Shabbat* before *Yom Kippur* we say:

וּכְתֹב לְחַיִּים טוֹבִים כָּל־בְּנֵי בְרִיתֶךָ.

וְכֹל הַחַיִּים יוֹדוּךָ סֶּלָה וִיהַלְלוּ אֶת־שִׁמְךָ בֶּאֱמֶת, הָאֵל יְשׁוּעָתֵנוּ וְעֶזְרָתֵנוּ סֶלָה. בָּרוּךְ אַתָּה יְיָ הַטּוֹב שִׁמְךָ וּלְךָ נָאֶה לְהוֹדוֹת.

אֱלֹהֵינוּ וֵאלֹהֵי אֲבוֹתֵינוּ, בָּרְכֵנוּ בַּבְּרָכָה הַמְשֻׁלֶּשֶׁת, בַּתּוֹרָה הַכְּתוּבָה עַל יְדֵי מֹשֶׁה עַבְדֶּךָ, הָאֲמוּרָה מִפִּי אַהֲרֹן וּבָנָיו, כֹּהֲנִים, עַם קְדוֹשֶׁךָ, כָּאָמוּר:

יְבָרֶכְךָ יְיָ וְיִשְׁמְרֶךָ. כֵּן יְהִי רָצוֹן.

יָאֵר יְיָ פָּנָיו אֵלֶיךָ וִיחֻנֶּךָּ. כֵּן יְהִי רָצוֹן.

יִשָּׂא יְיָ פָּנָיו אֵלֶיךָ וְיָשֵׂם לְךָ שָׁלוֹם. כֵּן יְהִי רָצוֹן.

שִׂים שָׁלוֹם בָּעוֹלָם, טוֹבָה וּבְרָכָה, חֵן וָחֶסֶד וְרַחֲמִים עָלֵינוּ וְעַל כָּל־יִשְׂרָאֵל עַמֶּךָ. בָּרְכֵנוּ אָבִינוּ כֻּלָּנוּ כְּאֶחָד בְּאוֹר פָּנֶיךָ, כִּי בְאוֹר פָּנֶיךָ נָתַתָּ לָנוּ, יְיָ אֱלֹהֵינוּ, תּוֹרַת חַיִּים וְאַהֲבַת חֶסֶד, וּצְדָקָה וּבְרָכָה וְרַחֲמִים וְחַיִּים וְשָׁלוֹם. וְטוֹב בְּעֵינֶיךָ לְבָרֵךְ אֶת־עַמְּךָ יִשְׂרָאֵל בְּכָל־עֵת וּבְכָל־שָׁעָה בִּשְׁלוֹמֶךָ.

On *Shabbat Shuvah* before *Yom Kippur* we say the following lines instead of the line below:

בְּסֵפֶר חַיִּים, בְּרָכָה וְשָׁלוֹם, וּפַרְנָסָה טוֹבָה, נִזָּכֵר וְנִכָּתֵב לְפָנֶיךָ,
אֲנַחְנוּ וְכָל־עַמְּךָ בֵּית יִשְׂרָאֵל, לְחַיִּים טוֹבִים וּלְשָׁלוֹם.
בָּרוּךְ אַתָּה יְיָ עֹשֵׂה הַשָּׁלוֹם.

בָּרוּךְ אַתָּה יְיָ הַמְבָרֵךְ אֶת־עַמּוֹ יִשְׂרָאֵל בַּשָּׁלוֹם.

MUSAF AMIDAH FOR *YOM TOV*

Adonai, open my lips that my mouth may declare Your praise.

אֲדֹנָי, שְׂפָתַי תִּפְתָּח וּפִי יַגִּיד תְּהִלָּתֶךָ.

בָּרוּךְ אַתָּה יְיָ אֱלֹהֵינוּ וֵאלֹהֵי אֲבוֹתֵינוּ, אֱלֹהֵי אַבְרָהָם אֱלֹהֵי יִצְחָק וֵאלֹהֵי יַעֲקֹב, הָאֵל הַגָּדוֹל הַגִּבּוֹר וְהַנּוֹרָא, אֵל עֶלְיוֹן, גּוֹמֵל חֲסָדִים טוֹבִים וְקוֹנֵה הַכֹּל, וְזוֹכֵר חַסְדֵי אָבוֹת וּמֵבִיא גוֹאֵל לִבְנֵי בְנֵיהֶם לְמַעַן שְׁמוֹ בְּאַהֲבָה. מֶלֶךְ עוֹזֵר וּמוֹשִׁיעַ וּמָגֵן. בָּרוּךְ אַתָּה יְיָ מָגֵן אַבְרָהָם.

אַתָּה גִּבּוֹר לְעוֹלָם אֲדֹנָי, מְחַיֵּה מֵתִים אַתָּה רַב לְהוֹשִׁיעַ.

On *Sh'mini Atzeret* and *Simḥat Torah* we say:

מַשִּׁיב הָרוּחַ וּמוֹרִיד הַגָּשֶׁם.

מְכַלְכֵּל חַיִּים בְּחֶסֶד, מְחַיֵּה מֵתִים בְּרַחֲמִים רַבִּים, סוֹמֵךְ נוֹפְלִים וְרוֹפֵא חוֹלִים וּמַתִּיר אֲסוּרִים, וּמְקַיֵּם אֱמוּנָתוֹ לִישֵׁנֵי עָפָר. מִי כָמוֹךָ בַּעַל גְּבוּרוֹת וּמִי דּוֹמֶה לָּךְ, מֶלֶךְ מֵמִית וּמְחַיֶּה וּמַצְמִיחַ יְשׁוּעָה. וְנֶאֱמָן אַתָּה לְהַחֲיוֹת מֵתִים. בָּרוּךְ אַתָּה יְיָ מְחַיֵּה הַמֵּתִים.

Adonai, open my lips that my mouth may declare Your praise.

Blessed are You, *Adonai*, our God and God of our ancestors,
God of Abraham, God of Isaac and God of Jacob.
Supreme God Who responds with kindness,
You remember the good deeds of our ancestors and
lovingly bring help to us.

Ruler, Supporter, Helper and Shield, praised are You, *Adonai*,
Who protects Abraham.

You are powerful, Almighty One.
You renew life with Your saving acts.

On *Sh'mini Atzeret* and *Simḥat Torah* we say:

You cause the wind to blow and the rain to fall.

You sustain the living with loving-kindness, and with mercy, renew life. You support the falling, heal the sick, free the captives and remember those who have passed on. Who can compare to You, Almighty God? Who resembles You, the Source of life and death, the Source of blossoming hope?

You are faithful in giving life to all. Praised are You, Who renews life.

MUSAF AMIDAH FOR *YOM TOV*

Adonai, open my lips that my mouth may declare Your praise.

אֲדֹנָי, שְׂפָתַי תִּפְתָּח וּפִי יַגִּיד תְּהִלָּתֶךָ.

בָּרוּךְ אַתָּה יְיָ אֱלֹהֵינוּ וֵאלֹהֵי אֲבוֹתֵינוּ, אֱלֹהֵי אַבְרָהָם אֱלֹהֵי יִצְחָק וֵאלֹהֵי יַעֲקֹב, אֱלֹהֵי שָׂרָה אֱלֹהֵי רִבְקָה אֱלֹהֵי רָחֵל וֵאלֹהֵי לֵאָה, הָאֵל הַגָּדוֹל הַגִּבּוֹר וְהַנּוֹרָא, אֵל עֶלְיוֹן, גּוֹמֵל חֲסָדִים טוֹבִים וְקוֹנֵה הַכֹּל, וְזוֹכֵר חַסְדֵי אָבוֹת וּמֵבִיא גוֹאֵל לִבְנֵי בְנֵיהֶם לְמַעַן שְׁמוֹ בְּאַהֲבָה. מֶלֶךְ עוֹזֵר וּפוֹקֵד וּמוֹשִׁיעַ וּמָגֵן. בָּרוּךְ אַתָּה יְיָ מָגֵן אַבְרָהָם וּפוֹקֵד שָׂרָה.

אַתָּה גִּבּוֹר לְעוֹלָם אֲדֹנָי, מְחַיֵּה מֵתִים אַתָּה רַב לְהוֹשִׁיעַ.

On *Sh'mini Atzeret* and *Simḥat Torah* we say:

מַשִּׁיב הָרוּחַ וּמוֹרִיד הַגָּשֶׁם.

מְכַלְכֵּל חַיִּים בְּחֶסֶד, מְחַיֵּה מֵתִים בְּרַחֲמִים רַבִּים, סוֹמֵךְ נוֹפְלִים וְרוֹפֵא חוֹלִים וּמַתִּיר אֲסוּרִים, וּמְקַיֵּם אֱמוּנָתוֹ לִישֵׁנֵי עָפָר. מִי כָמוֹךָ בַּעַל גְּבוּרוֹת וּמִי דוֹמֶה לָּךְ, מֶלֶךְ מֵמִית וּמְחַיֶּה וּמַצְמִיחַ יְשׁוּעָה. וְנֶאֱמָן אַתָּה לְהַחֲיוֹת מֵתִים. בָּרוּךְ אַתָּה יְיָ מְחַיֵּה הַמֵּתִים.

Adonai, open my lips that my mouth may declare Your praise.

Blessed are You, *Adonai*, our God and God of our ancestors,
God of Abraham, God of Isaac and God of Jacob,
God of Sarah, God of Rebecca, God of Leah and God of Rachel.
Supreme God Who responds with kindness,
You remember the good deeds of our ancestors and
lovingly bring help to us.

Ruler, Supporter, Helper and Shield, praised are You, *Adonai*,
Who protects Abraham and remembers Sarah.

You are powerful, Almighty One.
You renew life with Your saving acts.

On *Sh'mini Atzeret* and *Simḥat Torah* we say:

You cause the wind to blow and the rain to fall.

You sustain the living with loving-kindness, and with mercy, renew life. You support the falling, heal the sick, free the captives and remember those who have passed on. Who can compare to You, Almighty God? Who resembles You, the Source of life and death, the Source of blossoming hope?

You are faithful in giving life to all. Praised are You, Who renews life.

נַעֲרִיצְךָ וְנַקְדִּישְׁךָ כְּסוֹד שִׂיחַ שַׂרְפֵי־קֹדֶשׁ הַמַּקְדִּישִׁים שִׁמְךָ בַּקֹּדֶשׁ, כַּכָּתוּב עַל יַד נְבִיאֶךָ, וְקָרָא זֶה אֶל זֶה וְאָמַר:

קָדוֹשׁ קָדוֹשׁ קָדוֹשׁ יְיָ צְבָאוֹת, מְלֹא כָל־הָאָרֶץ כְּבוֹדוֹ.

כְּבוֹדוֹ מָלֵא עוֹלָם, מְשָׁרְתָיו שׁוֹאֲלִים זֶה לָזֶה אַיֵּה מְקוֹם כְּבוֹדוֹ. לְעֻמָּתָם בָּרוּךְ יֹאמֵרוּ:

בָּרוּךְ כְּבוֹד יְיָ מִמְּקוֹמוֹ.

מִמְּקוֹמוֹ הוּא יִפֶן בְּרַחֲמִים, וְיָחֹן עַם הַמְיַחֲדִים שְׁמוֹ עֶרֶב וָבֹקֶר בְּכָל־יוֹם תָּמִיד פַּעֲמַיִם בְּאַהֲבָה שְׁמַע אוֹמְרִים:

שְׁמַע יִשְׂרָאֵל יְיָ אֱלֹהֵינוּ יְיָ אֶחָד.

הוּא אֱלֹהֵינוּ, הוּא אָבִינוּ, הוּא מַלְכֵּנוּ, הוּא מוֹשִׁיעֵנוּ, וְהוּא יַשְׁמִיעֵנוּ בְּרַחֲמָיו שֵׁנִית לְעֵינֵי כָּל־חָי, לִהְיוֹת לָכֶם לֵאלֹהִים:

אֲנִי יְיָ אֱלֹהֵיכֶם.

אַדִּיר אַדִּירֵנוּ יְיָ אֲדוֹנֵינוּ, מָה אַדִּיר שִׁמְךָ בְּכָל־הָאָרֶץ. וְהָיָה יְיָ לְמֶלֶךְ עַל כָּל־הָאָרֶץ, בַּיּוֹם הַהוּא יִהְיֶה יְיָ אֶחָד וּשְׁמוֹ אֶחָד.

וּבְדִבְרֵי קָדְשְׁךָ כָּתוּב לֵאמֹר:

יִמְלֹךְ יְיָ לְעוֹלָם אֱלֹהַיִךְ צִיּוֹן לְדֹר וָדֹר, הַלְלוּיָהּ.

Leader:

לְדוֹר וָדוֹר נַגִּיד גָּדְלֶךָ, וּלְנֵצַח נְצָחִים קְדֻשָּׁתְךָ נַקְדִּישׁ. וְשִׁבְחֲךָ אֱלֹהֵינוּ מִפִּינוּ לֹא יָמוּשׁ לְעוֹלָם וָעֶד, כִּי אֵל מֶלֶךְ גָּדוֹל וְקָדוֹשׁ אָתָּה.

Each congregant while or after leader says above:

אַתָּה קָדוֹשׁ וְשִׁמְךָ קָדוֹשׁ וּקְדוֹשִׁים בְּכָל־יוֹם יְהַלְלוּךָ סֶּלָה.

בָּרוּךְ אַתָּה יְיָ הָאֵל הַקָּדוֹשׁ.

אַתָּה בְחַרְתָּנוּ מִכָּל־הָעַמִּים, אָהַבְתָּ אוֹתָנוּ וְרָצִיתָ בָּנוּ, וְרוֹמַמְתָּנוּ מִכָּל־הַלְּשׁוֹנוֹת, וְקִדַּשְׁתָּנוּ בְּמִצְוֹתֶיךָ, וְקֵרַבְתָּנוּ מַלְכֵּנוּ לַעֲבוֹדָתֶךָ, וְשִׁמְךָ הַגָּדוֹל וְהַקָּדוֹשׁ עָלֵינוּ קָרָאתָ.

וַתִּתֶּן לָנוּ יְיָ אֱלֹהֵינוּ בְּאַהֲבָה (שַׁבָּתוֹת לִמְנוּחָה וּ)מוֹעֲדִים לְשִׂמְחָה, חַגִּים וּזְמַנִּים לְשָׂשׂוֹן, אֶת־יוֹם (הַשַּׁבָּת הַזֶּה וְאֶת־יוֹם)

On Pesaḥ: חַג הַמַּצּוֹת הַזֶּה, זְמַן חֵרוּתֵנוּ,

On Shavuot: חַג הַשָּׁבוּעוֹת הַזֶּה, זְמַן מַתַּן תּוֹרָתֵנוּ,

On Sukkot: חַג הַסֻּכּוֹת הַזֶּה, זְמַן שִׂמְחָתֵנוּ,

On *Sh'mini Atzeret* and on *Simḥat Torah*:

הַשְּׁמִינִי, חַג הָעֲצֶרֶת הַזֶּה, זְמַן שִׂמְחָתֵנוּ,

(בְּאַהֲבָה) מִקְרָא קֹדֶשׁ, זֵכֶר לִיצִיאַת מִצְרָיִם.

אָבִינוּ מַלְכֵּנוּ, גַּלֵּה כְּבוֹד מַלְכוּתְךָ עָלֵינוּ מְהֵרָה, וְהוֹפַע וְהִנָּשֵׂא עָלֵינוּ לְעֵינֵי כָּל־חָי, וְקָרֵב פְּזוּרֵינוּ מִבֵּין הַגּוֹיִם וּנְפוּצוֹתֵינוּ כַּנֵּס מִיַּרְכְּתֵי־אָרֶץ. וַהֲבִיאֵנוּ לְצִיּוֹן עִירְךָ בְּרִנָּה וְלִירוּשָׁלַיִם בֵּית מִקְדָּשְׁךָ בְּשִׂמְחַת עוֹלָם, שֶׁשָּׁם עָשׂוּ אֲבוֹתֵינוּ לְפָנֶיךָ אֶת־קָרְבְּנוֹת חוֹבוֹתֵיהֶם, תְּמִידִים כְּסִדְרָם וּמוּסָפִים כְּהִלְכָתָם. וְאֶת־מוּסַף (יוֹם הַשַּׁבָּת הַזֶּה וְאֶת־מוּסַף) יוֹם

On Pesaḥ: חַג הַמַּצּוֹת הַזֶּה

On Shavuot: חַג הַשָּׁבוּעוֹת הַזֶּה

On Sukkot: חַג הַסֻּכּוֹת הַזֶּה

On *Sh'mini Atzeret* and On *Simḥat Torah*:

הַשְּׁמִינִי, חַג הָעֲצֶרֶת הַזֶּה

עָשׂוּ וְהִקְרִיבוּ לְפָנֶיךָ בְּאַהֲבָה כְּמִצְוַת רְצוֹנֶךָ.

On *Shabbat* we say:

יִשְׂמְחוּ בְמַלְכוּתְךָ שׁוֹמְרֵי שַׁבָּת וְקוֹרְאֵי עֹנֶג. עַם מְקַדְּשֵׁי שְׁבִיעִי, כֻּלָּם יִשְׂבְּעוּ וְיִתְעַנְּגוּ מִטּוּבֶךָ. וְהַשְּׁבִיעִי רָצִיתָ בּוֹ וְקִדַּשְׁתּוֹ, חֶמְדַּת יָמִים אוֹתוֹ קָרָאתָ, זֵכֶר לְמַעֲשֵׂה בְרֵאשִׁית.

וְהַשִּׂיאֵנוּ יְיָ אֱלֹהֵינוּ אֶת־בִּרְכַּת מוֹעֲדֶיךָ לְחַיִּים וּלְשָׁלוֹם, לְשִׂמְחָה וּלְשָׂשׂוֹן, כַּאֲשֶׁר רָצִיתָ וְאָמַרְתָּ לְבָרְכֵנוּ. אֱלֹהֵינוּ וֵאלֹהֵי אֲבוֹתֵינוּ, (רְצֵה בִמְנוּחָתֵנוּ) קַדְּשֵׁנוּ בְּמִצְוֹתֶיךָ וְתֵן חֶלְקֵנוּ בְּתוֹרָתֶךָ, שַׂבְּעֵנוּ מִטּוּבֶךָ וְשַׂמְּחֵנוּ בִּישׁוּעָתֶךָ, וְטַהֵר לִבֵּנוּ לְעָבְדְּךָ בֶּאֱמֶת. וְהַנְחִילֵנוּ יְיָ אֱלֹהֵינוּ (בְּאַהֲבָה וּבְרָצוֹן) בְּשִׂמְחָה וּבְשָׂשׂוֹן (שַׁבָּת וּ)מוֹעֲדֵי קָדְשֶׁךָ, וְיִשְׂמְחוּ בְךָ יִשְׂרָאֵל מְקַדְּשֵׁי שְׁמֶךָ. בָּרוּךְ אַתָּה יְיָ מְקַדֵּשׁ (הַשַּׁבָּת וְ)יִשְׂרָאֵל וְהַזְּמַנִּים.

רְצֵה יְיָ אֱלֹהֵינוּ בְּעַמְּךָ יִשְׂרָאֵל וּבִתְפִלָּתָם, וְהָשֵׁב אֶת־הָעֲבוֹדָה לִדְבִיר בֵּיתֶךָ, וּתְפִלָּתָם בְּאַהֲבָה תְקַבֵּל בְּרָצוֹן, וּתְהִי לְרָצוֹן תָּמִיד עֲבוֹדַת יִשְׂרָאֵל עַמֶּךָ. וְתֶחֱזֶינָה עֵינֵינוּ בְּשׁוּבְךָ לְצִיּוֹן בְּרַחֲמִים. בָּרוּךְ אַתָּה יְיָ הַמַּחֲזִיר שְׁכִינָתוֹ לְצִיּוֹן.

מוֹדִים אֲנַחְנוּ לָךְ שָׁאַתָּה הוּא יְיָ אֱלֹהֵינוּ וֵאלֹהֵי אֲבוֹתֵינוּ לְעוֹלָם וָעֶד, צוּר חַיֵּינוּ מָגֵן יִשְׁעֵנוּ אַתָּה הוּא לְדוֹר וָדוֹר. נוֹדֶה לְּךָ וּנְסַפֵּר תְּהִלָּתֶךָ, עַל חַיֵּינוּ הַמְּסוּרִים בְּיָדֶךָ וְעַל נִשְׁמוֹתֵינוּ הַפְּקוּדוֹת לָךְ וְעַל נִסֶּיךָ שֶׁבְּכָל־יוֹם עִמָּנוּ וְעַל נִפְלְאוֹתֶיךָ וְטוֹבוֹתֶיךָ שֶׁבְּכָל־עֵת, עֶרֶב וָבֹקֶר וְצָהֳרָיִם. הַטּוֹב כִּי לֹא כָלוּ רַחֲמֶיךָ, וְהַמְרַחֵם כִּי לֹא תַמּוּ חֲסָדֶיךָ, מֵעוֹלָם קִוִּינוּ לָךְ.

וְעַל כֻּלָּם יִתְבָּרַךְ וְיִתְרוֹמַם שִׁמְךָ מַלְכֵּנוּ תָּמִיד לְעוֹלָם וָעֶד.

וְכֹל הַחַיִּים יוֹדוּךָ סֶּלָה, וִיהַלְלוּ אֶת־שִׁמְךָ בֶּאֱמֶת, הָאֵל יְשׁוּעָתֵנוּ וְעֶזְרָתֵנוּ סֶלָה. בָּרוּךְ אַתָּה יְיָ הַטּוֹב שִׁמְךָ וּלְךָ נָאֶה לְהוֹדוֹת.

אֱלֹהֵינוּ וֵאלֹהֵי אֲבוֹתֵינוּ, בָּרְכֵנוּ בַבְּרָכָה הַמְשֻׁלֶּשֶׁת, בַּתּוֹרָה הַכְּתוּבָה עַל יְדֵי מֹשֶׁה עַבְדֶּךָ, הָאֲמוּרָה מִפִּי אַהֲרֹן וּבָנָיו, כֹּהֲנִים עַם קְדוֹשֶׁךָ, כָּאָמוּר:

יְבָרֶכְךָ יְיָ וְיִשְׁמְרֶךָ. כֵּן יְהִי רָצוֹן.

יָאֵר יְיָ פָּנָיו אֵלֶיךָ וִיחֻנֶּךָּ. כֵּן יְהִי רָצוֹן.

יִשָּׂא יְיָ פָּנָיו אֵלֶיךָ וְיָשֵׂם לְךָ שָׁלוֹם. כֵּן יְהִי רָצוֹן.

שִׂים שָׁלוֹם בָּעוֹלָם, טוֹבָה וּבְרָכָה, חֵן וָחֶסֶד וְרַחֲמִים עָלֵינוּ וְעַל כָּל־יִשְׂרָאֵל עַמֶּךָ. בָּרְכֵנוּ אָבִינוּ כֻּלָּנוּ כְּאֶחָד בְּאוֹר פָּנֶיךָ, כִּי בְאוֹר פָּנֶיךָ נָתַתָּ לָּנוּ, יְיָ אֱלֹהֵינוּ, תּוֹרַת חַיִּים וְאַהֲבַת חֶסֶד, וּצְדָקָה וּבְרָכָה וְרַחֲמִים וְחַיִּים וְשָׁלוֹם. וְטוֹב בְּעֵינֶיךָ לְבָרֵךְ אֶת־עַמְּךָ יִשְׂרָאֵל בְּכָל־עֵת וּבְכָל־שָׁעָה בִּשְׁלוֹמֶךָ.

בָּרוּךְ אַתָּה יְיָ הַמְבָרֵךְ אֶת־עַמּוֹ יִשְׂרָאֵל בַּשָּׁלוֹם.

FOOTNOTES

p. x: *Ahad HaAm, HaShiloah* 1898 III.6, *Al Parshat Derachim*, III.79.

p. x: "I have a precious gift..." *Talmud, Shabbat* 10b.

p. xi: The Sabbath is the choicest fruit..." Judah Halevi, *Kuzari,* 3.5.

p. xi: "How does one honor..." *Bamidbar Rabbah* 10.1.

p. xi: "The Roman Emperor Hadrian..." *Talmud, Shabbat* 119a.

p. 6-7, 13-14, 16-18: The translations for all blessings recited at home are based on translations by Shoshana Silberman in *A Family Haggadah*. Kar-Ben, Inc. 1987.

p. 2: Peninnah Schram. *Jewish Stories One Generation Tells Another*, pp. 208-209.

p. 4: "Prayers before Hadlakat Nerot," Chaim Raphael. *The Sabbath Eve Service*. Behrman House, Inc. 1985, p. 89.

p. 4: "Sabbath Eyes" by Nancy Lee Gossels in *Vetaher Libenu,* a *siddur* published by Congregation Beth El, Sudbury River Valley, 1980.

p. 5: *"T'khine* for Lighting Candles," Tracy Guren Klirs. *The Merit of Our Mothers*. Hebrew Union College Press, 1992, p. 86.

p. 8: "Blessing the Children: II," Danny Siegel. *Nine Entered Paradise Alive*. The Town House Press, Spring Valley, NY. 1980, p. 32.

p. 12: "*T'khine* of *Sora, Rivka, Rokhil* and *Laye*," Tracy Guren Klirs, p. 84.

p. 31: "For *Kabbalat Shabbat*," Ruth Brin. *HARVEST: Collected Poems and Prayers*. Reconstructionist Press, NY, 1986, p. 135.

p. 33: "An Evening Prayer for *Shabbat*," translation by Robert Abramson.

p. 39: "By the Shores" (abridged) by Geela Rayzel Raphael.

p. 40: "The darkness parts...," in Richard Lewis, *MIRACLES: Poems by Children of the English-Speaking World*, p. 214.

p. 42: "Watchful Anticipation," adapted from *Shabbos* by Shimon Finkelman, p. 89.

p. 42: "Every day of the week..." *Bereshit Rabbah* 11,9.

p. 50: "The Creation of the World," Madeleine L'Engle. *Ladder of Angels, Stories From the Bible Illustrated by Children of the World*. Keter Publishing House of Jerusalem, Ltd., 1979, p. 8.

p. 56: "Pass the Peace," Joel Lurie Grishaver. *Shema Is For Real,* p. 45.

p. 60: "Creation of Fish, Fowl, and Cattle," Madeleine L'Engle. *Ladder of Angels,* p. 11.

p. 72: "The House that Expanded" adapted from Adele Geras, *My Grandmother's Stories*, pp. 77-85.

p. 74: "As We Bless...," Faith Rogow.

p. 77: "Where Heaven and Earth Touch," Danny Siegel. *A Hearing Heart.* The Town House Press, Pittsboro, North Carolina, 1992, p. 62.

p. 83: "King David and the Frog," *101 Jewish Stories*. Board of Jewish Education of New York, pp. 163-166.

p. 89: "All words..." *Zohar* 43a, 192.1.

p. 91: "Morning Has Broken" by Eleanor Farjean.

p. 116: "Rabbi Simon and The Pearl," Board of Jewish Education of New York, p. 96.

p. 128: *"Shalom Ba'olam,"* Binyamin Yaakov Ruzinah in *Tov Lichtov*. Histadruth Ivrith of America, p. 51.

p. 148: "Reflections V," Danny Siegel. *Munbaz II And Other Mitzvah Heroes*. The Town House Press, Spring Valley, NY, 1988. p. 58.

p. 150: "The Challenge," Board of Jewish Education of New York, p. 53.

p. 169: "Portions," Rami M. Shapiro, p. 9.

p. 178: "Merger Poem," Judy Chicago.

BIBLIOGRAPHY

Bamberger, David. *When a Jew Prays: A Functional Guide.* Behrman House, New York. 1973.

Baron, Joseph L. *A Treasury of Jewish Quotations.* Jason Aronson Inc., USA. 1985.

Brin, Ruth F. *Harvest: Collected Poems and Prayers.* The Reconstructionist Press, New York. 1986.

Chanover, Hyman, ed. *A Prayer Curriculum for the Lower Grades, Book I.* BJE, Baltimore. 1991.

Chanover, Hyman, ed. *A Prayer Curriculum for the Lower Grades, Book II,* BJE, Baltimore. 1991.

Colodner, Solomon. *Lessons in Jewish Prayer.* Bloch Publishing Co., New York. 1968.

Dresner, Samuel H. and Byron L. Sherwin. *Judaism: The Way of Sanctification*. United Synagogue, New York. 1978.

Finkelman, Shimon and Nosson Scherman. *The Sabbath — Its Essence and Significance.* Art Scroll Mesorah Publications LTD., Brooklyn, New York. 1991.

Glatzer, Nahum. *The Judaic Tradition*. Beacon Press, Boston. 1969.

Goodhill, Ruth Marcus, ed. *The Wisdom of Heschel.* Farrar, Straus and Giroux, New York. 1986.

Goodman, Robert. *A Confluent Approach to the Teaching of Prayer*. BJE, Chicago. 1980.

Grishaver, Joel. *Shema is for Real.* Olin-Sang-Ruby Union Institute, UAHC, Chicago/Oconomowoc. 1980.

Grunfeld, I. *The Sabbath Day*. Feldheim Inc. New York. 1981.

Heschel, Abraham Joshua. *God in Search of Man.* Farrar, Straus and Young, New York. 1951.

Jacobson, Burt. *Teaching the Traditional Liturgy.* The Melton Research Center, New York. 1980.

Katz, Michael and Freedman, Joseph L. *Seder Shabbat: A Guide to Shabbat Observance.* LTF, New York. 1978.

Kirzner, Yitzchok. *The Art of Jewish Prayer.* Jason Aronson Inc., Northvale, N.J. 1993.

Klirs, Tracy Guren. *The Merit of Our Mothers.* Hebrew Union College Press, Cincinnati. 1992.

Kon, Abraham. *Prayer.* Soncino Press, London. 1971.

Millgram, Abraham E. *Sabbath: the Day of Delight.* JPS, Philadelphia. 1944.

Miller, Avigdor. *Praise My Soul.* Bais Yisrael of Rugby, New York. 1992.

Moskowitz, Nachama Skolnik. *A Bridge to Prayer,* Vol. I. UAHC Press, New York. 1988.

Moskowitz, Nachama Skolnik. *A Bridge to Prayer,* Vol. II. UAHC Press, New York. 1988.

Peli, Pinchas H. *The Jewish Sabbath: A Renewed Encounter.* Schocken, New York. 1988.

Raphael, Chaim. *The Sabbath Eve Service.* Behrman House, Inc., New York. 1985.

Shapiro, Rami M. *Tangents: Selected Poems, 1978-1988.* ENR Wordsmiths. Miami. 1988.

Shiovitz, Jeffrey, ed. *B'Kol Ehad: In One Voice* (a songster and audiocassette). United Synagogue of Conservative Judaism, New York. 1986.

Siegel, Richard, Michael Strassfeld and Sharon Strassfeld. *The First Jewish Catalogue.* JPS, Philadelphia. 1973.

Siegel, Seymour. *When a Jew Prays: Conceptual Guide.* Behrman House, New York. 1973.

Stampher, Nathaniel, ed. *Prayer Instruction in the Elementary Hebrew School: Teaching Guide for Second Year Classes.* BJE, Chicago. 1970.

Wenkart, Henny (ed.). *Sarah's Daughters Sing.* KTAV Publishing House, Inc., New York. 1990.

Wolfson, Ron. *The Art of Jewish Living: The Shabbat Seder.* Federation of Jewish Men's Clubs, New York. 1985.